CHRISTOPH STRASSER

STRASSER'S ROAD

THE STORY OF THE RECORD-SETTING RACE ACROSS AMERICA WINNER

CHRISTOPH STRASSER

STRASSER'S ROAD

THE STORY OF THE RECORD-SETTING
RACE ACROSS AMERICA WINNER

Christoph Strasser

IMPRINT:

Published by Christoph Strasser, English Language Edition

June 2019

Originally published in the German language:

Christoph Strasser: *Der Weg ist weiter als das Ziel,* eogth Verlag GmbH (Austria), August 2018

© Christoph Strasser | christophstrasser.at

ISBN: 978-1-64234-005-1

ISBN E-Book: 978-1-64234-006-8

North American Distribution: Octane Press, 815A Brazos Street, Austin, Texas, 78701.

www.octanepress.com, 512-334-9441, sales@octanepress.com.

English translation and editing: Vic Armijo | RAAM Media Director

Proofread: Ebony Roberts

Book Design and Layout: Das Buero ohne Namen, dasbueroohnenamen.com

Infographics and statistics: Michael Fetz | fetzdesign.com, Michael Pletz | vonnebenan.at

PHOTO CREDITS:

Cover: Alexander Karelly · **Back cover:** Manuel Hausdorfer | lime-art.at

Content pages: Alexander Karelly (all pictures, unless otherwise stated) · Pete Penseyres archive: page 6 · Dave Nelson: page 9, right side · Vic Armijo | RAAM Media: pages 9 (left side), 154–157, 273 · Manuel Hausdorfer | lime-art.at: pages 10, 19, 21, 26–29, 61, 64, 68–69, 110, 117, 124–128, 130, 146, 169–179, 186, 188, 243–244, 247–249, 257–269, 272, 283, 305, 317, 324–326 · Harald Tauderer | haraldtauderer. com: pages 55, 59, 75–79, 98, 217, 239 · Jürgen Gruber | groox.com: pages 54, 103 · Lorenz Masser | lorenzmasser.com: pages 119, 120 · Marion Luttenberger: page 145 · Race Around Austria: pages 129, 133 · Race Around Slovenia: page 48 · private archive Christoph Strasser: pages 33–47, 150, 196–209, 224–235, 284, 290

Printed in Austria

· · ·

TABLE OF CONTENTS

Pete Penseyres setting the 1986 RAAM speed record

...

FOREWORD

BY FORMER RAAM RECORD-
HOLDER PETE PENSEYRES

Every top athlete learns the finer points of their sport by observing those who came before. It's a safe bet that current leading tennis star Roger Federer knows much about the career, training, and techniques of Andre Agassi, the top star of 20 years ago. And so it is with 5-time Race Across America winner Christoph Strasser, who has admired and learned from the careers of 5-time RAAM winner Jure Robic (Slovenia), 3-time winner Wolfgang Fasching, and 2-time winner and long-time average speed record-holder Pete Penseyres (USA), among others.

At the finish of RAAM 2013, fans caught a glimpse of Strasser's admiration for the American, Penseyres. Strasser had just broken the RAAM average speed record of 15.40 miles per hour (24.8 kph) that Penseyres had set 27 years prior. Strasser's 2013 average overall speed was 15.58 miles per hour (25.07 kph), and as Strasser was being interviewed on the finish stage, RAAM president Fred Boethling handed Strasser a cell phone and said, "There's someone on the line who'd like to congratulate you. It's Pete Penseyres." Strasser's emotion overflowed and he beamed with pride, jubilance, and admiration at his accomplishment and at having it recognized so graciously by the man whose record he'd broken.

Penseyres was equally honored when Strasser asked him to pen the foreword to this book. His thoughts and feelings on the young man currently on the top of the ultra-cycling world appear below.

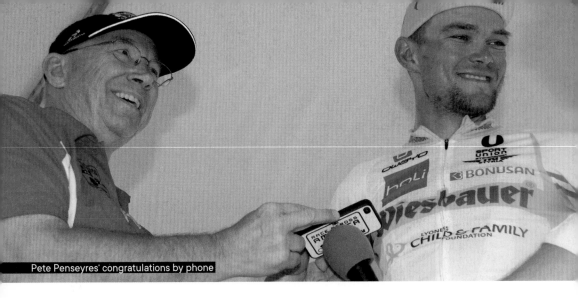
Pete Penseyres' congratulations by phone

"If That admiration was absolutely mutual. I was so happy for
him. After reading this, I now understand how he has turned
this race into a profession. He is so focused on every facet of the
physical, mental, and nutritional needs during training and in
the actual race, but also recognizes the absolute necessity for an
experienced and devoted crew. He has taken every component
of preparation for and execution of RAAM to a level far beyond
what anyone has done before. And he has created a roadmap for
others to follow if they want to be competitive with him. Very
few, if any, will be able to keep up, and even if they do, they will
have to adjust to his next advances. He never stops trying to improve each year. This requires those who would challenge him to
go beyond his previous year's performance."

"Yet he's always been really open about the things he's done.
When I was doing the race, I never tried to keep any of the
things I was doing secret, and he doesn't either. He took a lot of
the ideas that I had and took them to a whole new level in pretty
much every aspect of the race."

"I loved the book's introduction where he had to rely on his crew
to explain what he needed to do when he had temporary amnesia.
It was so similar to my experience in 1984, and probably many
other RAAM racers. They will be able to identify with his story,
but the majority of readers will be shocked and enthralled by his
ability to press on without even understanding what he is doing
and why."

"He's pretty amazing, but on top of all of his accomplishments, he's also a really nice guy. I'm always the RAAM escort rider that goes out with the previous year's winner, so I've gotten to do that and ride with him a few times and have had some really good chats."

"I wanted to live long enough to see someone break my record. It was set at a time when the course was easier, I think, in a lot of respects.[1] That's one of the reasons that it took so long. I knew that Christoph had an amazing ride and I was really happy to congratulate him right there at the finish. And of course when he managed to break the average speed record again, he put that record out of reach."[2]

EDITOR'S NOTE:

[1] *RAAM 1986 finished in Atlantic City and the final few hundred miles didn't have as much climbing as the current route to the Annapolis finish. The 1986 course also bypassed all of the Colorado passes and used much flatter Interstates for much of California, Arizona, New Mexico and Texas.*

[2] *In 2014 Strasser broke his own record with an average speed of 16.42 mph (26.42 kph).*

. . .

INTRODUCTION

"Now you have recovered, now you have slept well. Come on, get on the bike," says a man who seems so familiar, and yet so strange to me.

And, because I do not know why I'm here even where this "here" is, or what I should do—I stare at him, and the other people around me, this night in the middle of the Appalachian Mountains, just dead tired.

"We're in the middle of a bicycle race and you're in the lead. We are on record pace!" another tells me.

"Bike race? Do you want to scare me? I have not seen another cyclist for five, six days. What kind of a shit race is this?!"

Clearly, something is wrong. With me? With the others? If only I knew what exactly is expected of me. What is right or wrong in this moment? I vaguely remember riding through the USA, through the Appalachians, up and down. I know it's important to put pressure on the pedals, uphill and downhill, to ride quickly. But, why? What is the goal? It's as if my mind had taken its leave, and my memory with it. It's like being trapped in a bad dream, one that you want to wake up from as quickly as possible.

The men around me are friendly but determined. They push the bike away from me and onto the road, supporting me on both sides as I totter to the bike. "Once you start pedaling, everything will be easier again," they say, or words to that effect. I hear the words in my ears, but I do not understand the context. Deep inside, subconsciously, I know that I've worked on this thing all my life, but in the moment I could not explain what that "thing" is. It is incredibly important to me; I do not want to lose everything that I have built up over the years—even if it seems I have to go through hell. Physically, I am spent, mentally already at the end. "A bicycle race? Are you kidding me?!"

How I would like to simply not get on the bike now, to not continue. I imagine myself pouting on the ground, demanding explanations like a small child. I do not do it because the men's faces are familiar. I think, no, I'm sure, we have a common past. And apparently, everything has always gone well.

So I force myself onto the bike and begin to pedal. "There's a red traffic light in front," I hear from the loudspeaker of the car that follows behind me. "We turn right there." The words shake me up; I have heard that voice many times. It gives me security and motivates me. Without the support of this group, I would be lost, and I vaguely remember going through thick and thin with them, helping me, because I do not stop fighting for our common cause—my cause. You will already know what it is all about. I trust them and would do so even if my life was at stake. They will not let me down.

"Sabi, I love you" is written on a piece of paper that one of the men wrote at my request. I hold the piece of paper toward a camera, and I'm sure that my life part-ner Sabine will see it and cry with emotion. No one will know, just as no one sees how I am suffering on my long journey through America.

I keep fighting—fighting for whatever. We all want the same thing, to continue in the same direction. I could question where we are, because I myself, do not know in these hours. I do what I'm told because I know it's the right thing to do. Down-hill, I fall down the roads, uphill, I kick my soul out of my body. "What's this crap?" I think over and over. The tiredness lies like a veil before my eyes. The sweat blurs the next curves. I am crying and suffering, but for some reason, it must be so. It goes on, and on, and on, and on. But hopefully, it will be over soon. I know this, my companions deserve it.

And finally, the fog in my head lifts, and it is all crystal clear in front of me. I know why I do all this, and accept the pain and chaos in my head: Because cycling is my life and because these moments are the price I pay for my dream.

This book is about me, an ultra-cyclist who has achieved quite a bit in life. And it's about all those who stand by my side, who made my successes possible, and supported me through the worst crises. Friends inspire. Without them, I would have nothing to tell.

And so, even before the first chapter: Thank you to all of you who exist, and who are about to learn my story.

Christoph Strasser

RAAM 2014, we have dinner together on the last evening before the start: steaks for the crew, liquid food for me.

I

"I WOULD WANT TO BECOME A LEGEND!"

RACE ACROSS AMERICA, PREPARATION

It was one of those sunny days that I love so much. I walked with my crew to the beach at Oceanside, a drink in hand, and goosebumps running down my spine. It was RAAM time again—time to implement what I had been training for months.

I'm known and recognized in the ultra-cycling scene, but in Southern California, where the Race Across America begins, only a few people know me or my accomplishments. We went to a bicycle shop, "I don't know who you are," the salesman said when one of my crew suggested, against my will, that a special cyclist was standing before him.

I had to grin and was a bit embarrassed. "I'm racing RAAM this year," I replied. "That's this long bike race across the US. Actually, I've done it before and have even won a few times," I understated, in hopes that no one engaged me in a typical American "Yeah, good job!" kind of conversation. So close to the start, I wanted to spend the short remaining preparation time in peace with my team.

No, I'm not famous, and I like to stay away from situations outside of my professional life where I could be recognized. And yes, I admit that I feel very comfortable in Oceanside. My homes are in the little village of Kraubath and Graz, Styria in Austria. But Oceanside, California and Annapolis, Maryland sound familiar. I don't think of myself as a star. I'm just following my passion: to go as far as possible and as fast as possible by bike. I am glad that I have become a role model and a "star" for many people, but my attitude to myself hasn't changed as a result.

At RAAM, I am one who continues and strengthens the Austrian tradition. In 1988 Franz Spilauer became the first winner from outside of The USA. He inspired Wolfgang Fasching, who won in 1997, 2000 and 2002. Fasching was my first big role model. Later, Jure Robic ushered in a new era of ultra-cycling. Since Robic's first RAAM success in 2004, all other winners have come only from Slovenia, Switzerland, Germany or Austria. No American has won since 2003.

The Race Across America receives the attention it deserves in Central Europe due to its top performers. While almost every sports enthusiast in Austria knows of this race, in America it leads a shadowy existence. Once a year for two maybe three weeks, it is on the minds of its fans and of the public in those regions where the participants come from. But that too is peripheral. In the USA, RAAM is light-years away from major sports such as American football, tennis or NASCAR. So it goes without saying that in the US, ultra-cyclists who race RAAM do not get the attention they deserve.

RAAM is not a therapeutic US vacation, where you get to know the country and its people, riding through the most beautiful places in America. On the contrary, to successfully compete in RAAM means to spend the whole year with it. I think and act, I sleep and dream, I train and eat for RAAM. I live RAAM.

This race is so much more than a few words can say. The facts are clear: The Race Across America is some 3,089 miles (4,900 kilometers) long, with up to 110,000 feet (50,000 meters) of altitude gain, and it goes from the Pacific Ocean in Oceanside, California, to the Atlantic Ocean in Annapolis, Maryland. Its organizers rightly refer to it as the "World's Toughest Bicycle Race." Nonstop participants ride across the continent, taking breaks or power naps when they want to—or when they need to—all in less than two weeks. Racers who finish after twelve days are not listed in the official results. A rider who does not make it in less than ten days usually has no chance for a top finish position. Only one racer has ever made the journey under eight days. That was me in 2013 and 2014. There is no prize money in RAAM, and that's a good thing because it raises the opportunity to experience a fair and doping-free race. I consciously choose the word "possibility" because you can never be sure, except about yourself.

Every time the competition brings me to my physical and mental limits. I lose between 4 to 8 pounds (2 to 4 kilograms) during RAAM. This fact can be traced back to a simple mathematical calculation: one kilogram of body fat equals about 8,000 calories. During RAAM there is a deficit of 4,000 calories per day in food intake. Ideally, I lose half a kilogram of weight every 24 hours. But if it does not go well, you can even gain weight through water retention—something that I have experienced. Despite the calorie deficit, which is offset by the burning of fat reserves, my body gets enough food to function. The 15,000 calories I need daily are equivalent to thirty plates of spaghetti. Conventional food intake is, therefore, a physiological impossibility, and would also cost valuable time—the clock is always running during RAAM. My physical strength is therefore kept alive by liquid food, while my sports doctor keeps records of what I have taken. The amount and timing of food intake isn't my choice—my crew chief decides. My participation in my calorie intake is limited to choosing the flavor of the thick drink: chocolate or vanilla.

RAAM is a mentally challenging and gruelingly monotonous affair. It's all about turning the cranks steadily and forcefully, day after day, night after night. After 48 hours the body begins to feel the lack of sleep and efficiency decreases. The mind rebels, then I experience phases of disorientation and hallucinations begin to form in the convolutions of the brain.

This is the amount of food and liquids you would theoretically need for a day on RAAM.

Once, in an interview, I said that the key to success in Race Across America was in the noiseless two-way radios and that I have the utmost respect for the winners in the 1980s and 1990s who did not have these valuable tools.

The radio is my connection to the outside world. My outside world in RAAM is my crew, which I trust unconditionally and whose instructions I follow without discussion. From the outside, I'm the focus around which everything revolves. From the inside, I'm part of a team, like the racing driver in Formula One, who needs his mechanics to plan and execute the pit stops, develop the strategy, and keep an eye on the entire race to make important decisions for the driver.

All year long, I live RAAM; I train hard following a precise plan. Regardless of whom my toughest opponents might be, I want to be in top form, I want to arrive at the RAAM start with certainty that I will be able to finish the race quickly. What good would come from sitting in the saddle for hours or days longer than necessary? Why would I waste time at the time stations shooting photos and signing autographs? Yes, I live RAAM, but still, I want to get out of this bubble as soon as possible.

I am constantly connected to the crew through the Terrano ™ radio communication system.

Different bikes help me with the task: I have an aerodynamic bike for the long flat sections in Kansas that go on for hundreds of kilometers. A time trial bike can really be an advantage there. I have the right equipment for the passes in the Rocky and Appalachian Mountains, which is a much lighter road bike, that I change to depending on the route. Watt is the unit of measure of energy expenditure per period of time. At RAAM, I achieved an average of 164 watts during my record run of 2014 over 183 hours, which corresponds to 16.4 miles (26.4 kilometers) per hour.

My team usually consists of two mechanics, a sports doctor, a physiotherapist, three drivers for two cars and an RV, a photographer, a cook, a cameraman, and a media officer. But everyone is much more than what their job description says. We are all "Team Strasser," and we all have the same goal—namely to get from west to east as fast as possible—with individual and team tasks. My only duty is to pedal. Everything else is taken care of by my team. Not only do they feed and inform me, but they also light up the road and look for the next resting place at night. The team keeps me awake and amused by asking me questions or giving me arithmetic tasks. When they need to, they yell, "Stay awake!" through the speaker, followed by honking the car's horn if they see that I'm about to fall into instant sleep. My team reads me email or Facebook posts from friends and fans from the homeland, they tell jokes, play the music I like, or they drive ahead, stand by the roadside and do the "wave" when I pass.

Without my people, I would be quite lost.

But many of us know the challenge of putting together a working team, be it in a sports club or in another professional environment. This beautiful quote from Antoine de Saint-Exupéry is valuable, inspired, and yet, does not go far enough:

"If you want to build a ship, do not drum up men to get wood, assign tasks, and divide up the work, but teach the men to long for the vast, endless sea."

Mere longing is not enough to ride across America as fast as possible. It takes knowledge and experience, communication, and crisis management to succeed. It takes an overwhelming faith and will to achieve the goals set. The first priority each year is to reach Annapolis. When I won in 2014, I relied on a team with a combined total of 42 RAAM appearances—a priceless level of experience. A year later, with a partially new crew, the subconscious played a trick on us: some probably thought a bit arrogantly, that "Team Strasser" would only have to compete to get the victory. But, it turned out differently: I fell short. We all fell short.

Teams are not thrown together in the US, but found and shaped during the months prior to the race. There are team meetings where everyone gets to know each other better in preparation of what is to come later: eight or nine days under extreme conditions and in confined spaces. The race is not only a challenge for me but also for each of the crew members. The day/night barrier is lifted and sleep schedules change to go with a crew member's assigned shift. Their food intake may be more diverse than mine, but certainly not healthier. The follow cars must be cleaned every day or they will turn into moving garbage dumps. As if all these challenges are not enough, factor in everyone's own character and personal quirks. Welcome to RAAM!

The fact that I have no women on the team has nothing to do with sexism; it's purely practical. It's about sleeping situations and toilets, but it's also about cockfights between the boys and flirting with the others. There is also another aspect: women, I feel, tend to be more empathetic and compassionate, especially when someone is feeling bad. In these moments, I especially do not need coddling or sympathy, but instructions and support, because everything else distracts me from the actual mission, namely, to guide me across the USA as fast as possible.

Team meeting in May 2017

One day in the spring of 2014, I sat with my team in the garden house of my parents in Kraubath and we all discussed the upcoming task: the Race Across America 2014. Our team leader, Rainer Hochgatterer, who had mentored me since 2011, questioned me about my motivation. As usual, I practiced understatement, talked about a possible victory, about the importance of staying humble and of doing my best.

21

Rainer grinned. He knew that his questions irritated and provoked me. And then he cracked me hard, "If I were you, I'd want to become a legend in my sport."

It's so easy to get things straight to the point.

Rainer is the person I owe the most to during my ultra-sport career. As my sports doctor and team leader for years, he combined the two most important functions of my crew, which meant that possible conflicts could not occur. There would not be an instance in which the doctor pleaded to not finish the race for health reasons, only to have the team leader disagree, as had actually happened in my first RAAM.

Having someone like Rainer by my side gave me confidence, motivation, and perseverance. After my record race in 2014, which I finished in 7 days, 15 hours, 53 minutes, he wrote me a humorous message: "Didn't we agree to shoot for 7 days, 12 hours? I think you should try a little bit harder next time." There is a grain of truth in every joke, and I understood what he meant. He was saying," Do not rest on your laurels, you have not achieved everything. "

At RAAM 2014, he led me and all of us to success, but I sensed that his thoughts were not always one hundred percent focused on the race. So it did not surprise me when he announced to me, with a heavy heart, that he was no longer available in the future.

Seven RAAM races—once with Fasching, twice with Gerhard Gulewicz, four times with me—was enough for him. He set new goals in life and wanted to spend more time with his family. As much as his departure hurt, it was still crucial for my future career. Rainer Hochgatterer had become a kind of father figure in my athletic life. Having to part from him was an important step in my personal development.

My entire team and I realized just how significant he was when he sent us all an e-mail three weeks after RAAM 2012. We'd finished second behind Swiss racer Reto Schoch, in an emotionally charged and frustrating race. And Rainer asked the question whether we felt ourselves lessened by our defeat, whether we had feelings of lost value. To "undervalue" in sports is a very daring statement. The results list is fact. One can still cite so many explanations, excuses, reflections, but still, it is unchangeable. But he brought our emotional status to the point: "The victory at the RAAM belongs to Austria, to Styria. The victory at RAAM belongs to Christoph Strasser," Rainer wrote, and in my mind, I saw all my teammates nodding at these lines, just as I did.

A mere three weeks after a Race Across America, which had led us all to our physical, mental, emotional limits, Rainer began to motivate us for an event that would take place in about 340 days:

"In 2013, he should again take back the victory. And in a manner that has never happened before, so that the opponents do not even come up with the idea to attack him."
"With our help, Christoph can ride a time of well under eight days at RAAM."
"And I mean well under eight days."
"If you add up the best stage times in 2011 and 2012 and still include the usual sleep breaks, he could complete it less than seven days and twelve hours!"
"I believe in it, I'm sure, I promise he can do it; with our help. I think we should immortalize him, we should make Christoph immortal."
"So what do you say?"

There are so many motivational speeches that can produce an impact, but yet miss the hoped-for result. The words of Rainer Hochgatterer went directly into my heart. And I sat on the bike for a training session 340 days before the next RAAM.

"What would it mean to you in the big picture to complete RAAM?" a cycling friend asked me, as I first toyed with the idea. He wasn't sure what would motivate me to take on something so hard, so monumental.
"I do not know," I answered. "It would be cool though, right?"
That was at a time when I was torn between my humble approach to being satisfied

with what I had and what I was, and my ambition to become a really good cyclist. When I met Wolfgang Fasching at a training seminar in 2004, he talked about RAAM and about mental strength; I presented myself in the introductory round as one who "maybe one day will attempt the Race Across America." Three years later we sat together at an interview for an Austrian sports magazine. Fasching was about to end his career and I was about to follow in his footsteps. It was the first time we could talk at length, and it was the beginning of a friendship that continues today.

I am often asked what it takes to participate in RAAM again and again, and what I still want to achieve there—if I am out for records. The reality is somewhere in the middle, but above all, I love this sport, the "Weitradlfoan," or "far-biking" as I call it in my Styrian dialect. I love cycling and adventure. But the answer is also simple when I'm asked about victories and records: it feels good to be the most successful or the best athlete in a discipline. No athlete will ever deny this fact, not even me.

> Personally, it's not primarily about records. To be honest, they are not really important to me. Of course, I would like to win the races, but in the preparation time, this prospect as motivation would not be enough for me. Achievements are ultimately the result of doing that which fulfills you every day— because only then are they even possible.

The Race Across America still kindles a fire in me, along with the will to work even harder, to keep improving myself and to learn from my past mistakes. If this will and the hard work are then rewarded with a victory, then, of course, it's all for the better. But the joy of a victory disappears quite quickly. What remains is the joy, the zeal and the hard work that led me to victory. Nowhere else but RAAM does the sentence apply better, that the journey is the goal. It's a damned long journey, twelve months earlier, under the finish arch in Annapolis, it all starts over again. Because one thing is clear: the harder I train in advance and the more meticulous I prepare myself, the easier it will be for me later in the USA. However, if I am inconsistent in the preparation time, shorten training and make myself more comfortable and take things easier, I will lose it in the race because I will be all the more challenged by the difficulties of competition: the wind, the weather, the physical issues.

"You have it easy as a professional, you can train all day and you do not have to work," I sometimes hear from cycling colleagues struggling to bring their family life, work and training under one roof. I do not agree with this perception. Yes, it is easier to organize your day flexibly around the training. But somehow, it is too often overlooked that I am in a sports discipline where there is no prize money. Sponsors cover expenses. I need lectures at institutions and companies to generate sales and a well-running online shop for cyclists. All this means a lot of organization and work along with the training. The assumption that I'm just sitting on the bike and will be royally rewarded is wrong.

Cycling is my life and I make my living with it. My dedication and fire for the Race Across America is compounded by the fact that it is part of my livelihood at this stage of life. If my livelihood or career depends on it, giving it up is simply unthinkable. If the sense of achievement remains, to which the professional life also depends, the drama of a defeat is greater. If it's just a costly hobby, life goes on as normal. When it comes down to it, who wants it more, the one for who ultra-cycling is a hobby, or as in my case, the one who depends on ultra-cycling success to make a living?

At Oceanside, nobody questions my motive to do the Race Across America. Even if not everyone recognized me, I was pretty sure that all 170,000 inhabitants knew what RAAM was. After all, it starts on the Oceanside Pier, built in 1888; at 1,942 feet (592 meters), this is the longest wooden pier on the US West Coast and thus a monument in itself.

In the Race Across America, each participant receives a start number that lasts a lifetime. These number designations are assigned in succession: the original "founding fathers" were John Marino, #1; Michael Shermer, #2; Lon Haldeman, #3; and John Howard, #4. Pete Penseyres, whose record stood for 27 years before I broke it in 2013, is and will always be #11.

Were he still racing, Franz Spilauer, Austria's first winner, would now be wearing #66. The great Seana Hogan was assigned #161 back in 1992, and still proudly wears that number today (yes, she's still racing!). The great Jure Robic raced with #273. The American, David Haase is #288. And me, I was assigned #377 at my RAAM debut in 2009. Ten years later, the numbers given to the 2019 rookies are in the 600's. The days before the RAAM start are characterized by hectic pace and activity. The organizers finalize the Route Book, which in great detail shows the nearly 55 Time Stations and the route the participants have to follow meticulously.

My team organizes all the materials that might be needed for our long trip: cables, tape, tools, bike parts, water, food and so on. At our rented house in Oceanside, the necessary radio and communications components are installed in the rental cars.

Preparing the rental cars in Oceanside before the race.

The cars also get speakers and auxiliary lights, and roof racks for the bicycles and the RV are readied for use. In the evening we sit together for dinner and discuss the last tactical details. Incidentally, there is no dinner for me, I change my diet to liquid food three days before the start, so that my digestive tract is already used to the race menu.

Of course, the 14-day acclimatization includes light training rides. It's not so much about getting the finishing touches or increasing my fitness even more—I spent a year preparing, and if I did not make it in that span, the last two weeks would not be able to improve anything—but rather, acquainting myself with first sections of the route and with the prevailing weather conditions.

Like every top athlete, I also take a break from my annual training schedule in the fall. In November, the first kilometers of training begins, and over the winter, the eight-month-long build-up becomes really hard and intense. Winter in Austria means that it is storming and snowing, or that it is raining and slippery. That's why I sit on my ergometer six days, and usually well over thirty hours, a week.

Since I have set up my training room so that I can also telephone and work while doing my physical activity, sometimes I find that these long periods of endurance work are not so bad. I'll pass the time watching skiing, tennis at the Australian Open, or watching music videos. But the training plans also include many high-intensity tempo or force intervals that push me to the limit. Often, I am completely exhaus-

Heat acclimation training before RAAM is very important in enduring the desert heat of the first days of the race.

ted in the evening and not of much use anymore. Besides the race, I pedal about a thousand hours a year on the bike—which equates to just over thirty thousand training kilometers.

It may sound paradoxical, but if I had to describe the hardest moments of RAAM, then it is these weeks in winter. It's snowing outside, in the morning my legs hurt from the work of the past few days, and I'm alone with myself, knowing the plan today is once again seven hours on the stationary trainer. Only when it's dark outside again will I get off the bike. For that, I need all my motivation. Sometimes I have to fight with myself to endure this life every day. But I know that I will only do the best at RAAM if I go through this training. In the spring, the training shifts more and more outdoors. I meet up with my training colleagues again and the fun factor increases enormously. The weeks go by insan ely fast as the RAAM start moves closer and closer.

From the moment I start RAAM, there are finally no more questions, no thinking, no brooding, no decision making. Everything has already happened by that moment. A year full of meaningful questions, full of self-motivation, full of Aufbäumen (picking myself up)—and sometimes laziness full of a guilty conscience—is already behind me. All questions have long since been answered: Is the team prepared well enough? Am I technically well organized? Is the bike alright? Did I do everything for the sponsors and start the media work? Is everything thought of and are all the thousand puzzle pieces in the right place?

When the starting signal comes, it is all about riding, kicking, fighting and digging deep. The question of meaning is clarified, the team is there. There will be phases in which, because of exhaustion, I almost fall off the bicycle, knees buckling, my butt burning like fire, my toes falling asleep, my fingers becoming numb, my tiredness clouding my mind. It may happen that my head is buzzing, my skin is burning from the sun, my stomach is rebelling, my gut is crazy and I get diarrhea. But there is no more discussion. The task is as clear as nothing else in life: no matter what comes, continue until the finish line is crossed.

As a reward, there are periods when I get intensely into the flow, where endorphins flood my body and I almost cry with happiness when with my team, we overcome all the difficulties. Before every RAAM, I know that I will experience sunrises like so-

Winter training & multi-tasking: During these indoor rides I do some of my organisational tasks by working on the computer while also preparing myself for RAAM.

mething from a picture book, get motivating messages, and serve as a role model for other people.

This race has its ups and downs, but in the end, the positive always prevails. That's the appeal of this mix of adventure and competition. In my mind's eye, I see myself entering Annapolis, visualizing the last kilometers and meters, and feeling the emotion of standing under the RAAM finish arch. I look forward to it. My team is ready to go.

#longdistancecycling #trainhard #roadtoraam #raamfever #raceacrossamerica #jawui

One more night of sleep, then it starts!

24-Hour race in Fohnsdorf, Austria, 2003

II
"WELL, JUST TRY IT."
BREAKING THROUGH, 2002 TO 2007

"How far behind me is he?" I asked my crew.

"Way too far, go on!"

"But we agreed ..."

"You are controlling the race now!"

"But ..." I was not sure what to do, and my team just gave me strict instructions. To some extent, I was too shy to shake off Marko Baloh.

"Keep riding! Full throttle!"

I pedaled on as instructed. I did not wait any longer, though I thought I was breaking a deal: my competitor and I had agreed on a common approach and I no longer stood by it. The Glocknerman 2007 became a triumph for me, and a success I did not really want to happen the way that it did.

Was I afraid of winning? Perhaps.

I had done everything in advance of the competition to be in contention for the Glocknerman, the ultra-cycling marathon world championship. In the previous years, I had made a name for myself in the scene with my results in smaller races. I had worked according to my own training plans (meaning "many miles"). I also worked with mental coach Thomas Jaklitsch on important personal issues, like whether I want to make my living from cycling or how I could positively shape my life and my sport. I had already qualified for the Race Across America, and all doors seemed open to me.

Not only was I psychologically and physically prepared, but I also presented myself coolly, almost casual, at the starting line. In past years perhaps, I stood out from the others with my deliberately chaotic and unprofessional appearance that I played up. But now I put emphasis on projecting a more coherent overall image. I had designed my cycling jersey myself and placed the logos of my sponsors Wiesbauer, Specialized, Panaceo and the local bank from my home town of Kraubath. My motivation was fueled by the presence of a camera crew from groox, a small Austrian video production company, who wanted to make a movie about my Glocknerman. While we were not sure if a DVD was going to be released, or even who would be interested in the story, I said with a hint of skepticism, "Let's work on it first, then we'll see."

Interview with "groox" shortly before the Glocknerman start in 2007

The Glocknerman is a cycle race over 627 miles (1,010 kilometers) long, with 52,493 feet (16,000 meters) of climbing. It leads from Graz through Southern Austria and back. The most difficult section of that race is the loop over the Iselsberg Pass, the Felbertauern Pass, and the highest mountain pass in Austria, the 8,218 feet (2,505 meter) high Grossglockner High Alpine Road, which has to be ridden two times, before heading back to Graz, the capital of the Austrian state Styria. It is one of the toughest events extreme cycling has to offer. The event, which takes place every year in early June, is one of Europe's oldest ultra-cycling events. Even though there are lots of other competitions that are longer, more demanding, have more entrants, and are more prestigious than "Graz-Glockner-Glockner-Graz," it is referred to by the organizers as a "World Championship," (which is kind of a strange declaration, but nice for marketing).

The race started in Graz around noon, with the Slovenian, Marko Baloh, as the declared favorite. Another Slovenian, who would have been an even bigger favorite, was absent: Jure Robic had just done the Race Across America (and won it for the third time in that year). But there were other prominent faces on the scene, for example, Thomas Ratschob from Switzerland, the Turnowsky twin brothers, and Franz Preihs from Austria.

The pace of the competitors was extremely high from the start, and it felt like a criterium race. The number of riders in the leading group melted quickly. When we climbed the Glockner High Alpine Road for the first time, Baloh pulled away, but he could not defend his lead over me and I rejoined him. "Marko is just human too," I thought to myself as I watched him fight. Still, before the start he had been the one I had thought was likely to win. Over a 24-hour period, The Slovenian had a lot of experience and world records, and for that duration of racing was probably the best in the world after Jure Robic.

"We're being chased by four pursuers," Baloh told me, "I think it would be better if we worked together and continued together."

I was surprised and honored. I thought it was crazy that he suggested this tactic to me! I gladly agreed. I was sure that it would be an advantage for both of us.

We rode the beautiful, high-alpine Felbertauern section together, but on the second Glockner round, I pulled out a lead of three minutes on Baloh. Thinking of our agreement, I waited for him—just as he also slowed his pace when I had to take short breaks twice for gastrointestinal problems. Although we were not consistently at our performance limits, we'd calculated that our chances were good to break the course record set by Swiss ultra-cyclist Daniel Wyss.

Glocknerman 2007: Marko Baloh and I on the climb to the Grossglockner High Alpine road

But we did not reach the destination together. On the ten percent steep climb to the Soboth, the Slovenian's strength seemed to have left him, and this time maybe for good. I felt tied to the deal with Baloh, but at the same time, my supervisors spurred me on, "Keep going. Go on!"

"How far back is he?" I asked.
"Too long to wait," they said. "Get going!"

As an ultra-cyclist, you are committed to yourself and your team. I let myself be infected by my crew's will to win and despite my bad conscience over Marko, I pressed harder and harder on the pedals, hid my fatigue and pain, and again gave it my all. I almost escalated into an ecstatic state that resulted from a combination of euphoria on the one hand, and the fight with my bad conscience on the other. For the last 62 miles (100 kilometers), I put a hundred minutes on Marko Baloh. My winning time of 36 hours and 19 minutes, was four minutes faster than the course record and made me the most recent ultra-cycling marathon world champion to date. In the Glock-nerman, drafting is allowed, unlike almost any other endurance race, and because I had been riding together with a competitor for much of the route, I still felt relatively strong after all my efforts to reach the finish—just past midnight on the second day of racing.

At the award ceremony, we looked each other in the eye.

"Sorry, Marko," I said, honestly.
"Don't worry, you were better today," he answered. Baloh was, and is, a great and fair sportsman. Unfortunately, he has never managed to win the Race Across America, even though he's deserved to win it.

By the way, the DVD, the one that we were not sure should be produced at all, sold hundreds of copies and the groox company became an integral part of my crew.

Three years later I was back at the start of the Glocknerman. The Race Across America was not on my calendar for the season, mainly due to economic reasons, so I had looked for other challenges. The Ultra-WM not only delivered a prestigious title in this case but also took place on my doorstep. Even though the race distance and altitude were the same, it's hard to compare the 2007 race with that of 2010. From the beginning, we racers had to fight bad weather; on the high alpine road not only were there high snow walls to our left and right, but we also had to suffer through sleet.

My tactic was clear: I did not want to waste energy or attack unnecessarily—I'd wait until the really dif-

Wow, I can hardly believe it. What has happened in the past few hours has been incredible. I had been working very hard right from the start, always keeping up with the pace of the lead group, although I knew that my pulse was at redline on the first three mountains. But I knew that the others were also on the limit and were about to break. The fact that I was doing so well, in the end, was a matter of mental ability and a firm belief that I could race to victory.

ficult climbs. So I stayed in the front group during the descent from the Felbertau-ern. But, on the first ascent to the Hochtor, the highest point of the Grossglockner High Alpine Road, there was no stopping me. From that moment, I only looked forward; what happened behind me was no longer in my focus. My crew could tell me if anything important was happening behind me. And their news pleased me: within one climb I had put ten minutes between me and my first pursuers.

Obviously, my comrades had to fight not only with my pace, but also with the cold, and their fatigue in the night hours.

As important as it is to set realistic goals and plans for your own actions, it is also important to anticipate what else can happen. When my three-man crew and I stopped for a while at the Grossglockner summit and I put on an extra thermal jacket for the downhill, we discussed our options regarding the speed we needed. I could wait, conserve my energy and then catch up with the others to attack again in the second round. Or, I could do the remainder of the race, some 550 kilometers, solo, risking wearing myself down in the wind and being caught by a cohesive chase group later. My supervisors, Christian "Scheb" Schebath, Jürgen Gruber, and Roland Stuhlpfarrer, thought as I did; the second option was better. I'd take short breaks, or better still, no breaks, and keep my highest concentration for the remaining 20 or so hours. We agreed that we wanted to do it this way. My condition was strong enough to gamble on me riding the remaining miles solo.

The trio, with whom I wanted to win the second world title, was as well-rehearsed and as ambitious as me. When I noticed at the end of the race that I was always handed

Winter weather at the Glocknerman 2010

the bottle by Jürgen, I also realized that the three colleagues had never had a driver change and Scheb was behind the wheel the entire time.

"Are you crazy?!" I asked. I was bothered by the risk the team was taking.
They laughed from the car. "That's why we did not tell you. We knew you'd just get excited."

Teamwork works when everyone knows what he has to do and can do. My job was to push as hard as possible on the pedals. I didn't I draw up a timetable before the Glocknerman and distribute precise tasks to the three supervisors, nor could I. I knew that I had people with me who were always up to the challenge. While on a descent from the Grossglockner in the middle of the night, a marmot ran across the road and I had to suddenly slow down from 44 miles (70 kilometers) per hour to half that speed, they reacted perfectly and avoided a collision. A descent from a high alpine road is challenging enough in daylight—at night it becomes a dangerous balancing act.

Cyclists and their follow car crew must be able to form a unit, to be able to judge and estimate speeds. Without the light of the follow car, I would be flying blind. Nevertheless, the car—with obliquely adjusted auxiliary headlights—must be steered to one side, so that in the event I need to brake hard, or I fall, an even greater calamity doesn't happen. Incidentally, I had encounters with animals again and again. Once, at a training camp on the Italian Island of Elba, a wild boar family crossed in front of me. I was going 37 miles (60 kilometers) per hour and was too perplexed to slow down in time. Fortunately, I slipped through between the mother and a piglet, which was good all around. Avoiding a crash is always good—no one wants injuries or damaged equipment. But in this case, avoiding the baby boar was vital because mother boars become very aggressive and protective of their babies. Imagine being down on the pavement, scraped, dazed, and possibly injured, and then having an angry mother boar come after you with her teeth and tusks.

One night, a mighty stag stood in my way on the Race Across The Alps (RATA) and only moved leisurely aside at the very last moment, when I had already seen the crash in my mind's eye.

Our strategy to go solo was working well. When I arrived at the Hochtor for the second time, my lead was just over an hour. The racing that followed on the way back to Graz was perfect. Although Gerald Bauer and Franz Preihs worked together behind me and ultimately finished second and third, I was able to extend my lead on each section. With very short breaks, loud music, and lots of caffeine, my lead at the end was two and a half hours. I was happy about the win, congratulated the two runners-up and waited for one of my best friends the next day after I was feeling human again. Alexander "Lex" Karelly was, and still is, a fixed part of my crew as a photographer, but our collaboration had a side effect: he too became infected with the cycling virus. He participated in the 2010 race and battled through the wind and weather, in between having a fun time and enjoying the experience. His last hours of the Glocknerman were torture. He suffered so much knee pain that he had to push his bike up the Soboth climb, then cranked part of it with only one leg. He managed to finish just one minute before the cut-off. We hugged with tears in our eyes at his being the last rider back to Graz—he earned 10th place. To understand how Lex is put together, all you have to do is remember this anecdote: Instead of celebrating a tenth place at the "World Cup," he preferred to enjoy the self-irony of being the "lanterne rouge," that is, the last place rider. Yes, only ten riders reached the finish goal within the allotted time, and he said with a laugh that he was proud to be the slowest finisher at Glocknerman.

Looking back changes the value of things. The two Glocknerman triumphs are not the most important ones in my career, but they are two competitions I do not want to forget. Every competition, every training, brings new stimuli, impulses, and experiences. The Glocknerman twice presented me with special challenges and prepared

At the finish of the Ultra-Cycling Marathon World Championships

me for the times after. In 2010, I was exposed to external pressure that I had not experienced before. "You set a new record already," I was told. "You only need to pick up the win." Statements like these upset and annoyed me. So much can happen with a continuous load of over 36 hours—knee problems, stomach upset, a fall, a technical issue with the bike. And yet, there are people who babble on as if I had already won.

If I could see a positive side of the pressure in 2010, which I did not like at all, it was this: At this time, I did not yet have a single win in the Race Across America, only one DNF ("did not finish"), but still, I was already recognized in the ultra-cycling scene.

But don't misunderstand my meaning. It is not my conviction that someone becomes a better or happier person just because he achieves success. On the contrary, I belie-ve that if someone is too focused on achieving the goal, he may lose sight of the real importance that comes with the journey to reach that goal. Reaching the goal satisfies only for a moment. The way to my goals—the daily work I put in—satisfies permanently... and makes me happy. My quest for making a name for myself in ultra-cycling began in 2002. I had just completed my year as a civil servant in a nursing home in Knittelfeld, had stopped playing football (my first sporting passion), and concentrated entirely on cycling. I commuted between Kraubath, my hometown, Leoben, where I tried to study, and Knittelfeld, my workplace, which was all within a radius of about 25 miles (40 kilo-meters). As a 20-year-old, long-haired, environmentally conscious world improver, my bike was my favorite thing, and my longest tour had been from Leoben to Villach and Salzburg to visit with university friends and enjoy a few cold beers. After a necessary rest day, I rode the 147 miles (236 kilometers) back to Leoben.

In Fohnsdorf, Styria, a 24-hour competition took place in those years, even attracting some big ultra-cycling names. The star of the event was local hero Wolfgang Fasching, who had won the RAAM in 2002 for the third time; he'd also won in 1997 and 2000 (and had landed on the podium in each of his eight RAAM's). He probably considered the event in Fohnsdorf to be a training session under competitive conditions, or perhaps since he was racing on a 4-person team, it was just for fun. I also wanted to compete with three friends as a team, but that didn't matter because two withdrew. The entry fee was 35 euros—not a small sum considering it represented more than ten percent of my monthly salary. And so, I opted to race solo.

24-Hour Race Fohnsdorf 2002, 2003, 2005, 2006

There I stood: with long hair under my baseball cap, legs unshaven (unusual in the bike scene), wearing a T-shirt, soccer shorts, and running shoes. I brought the mountain bike I had gotten from my grandfather for my confirmation and the others just laughed at it. I wanted to be different from those whose bikes flaunted luxury. I did not like swimming with the current—those who seemed to place less emphasis on intrinsic value and more on having a thick wallet. To have good, expensive bikes, I'd have to work more and have less time for training, I thought. I said to myself, "I am holding up a mirror to them through my demeanor and my approach," and I felt morally superior.

My attitude changed over time. Also, I have realized that good racing machines do not necessarily speak of a bad character. Nevertheless, I felt comfortable during this time because I wanted to pursue a cool hobby and not be part of some ostentatious scene. To put it bluntly, I wanted to blow the others away with the shabbiest, simplest bike, and with my unconventional looks.

This was not possible in Fohnsdorf in 2002. I completed 261 miles (420 kilometers), which meant ninth place, though I surely would have done better had I not taken six hours of sleep breaks. Wolfgang Fasching passed me a few times, but out of sheer cowardice, I did not even dare to say hello.

I remained faithful to the 24-hour competition in Fohnsdorf until 2006. One year after my debut, I managed 62 miles (100 kilometers) more and finished seventh, having reduced my number of sleep hours to two. A few months later my parents gave me a road bike as a birthday present, and at a student party in Leoben, I met two people who were to become my first cycling mentors.
Daniel "Hufi" Hufnagel and Johannes "Johnny" Reiser are Styrians like me and members of small cycling clubs. At that party, we started talking and I was grateful to them

for inviting me to train with them and to explain a few basics to me. Until that time, "basic endurance and interval training" were foreign words for me, and I was unclear on what I should pay attention to in my diet. I went with them to the training camp in Lanzarote in 2005, where we put in six hours a day on our bikes, where of course, my two friends were always faster than me.

In Fohnsdorf, I had finished third the year before, riding 373 miles (600 kilometers), and climbing 19,685 feet (6,000 meters). With this result on my sports resume, I applied to the race organizer for a starting place at the Race Across The Alps. This is a race of over 326 miles (525 kilometers) and 44,783 feet (13,650 meters) of climbing; it goes over 14 alpine passes and is referred to as the toughest one-day race in the world, due to the terribly steep and numerous climbs. When I sent the email from an internet café in the Canary Islands where I was having a training camp on Lanzarote, I assumed that I would not be granted an entry. But when I unexpectedly received the approval, I was astonished and even a little bit desperate. "What should I do now?" I asked Johnny.
He grinned, shrugged, and told me in his pragmatic way, "Well, just try it."

Life can be so easy.

In Fohnsdorf, things went better from year to year; in 2005 I finished second, in 2006 I won with 416 miles (670 kilometers) and 22,309 feet (6,800 meters) of altitude gain. That was 150 miles (250 kilometers) and 8,202 feet (2,500 meters) more than on my first start.

Until a few years ago, I was the youngest participant to finish RATA. In 2005, I finished in 14th place after 27 hours and 32 minutes, and as a 22-year-old. I was already breaking down the myth that ultra-cycling was just something for older athletes with years or decades of training kilometers. I found myself confirmed in my little rebel world. Here was this "young savage," parked in the paddock with his rusty 1978 camper van who flaunted himself with a touch of flippancy, and who had begun to keep up with the fastest.

A LANDMARK PODIUM FINISH

Because I was, in principle, the youngest participant not only at RATA but also elsewhere, I was also noticed at the 24-hour Kraftwerktrophy in Theiss, Austria. It was there, that I not only first met Jure Robic and Marko Baloh, but it was also the first time I competed with them. And just a year later, in 2006, I was third with them on the podium; Robic and Baloh had crossed the finish line hand-in-hand, and so were both credited with first place, with me in third. That was the biggest moment for me as a cyclist so far; the two Slovenians were the measure of all things and their feats seemed absolutely unattainable. Being on the podium next to them felt like a victory.

The result in Theiss was trend-setting for my career. From that moment on, the ultra-cycling world knew that "there is the Strasser." As a result, not only did I feel joy and satisfaction in my work, but I also saw the opportunity to make a living from it. I stopped going out to have a beer or two, as I had been regularly. I became more professional and incorporated myself into the ultra-scene by appearance and deed. And it was possible for me to get my first carbon bike and get excited about getting my first sponsors. At the company Wiesbauer, which supports me to this day, I was even able to negotiate getting an additional bonus for a victory at the 2007 Kraftwerktrophy in Theiss. Although that event was canceled, I succeeded in others.

At the RATA, I finished sixth with Hufi, who brilliantly mastered his one-time trip to Ultradium. It was also the race in which I first got into a conversation with Wolfgang Fasching, who took second place. At this time, I had already met him at one of his lectures, and my inhibition threshold had dropped in comparison to Fohnsdorf 2002. And over the years, we got to know and understand each other better.

Another event from 2006 has remained in my mind: in Kelheim I won the 24-hour race. My brother Philipp, then 14, and my cousin Michael "Kougi" Kogler, 17 at the time, came along for that race. They were not mechanics or experienced crew, and they did not have driver's licenses. So I was at the wheel when we drove in that morning. After we had positioned the ice chests in the paddock, with the racing food consisting of cereal bars, polenta, rice waffles, and the usual sugary drinks, the starting signal was fired at 14 o'clock. Twenty-four hours, 472 miles (760 kilometers) and 27,230

Jure Robic and Marko Baloh both won the 2006 24-Hour Kraftwerktrophy
(they crossed the line hand-in-hand) with me finishing in third place.

feet (8,300 meters) of climbing later, I was at the finish with a performance that was
a new track record. "Keep me awake," I'd told them as I sat back behind the wheel
for the drive home. We had not gotten very far when I realized that I was fighting off
one microsleep after another. At a highway rest stop, I slept for half an hour, then we
went on relatively safely. The trip to Germany had shown me that even though I was
getting better and better as an athlete, it was time to make my environment and my
nutritional strategy more professional.

At times, I am asked if I am addicted to cycling or if I traded a possible past addiction
for another. It is known that some sports greats have had drug problems or an un-
settled life before their sporting career, and then broke out of these circumstances
through their sport—the sport, therefore, taking the place of the former addiction.

RATA 2005

24-Hour Kelheim, 2006

In my teens, I was not addicted to alcohol, drugs, or sports. I was probably a very ordinary teenager, who liked going to parties and my coming of age had certainly led to a beer (or two) too many. Is this addiction or a natural testing of your own limits?

Where my excessive athletic ambition originates from, I cannot answer. My parents did not do much sport and never forced me to achieve athletic goals. They gave me a free hand in choosing what to do with my free time, whether it was sports, or whether I wanted to go out and celebrate on the weekend. Instead, they taught me a healthy lifestyle and demonstrated to me that the realization of one's dreams requires careful handling of money and diligence. I am thankful for this freedom because it has made me a reasonable and responsible person. Since I was allowed to live my life, as an adult, I had no need for parties or alcohol excesses. I experience my intense moments on the bike.

I do not consider cycling as an addiction. I live my greatest passion with energy, commitment, motivation and an iron will. That may seem like an addiction to many from the outside, but it is not. I can live well even without my bike. I love the training-free time of the year, in which I'm able to relax a little and shift down a gear.

When I discovered my irrepressible passion for cycling, I soon found out how much more satisfying it was to be able to start a training ride or head out for a mountain tour at 5:00 am, rather than falling into bed at that time, exhausted after a night of celebration.

Cycling is a big part of my life. My biggest passion was making a career out of it, and I've put a lot of time and energy into this job. Nevertheless, I do not want to go so far as to equate this extreme passion with an addiction, something negative, harmful, and uncontrollable.

In any case, in 2007, I could not get enough of cycling and racing. Only two weeks after the Glocknerman, the duel with Marko Baloh, and the discussions with my crew, I took part in the Race Across The Alps. It was a phase in which I thought I was almost immortal, and I wanted to prove myself every month: in Schötz in Switzerland, in Kelheim, in Hitzendorf in southern Styria at the Kainachtaltrophy, at the Glocknerman, and at the RATA. I kept up with the fastest at that race, ultimately staying below the 23-hour mark at 22 hours and 59 minutes, taking second place 14 minutes behind Austrian, Rene Fischer. Ten years later, a time under 23 hours would barely bet enough for fifth place. In 2017, Robert Petzold from Germany needed less than 21 hours (exactly 20 hours, 40 minutes) to win. It may take some time, but sooner or later, the RATA winning time will start with "19".

Jure Robic and me at the 2009 Race Around Slovenia

III
"YOU WILL WIN RAAM SOMEDAY!"
THE RACE AROUND SLOVENIA

I finished third in the 2007 Race Around Slovenia, and had even more cause to celebrate: I'd qualified for the Race Across America. What a cool outcome!

It was love at first sight: cheering people on the roadside in every small village, groups of 30 to 40 people at each time station, and at the checkpoints where the participants have to come by and sign in. This race features a long course with so much climbing, plus an additional special challenge: the starting time was between 9:00 pm and 10:00 pm, which meant you would start the race at a time when you would normally go to bed, but then have another two nights of staying awake —at least if you have thoughts of winning or making the podium.

A second night at the RAS is like a seventh night at the Race Across America. You start RAS at night and then try to do the second night without sleep; In RAAM you begin with power naps earlier.

> Such a great start to the season is immensely important. Now I have less pressure to succeed, the media and the other competitors have become aware of me, and I can be loose and relaxed at the start of the next competitions.

What's more, the former RAS was the home race of Jure Robic, the dominant racer of the international ultra-cycling scene of his time. The man from Jesenice, Slovenia was one of my role models. He was the epitome of strength and perseverance, winning nearly every race he attempted except for his first RAAM. This surrounded him with an aura of invincibility, which was enhanced by his appearance as a major in the Slovenian army. But I dreamed of competing on an equal footing with him, knowing that I really would not have a chance. How could I accomplish something that not even Wolfgang Fasching had done? He, too, had been unable to win in head-to-head duels with Robic.

"Do you think you could beat him?"
Amazed, I looked up. Rainer Hochgatterer and I had met in spring 2008 in a coffee-house in Judenburg, a small city not far from my home village. I was looking for sports medicine support and he had been recommended to me by Wolfgang Fasching. He was an expert and insider, had cared for Fasching at the 2007 Race Across America and was part of Gerhard Gulewicz's crew in 2008 and 2009.

Rainer did not want to work with any athlete who would be satisfied to merely push through to finish a doubtlessly tough race. He wanted to spend his time with riders of character who had the goal of victory. And I wanted a doctor on my team who encouraged, supported, and challenged me, and not one who would throw in the towel for me at the first sign of weakness.

"Who will win RAS?" He asked.

Thoughtfully, I stirred my coffee. "I'll ride for victory. If I did not believe that I could win, then why would I even compete?" I said in a confused voice, perhaps not fully convinced of my own words, but aware that they were the ones he wanted to hear. Hochgatterer laughed. I had passed his first test before our collaboration had even really begun.

We fit well together and we stayed together until 2014—seven long years.

Even though we celebrated great moments of success together, our collaboration began with a second place that bore the weak taste of near success, but at least I was closer to Robic than the other competitors in that race. Jure Robic led, but on the second night, on the flats of the Slovenian-Austrian border, which I knew very well, I reduced the gap from around 60 minutes to 14. 800 kilometers were behind us, 350 still ahead. The local hero and his team seemed to get nervous. After all, Robic's crew watched me at sunrise to verify how I was doing. I seemed to be on a wave of euphoria, and broke in just at that moment in which the Slovenian struggled out of his temporary low and moved away.

My frazzled nerves finally broke completely, over one of the few mistakes in the route book. After taking the momentum of the last stretch well into the first hours of the new day, and continuing to make up ground on Jure Robic by my average speed of over 18 miles (30 kilometers) per hour, a big surprise came first for the entire crew and then for me as well: a supposedly short but steep and strenuous climb turned out to be a full-blown mountain.

The climb had not been correctly marked on the elevation profile for this stage in the route book. I could not mentally adjust to it, and this can mean failure for a rider so close to the edge physically and mentally, and especially for one who lives focused on goals. This unexpected challenge coupled with sleep deprivation was more than a small setback. I could handle it with the utmost difficulty, but the physical fatigue and overall tiredness after about 40 hours without sleep pushed my limits—and Jure Robic was able to extend his lead again.

Hochgatterer did not know me that well at the time, nor did I know him. But in Slovenia, I realized that he was the man who would always find the right words for me. During a break, he held my face in his hands, looked deep into my eyes and said, "You're doing great! And do not forget: the others are going through the same things. I saw Fasching and Robic at RAAM and these guys suffer the same way. You are not weaker than them, each one of you is going through tough times!"

Sixty-two miles (100 kilometers) from the finish, I was one hour behind Robic and the chase was over. Robic would not falter; he increased his pace again in a final show of power. We realized that trying to chase him down no longer made sense. Accepting that a set goal can no longer be achieved is a sign of strength, not weakness. This was a learning process for me and my team. Nevertheless, the missed victory bothered me.

Almost 43 hours after the start in Postojna, 736 miles (1,185 kilometers) and about 45,930 vertical feet (14,000 meters) later, I completed the loop. I was two hours behind Robic and my first reactions were of disappointment and sadness. I was so close and yet so far away from beating him! But then, legitimate joy prevailed. I had planned to improve my previous year's results at the RAS and was successful in that regard. I had fancy stuff from my sponsor Specialized, and an improved, liquid food-based diet concept. I caught Marko Baloh on the climb to the Vrsic Pass and shook him off in a technically difficult descent to Kranjska Gora. Except for Robic, all the established riders stayed behind me and I was able to confirm my previous season's results. And, I was also able to prove my musical talent. When a karaoke version of "Märchenprinz" by the group EAV boomed out of the loudspeaker of the follow car, I bellowed along.

Rainer Hochgatterer, Markus Kinzlbauer, and Markus Vogl did a great job and had a busy time during the one and a half day long race. On top of their support duties, they had to disassemble and reassemble all of the electronics of our sound and lighting system. The next day, after the initial disappointment over not winning had faded, above all, I felt appreciation and gratitude.

I can only say that I am overjoyed. It's just wonderful to be able to do what you love and be supported by everyone—be it my partner Sabine, my family (who even waited for me this year), my support crew, and all my friends and fans. Only then, are successes possible, and that's why you can enjoy them and be happy. And for that, thank-you!

I did the Race Around Slovenia a total of six times. I could not win as long as Jure Robic started. In 2010, we were at the start; it was very cold and rainy, and winter had reported back for this early May event. Every minute, another athlete rolled off the starting ramp, which was built in the main square of Postojna. In the minutes while we waited for the start, we racers were sheltered from the weather in an underground parking garage, just below starting area. While pretending to be calm and relaxed, we leaned on our bikes, made small talk, and sized each other up. General nervousness was clearly noticeable in the air. A thermo-jacket, leg-warmers, and over-shoes provided my protection from the cold. Many of the other 70 participants were dressed even warmer, ignoring the limits of aesthetics. Robic was conspicuous. The professional soldier wore a sleeveless vest over his short-sleeved jersey—the weather could not harm him. I was impressed.

During the race, Rainer Hochgatterer handed me his personal down jacket and his mountain jacket, and I admit that I would not have made it without them. Slovenian Army Major Robic won, and much later, after just under 47 hours on the bike, I finished four hours behind him. The attrition rate was 60 percent. Among those who had given up were top riders such as Marko Baloh, Franz Preihs, Eduard Fuchs and the Swiss racer Thomas Ratschob. One racer even ended up in hospital with hypothermia. Robic himself had toyed with the idea of packing it in. That was one of his toughest races, he later said—only once, at a RAAM, had he been so close to the limit.

RAS 2010: Winner Jure Robic was the first to congratulate me

Robic was already a role model for me; at the time of this race he was already a 4-time RAAM winner, and just five weeks later he took his fifth win. His performance in Slovenia solidified his position in my mind as someone to emulate. And besides, he was a nice, good guy—before the start and after the finish line, at least. But as soon as he got on the bike, whether in training or competition, Jure Robic was a fighting machine. He was one who did not look back and did not care how the other riders might fight to beat him—none of that concerned him. He simply rode on and let his legs demonstrate his dominance. Robic had spent his life fighting for the recognition of his father, never received that praise, but continued to fight for it. Born in 1966, he had experienced Slovenia's struggle for its independence, and for the rest of his life, embraced his country's mentality of fighting for freedom. At the zenith of his career, he allowed other riders to come closer, and could finally show his softer side.

I had been just about to get off the bike myself. Because of my lack of sleep, I had slight hallucinations and anxiety. I felt haunted. I almost wanted to smash my bike. My crew found the right words, at the right time, and somehow we managed to turn my aggression into pedaling and I continued.

At dinner in the hotel, the day after the race, he even invited me to his table and we ate together from his plate because he had ordered too much. We exchanged stories, discussed the race,and laughed at the funny anecdotes of our crews; we were both so grateful for their support. At that moment, the hardships of the two-day nonstop tour took a back seat.

I ignored that my whole body was still aching, muscles stiff, knees slightly swollen, fingers numb, and eyes red.

Nor do I ever forget that gesture of respect and fair play he had shown me in 2009, when our backup car had temporarily broken down. Robic instructed his crew to send one of his two cars back to hand some bottles to me, so that I could continue. However, because we lost our way three times that year and had also been given a penalty, I fell short of my expectations and took fifth place. Robic's attitude towards me as a competitor was overwhelming. That, along with his reputation for fair play, made me want to emulate him as I progressed in my career.

RAS 2009: The water bottle from Jure Robic

I was already registered for RAS 2011, eager to compete with him again, on his territory, and in a country where I was valued for my regular participation and good performance. "If you beat him," I told myself, "that's the biggest thing you can do. In 2008 and 2010 you have already finished second, in 2011 you are taking it!"

Then I received a message from a good friend of the organizing committee of the Race Around Slovenia: "Jure Robic training crash—dead."

It was September 24, 2010, and I do not remember today how long I looked at those five short words. I had fallen into a state of shock. It could not be. Robic dead?! Incomprehensible!

Facebook already existed in 2010, but at the time, I was still aloof about social media. So I searched online and found the information, in Slovenian, that I was looking for. While riding his mountain bike downhill on a gravel road in the forest near his house, Jure collided with a car being driven up the forest road by a local man who was out to cut firewood. Robic always trained as if he was in a race. Was he taking risks or had the driver been drunk? The answer did not interest me, and it was never publicized. Robic, the seemingly superhuman fighting machine, the human I had adored, was no more. Thousands of people came to Krajnska Gora, Slovenia for his funeral on a sunny, warm autumn day—half of them on bicycles, in cycling jerseys and wearing helmets. We all wanted to pay tribute to him, the dominator of the ultra-cycling scene. We all felt the same: we were shaken by the tragic loss. I looked into many familiar faces and met people with whom I was connected to through cycling. The many people expressing their deep sympathy once again made me realize what Jure Ro-

The climb to the Vrsic Pass

bic meant to Slovenia. I cried. I could not believe the loss and knew that ultra-cycling would not be the same without him.

There is nothing worse than having to accept condolences from those present at the funeral of a loved one. When it was my turn, Jure's partner Helena hugged me and whispered in my ear, "Jure has often told me about you. He said that he likes you and that he is sure that you will win RAAM at some point." I thanked her, said goodbye later, and walked home sadly, emotional and confused. My eyes were still wet and my heart was heavy. I still heard the voice of Helena in my ear. Jure Robic, my idol, had trusted me to win the Race Across America. I was honored and flattered, and at the same time afraid of failing this mission and disappointing him.

With the loss of my idol, and the challenge of beating him now gone, a sense of emptiness spread over me. "Does it still make sense to be in the RAS?" I asked myself. For me, it is better to race in an event with the strongest guy and only finish second behind someone like Robic, rather than choose other races with weaker racers and take a one-sided win. "Am I not doing the event and my competitors profoundly wrong if I'm fixated on Jure Robic?" I had convinced my sponsors that the RAS was a top-rated event, which was true. To make a comparison from the winter sports: RAS is like skiing's World Cup Downhill races, which attract all of the top racers. RAAM is more like the World Ski Championships, the biggest race a skier can win, but the field is limited to four racers from each county, so not all of the top racers are there. Meaning, RAAM is more prestigious than RAS, but for various reasons (financial mostly) not all of the top ultra-cyclists are able to participate.

Since my paternal grandmother comes from Slovenia, I also understand some of the language and have a special connection to this beautiful country. I was at every start since 2007 as a young, easy-going Austrian who courageously accepted the challenge of competing with the Slovenian stars. So I could count on the support of a community of ultra-cycling fans, who believed that I could succeed Jure Robic—that I could be the next dominant winner of RAS. But the legacy of the superstar who died about eight months earlier, was hotly contested. A handful of athletes were thought to be capable of winning: Marko Baloh for example, Eduard Fuchs, or Thomas Ratschob, and me. The "usual suspects," so to speak. It was clear that in a poll on the possible winner, I would not have received one hundred percent of the votes. There were at least two camps: Baloh's, and mine.

The fan enthusiasm was enormous. The RAS 2011 was both a big party and a Jure Robic memorial race. In addition to the grief over the passing of the nation's cycling hero, there was a certain tension and anticipation that the monotony will come to an end and that there would be a new winner. "Jure, I want you to be proud of me," I thought at the start, and I left no doubt how seriously I meant that. Right from the start, I immediately took the lead and rode as the solo leader through "Robic Land" on the Vrsic Pass, and through Kranjska Gora, the mountain ascent near Robic's home that he loved to use for training. I found my trained rhythm, balancing food intake and performance. My bike and body formed a unit, and I used the mental advantage,

"I love this race, I love the DOS (RAS),
I want to win for Jure Robic."

the "mental tailwind" you get when you're at the top of the field. In such phases you hardly feel the effort, pain is hidden from the conscious mind and you seemingly effortlessly roll toward the goal.

I defended my lead until late into the second night. Sleep deprivation then became apparent, but on the way to becoming a legitimate successor to Jure Robic, I refused to take a break. When sleep deprivation becomes too intense, memory and judgment diminish, the mental state becomes unstable, and hallucinations occur. The flow was past, and Robic's words seemed to fade.

Jure's words, which Helena had shared with me at his funeral, accompanied me.

The solid white line that separates the two lanes of the roadway, I thought, was un-rolled toilet paper. I told my team, "We have to make order here." This project was hopeless, however, because I realized that I would never manage to roll up kilometers of toilet paper. A little later, my memory reminded me that I had been a bicycle messenger in Graz (and that was not a hallucination), so I asked myself and my crew, "Where is the package?"

My people did not understand. "Please, what?"
"Well, the package we have to deliver. Where do we have to bring that to?"
"What?!"

Hallucinations come and go. They do not require answers, if answers don't come up. I kept pedaling, until I started looking in the various pockets of my jersey for the car key to my old camper bus...

It was not an easy night, not for me, and not for my crew. I was getting slower and starting to weave. Each descent became a suicide mission. A sleep break had become inevitable. Baloh passed me. Another break was needed. Ratschob passed me. After an hour of sleep, I woke up and looked around in bewilderment, trying to understand the situation and sort myself out. My crew stood in the parking lot, talking calmly and having cigarettes. At that moment, I realized that I would not win RAS. That would be Baloh. But this realization did not bring anger and disappointment; it brought relief. My experienced crew was no longer in racing mode, which made me realize that the race was over for us.

I realized that the top shape I was in was no guarantee of success. For the RAS and then in Slovenia, I had built up so much pressure that I wanted to force triumph with a crowbar. We failed. But only after the crew had taken it easy was I also relaxed, and able to hold onto a third place finish. Perhaps this circumstance was related to my fundamental attitude of not wanting to disappoint the people who are there for me.

I had to wait another year. On my last participation in the RAS in 2012, we acted smarter, I put in two planned power-naps of 20 minutes each, did not give in to fatigue, and completed the second fastest Slovenia round trip of all time.

From a purely sporting point of view, this was my best competition so far. Throughout the race, there were only a few situations in which I did not have full pressure on the pedals. Marko Baloh, who is known as a fast starter, took off a few minutes in the beginning, but after crossing the Vrsic, the outcome of the race was likely determined. If you cross this point of the race as the leader, the chance of winning is very high.

RAS 2012: On the way to the long-awaited success

The second night my crew was tactically perfect; we had the courage to take breaks in time to prevent the terrible hallucinations.

At the finish, Baloh was two hours and twenty-five minutes behind me. The Swiss racer Simon Ruff secured third place in front of Severin Zotter (of whom there is still much to tell). My finish time was scratching at the 40–hour mark, and my average speed was just under the 30 kilometers per hour sound barrier.

Only one racer had reached that number five years earlier, but even faster: Jure Robic.

I have been working for six years on this victory and am very proud now. I have been close to it several times, but my efforts have never been enough for full success in Slovenia. I am extremely satisfied and happy with the victory, but more important than the mere result is the way my team and I completed the race—no penalties, and no technical or physical problems.

The big moment has come: the start of the Race Across America

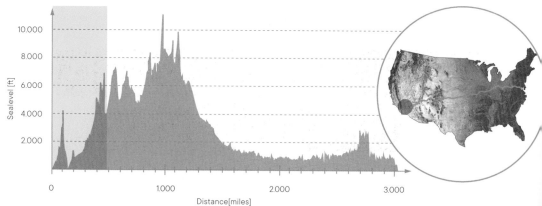

Sealevel [ft]

10.000

8.000

6.000

4.000

2.000

0   1.000   2.000   3.000

Distance[miles]

IV
MY BUSINESS CARD, HIS STICKER

RAAM, TIME STATIONS 0–8

"I want it, I can, I may, I'm worthy – RAAM win 2011" Always on mind: My goal for RAAM 2011

Gerhard Gulewicz's vehicles all had stickers reading "8:16," referring to his target finish time of 8 days, 16 hours. Gulewicz wanted to be on target after second-place
finishes in 2009 and 2010; he came back in 2011 wanting to be first. "I'll race RAAM
until I win it," he had once said in an interview, and I had wondered about this statement. The Race Across America is a competition, the victory is not given in turn to
those who try it again and again, but reading between the lines of Gulewiczs statement, I saw the hope that he had. Those who take part in the RAAM have had to
qualify, and whoever wants to win RAAM must be the fastest between the west and
east coasts. There are no gifts. Interpret it as you like, but my compatriot did not lack
self-confidence. He apparently also took The Gospel of Luke into account; from Luke
8:16: *Nobody lights a candle and covers it with a jar or put it under the bed. Instead,
one puts the light on the nightstand so that all who enter will see it shine.*

In 2011, Slovenia's Marko Baloh and Gulewicz were the declared favorites. A few
months earlier, five-time RAAM champion Jure Robic, my role model and idol, had
died in a training accident, and that same duo became the crown princes of RAAM.
For me, 2011 was my second participation in the race. In 2009, I had DNF'ed due to
health problems. As I strolled through Oceanside and chatted with my crew, I wanted

to emphasize that my plan was to stay healthy and get through it. If I could manage that, then I could also expect to be at the front. The most prominent ultra-cycling race in the world had once before shown me my limitations, so I was modest and humble. Nonetheless, I was not scared. My team's mood was good. I left the big talk to others and wondered how someone could set a certain finish time without knowing what to expect on the route or what the weather would be like. In my heart, I hoped to put Gulewicz in his place. It seemed to me that he believed that he only had to cycle through the USA in order to win, and that attitude was alien to me. Also, I had not forgotten that in 2008 he had mimicked my circumnavigation of Austria and had not completed it, but had greater media response than I. However, the psychological warfare before the start of the race was limited. We had booked the same motel, but we each went our own way.

The pier at Oceanside is always busy, but especially on the day that cyclists are sent on a journey across the continent. In the starting area racers and support teams, family members, fans, interested spectators, onlookers, and artists are bustling. There are obligatory hugs with other participants; we wish each other all the best. I stand with my team for the last time in a circle, we clap and we hug each other. These are rituals that I do not want to miss—moments in which I want to give a great deal of responsibility to others, knowing that I'll rely on them unconditionally.

Once again, there were these same but important moments. Some took pictures, others asked for permission to take selfies, others asked me for photos. An older cyclist with a white beard, a flag headscarf, a bare chest and "stars and stripes" shorts caught my eye.

The US flag is ubiquitous across the states. She hangs from every other house, in many shopping centers, and often entire boulevards or avenues are adorned with her. I've seen many tracts of land that look dirty and miserable, dwellings that need a major refurbishment, but the flags all seemed new or at least freshly washed. I have nothing against patriotism—I am a proud Austrian. How the flag and anthem are worshiped in the US, however, I find a little exaggerated. Before each RAAM, the national anthem is sung; at other major sporting events, it is an indispensable part of the program.

RAAM 2017: Relaxed mood before the start

"Oh say does that star-spangled
banner yet wave,
O'er the land of the free
and the home of the brave?"

The Race Across America begins with the last notes of the US national anthem. The tension increases, nervousness is present, but above all, it is fun to ride through a tunnel of fans.

There is no mass start; technically, RAAM is a time trial with racers departing at one-minute intervals. On 15 June 2011, I left the start at 15:57, five minutes ahead of Gerhard Gulewicz, and seven minutes ahead of Marko Baloh. My goal was to stay as long as possible in front of my compatriot, ideally the entire race. I did not know when we started our journey that it would play out the way that I'd hoped, but I only saw Gulewicz at the start and then again at the awards banquet in Annapolis.

The first seven and a half miles (twelve kilometers) are ridden neutralized with an escort of bike guides who take participants out of Oceanside on a wide bike path. There is no passing in this neutral zone and a rider's speed can't go over 20 miles (32 kilometers) per hour. Everyone is allotted twenty-four minutes for this section. If they go faster, then they need to wait at the end of the parade zone until this time has passed. Thus, the initial minute interval between the individual ultra-cyclists is maintained. RAAM does not forgive any periods of weakness, but the final outcome certainly will not be decided in the parade zone of the first few miles. At the end of the bike path, it reaches College Boulevard and the race is on.

"Good luck!" I called out to another racer whom I overtook a few kilometers after the start of the real race. That is the least I wish for others, but if I know the rider, then several pleasantries are changed. The rider, to whom my "Good luck!" was addressed, only nodded and sweated. We were on the first climb of RAAM, and already here, about 3,055 miles (4,900 kilometers) from the finish, I saw competitors suffering. The road climbs like a parabola on the outskirts of Oceanside. The four or five cyclists in front of me seemed to be standing still rather than moving.

For many, this account of the early miles may come as a surprise, just as I felt like I had entered the wrong movie when I first saw it in 2009. Before my first Race Across America, I had images of long, boring, flat, straight roads in my head. We had made a training trip that first year and when I rode the first section, and suddenly stood in front of this twelve percent grade, I asked my companions in disbelief, "What's that there? "What have I gotten myself into?"

This climb spoils the otherwise very positive impressions of the first hours of RAAM, as the route leads through avocado and orange groves. The vegetation is colorful and thriving, it smells good and it is fun to ride. I also always see other cyclists there, not just race participants, but also locals and tourists on bikes. But the US is not a "country of cyclists." Once outside of California, the bike is no longer a popular means of transportation. If all goes well, I won't see any of my competitors on their bikes anymore and the only cyclist that still exists in my perception is me.

It would take too much to describe all the key moments of a Race Across America. RAAM is one big challenge. The three climbs with a total of 4,900 feet (1,500 meters) in altitude before the first Time Station at Lake Henshaw give a first taste of what to expect.

Next is the so-called "Glass Elevator." In 10 miles this spectacular descent drops 3,626 feet (983 meters) down into Borrego Springs. Some have compared the views

RAAM 2014: Leapfrog support in the first ascents to Time Station #1

on the descent to those seen on one of those glass elevators that some builders put on the outside of high-rise buildings. With an average grade of eight percent, the winding road is extremely wind-prone due to the prevailing thermals. I carefully rode this technically demanding section in the last few days before the start and learned that in one of the long curves there is a tailwind, and the speedometer shows 50 miles (80 kilometers) per hour.

A turn later and the wind comes from the front and slows me down to 18 miles (30 kilometers) per hour. It's the toughest descent in the entire race and I've only been on the road for a few hours.

In 2014, German Stefan Schlegel crashed on the "Glass Elevator." I had just overtaken him when his front tire blew out; he crashed into the guardrail and was thrown back onto the road. Had he gone over the rails he would have fallen down a 300-foot (100-meter) scree slope. Schlegel was fortunate enough to only suffer bruises and abrasions. Moments after he stopped tumbling, he was helped by my crew who had been driving behind him. My crew stayed with him until his own crew arrived. It was a good outcome from what could have been a tragedy. Stefan was able to continue and reached the finish. But his accident had once again shown me how unexpectedly fast a RAAM can end.

The first miles of RAAM lead through vegetation that is much like we'd find in Central Europe, with pleasant temperatures in the mid 70's (25). After the "Glass Elevator," about four hours have passed since the start in Oceanside. It gets twenty degrees warmer in twenty minutes. The higher the temperature, the lower the performance, as the body uses much more energy to cool itself. This twenty degrees of air temperature increase results in a higher heart rate—up to twenty beats per minute more.

"Downhill you do not win the race, but you can lose it," they say. Might be. However, if I dig deep and work hard for every minute of a climb, I should not then lose that time by riding too slow on the downhill. That's my motto when I think of the Glass Elevator. That's why I ride downhill in a particularly ambitious way.

In 2011, I was spared the worst of the heat. I rode through the Mojave Desert at sunset and through the rising full moon. The thermometer was only 95 (35) that year, and yet it was pleasant compared to the conditions I endured in later editions. In 2015, after just 62 miles (100 kilometers), the heat hit me, my performance faltered and I suffered from cramps. On top of that, I could not drink any liquid food and my hormone balance went crazy. The antidiuretic hormone (ADH) is responsible in our body for controlling the water balance. ADH causes increased retention of water from the primary urine, thereby concentrating the urine and decreasing its volume. But, if it comes to inappropriate stress due to excessive disbursement of ADH, then this leads to a low fluid excretion via the kidneys because the body wants to protect against dehydration. The water accumulates in the body, which in extreme cases can lead to lung problems and edema if the fluid intake is still high.

Especially at the beginning of a Race Across America it is important to find the right rhythm. Physical fitness is one side of the coin, and without optimal preparation, there is nothing to gain. On the other side, is the mental component. Anyone who says that he is not nervous at the start—driven by anticipation, curiosity or fear of uncertainty—is only fooling himself. RAAM is a very special race, which is why the body's tension and the racer's thoughts are different than usual. So in those first few hours,

The "Glass Elevator" descent to Borrego Springs is a highlight of the race.

The cheering of my crew is very important for my motivation.

there is a risk of getting overanxious, going too fast and passing the competition too quickly. This is the classic problem with this race: to have to perform at the limit and at the same time make sure that you do not spend too much.

It's not just the heat, the nervousness, or the competitors that make the first 620 miles (1000 kilometers) of RAAM so challenging. At the beginning of the race, I and all of the other riders are riding alone. My motorhome has to take a different route to Borrego Springs, and only after that can it be available for me to use. What's more, the follow cars, which leave 300 yards (274 meters) behind me at the start, must also take other roads for the first 25 miles (40 kilometers). For this reason, I have to carry tools, in case I have a mechanical issue with my bike that I would need to fix myself. It is also important that I know the way or at least have it stored in my cycling computer. After all, it has already happened that a participant has lost his way, become dehydrated and had to give up at the first time station.

I'm used to my crew driving behind me in the follow car. But in the toughest race in the world, there are different rules for the first 1,300 miles (2,000 kilometers). The most important of these is called "Leapfrog Support," which means that I can only be assisted by my crew four times an hour, only from the roadside, and only from 7:00 am to 7:00 pm during the day. This prevents the formation of a motorcade behind

a RAAM racer. My team has to drive ahead, park the car on the side of the road, and hand up water and liquid food as I ride by. This scenario keeps repeating itself until after Kim, Colorado. Leapfrog Support wears me down. I want to be entertained, listen to music, feel the support of my people, and know they are nearby. My first challenge in RAAM, is thus, to survive the first day and to be glad that my team will be with me during the night—from 7:00 pm to 7:00 am. After Leapfrog Support is over, I have someone to complain to about how bad I am feeling and how hard the race is again this year. Before that, I have to deal with myself and my problems alone. One of these problems is that the situation will not change for three days.

As stringent as the daytime Leapfrog Support rules are, the nighttime rules are just as strict. These say that for reasons of protection and visibility, the cyclist may not ride a single yard (meter) without his follow car. That's why Team Strasser has a few basic rules: Before the start of the night, the car has to be gassed up, and food and drinks are to be purchased and stowed in the car. Every crew member must have been to the bathroom, because at night, we have to be able to drive twelve hours without a single stop.

When the Leapfrog phase is over, before assisting their rider, a crew must take the current traffic situation into consideration. A support vehicle may only impede two or more consecutive cars for a maximum of two minutes. Caravanning is prohibited and will be punished.

Statistics show that nine times out of ten, whoever reaches Congress Time Station 6 first, will win RAAM.

There are 54 Time Stations in this race; one of the most important is number six. After just over 370 miles (600 kilometers), the route climbs through from Salome to Congress, Arizona.

This checkpoint is run by The Bullshifters, an Arizona bike club, and is one of the most well-known and hospitable of the race. It is in front of the Sierra Vista Motel—the smallest motel in Arizona with only four rooms. The Bullshifters put up a temporary pool for participants and their crew; they put out snacks and drinks and also offer Wi-Fi service.

Now the route changes, the flat desert landscape changes to mountainous climbs. The time trial bike, which I've used since 2013 after passing Borrego Springs, will be replaced at this point by my climbing bike. And the next key point is Yarnell Grade. The earlier you get there, the better, because then this 6-mile (10-kilometer) climb, with 2,300 feet (700 meters) of elevation gain, is faced in the cool morning and not in the blazing midday sun or in the afternoon heat.

On these sections, I already felt comfortable in 2011 because they are reminiscent of my native hilly landscape. Toward Cottonwood, there's another steep climb, followed

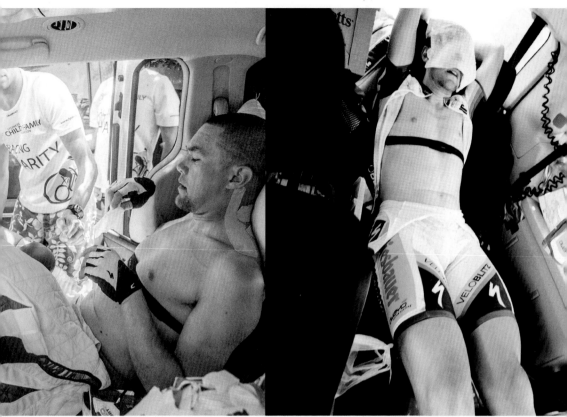

by my first power nap. As I stepped into the backseat of the follow car, my competitors came to my mind: Marko Baloh was still behind me but was about to overtake me in this race phase. But I had already left Gulewicz far behind. "It will be a tough and challenging race," my crew chief and doctor Rainer Hochgatterer told me, "So lay down, take a good rest and relax for a few minutes."

Before I closed my eyes, I thought of Gulewicz's cocky goal of winning RAAM in a time of 8 days, 16 hours. I thought of the business card that I had designed and printed for myself as mental preparation for this race. It said, "Christoph Strasser RAAM Winner." It hung on the whiteboard in my office and had been my screensaver for the past few months. Now I was thinking of actually ordering a box of cards of this design from the print shop. I placed a cool pad on my forehead and a wet towel over my head, closed my eyes, and fell asleep with a smile on my face.

Race Across Italy 2013

V
"MADNESS, ALL THOSE DEAD SHEEP..."

RACE ACROSS ITALY, RACE AROUND IRELAND

It's not like I turned away from the Race Around Slovenia after winning it. The RAS has a special meaning for me in every way: It was the home race of my idol. It was in this race that I first raced longer than 24 hours and where I earned my RAAM Qualification. It is one of the toughest ultra-cycling events there ever was, despite the manageable distance of 745 miles (1,200 kilometers). It is here where I have learned the most important lessons that have shaped me. My participation in this race alone changed me from a young, cocky newcomer to a professional athlete. And, it takes place in a country where I was appreciated and encouraged.

That I have not competed in RAS since 2012 is mainly due to one reason: it takes place in May and thus at a time when the Race Across America is not just at the door, but knocking loudly. In 2018, for example, RAS was held from May 16–20, and just three weeks later, on June 12, RAAM started.

Together with Rainer Hochgatterer, the man who designed my training plans and had been my competition coach since 2010, I decided to give up RAS. Emotionally, I made this decision with a heavy heart. But my mind told me, that in 2013 there is only one victory that counts—the one at RAAM.

Just this year, a new ultra-race was launched: the Race Across Italy. The route ran from the west to the east coast and back again, on a 391-mile (630-kilometer) route with 16,400 feet (5,000 meters) of climbing. While that amount of climbing sounds tough, the ascents were really not bad. They weren't steep and the small curves and easy downhills that didn't require much braking made it possible to get over these mountains quicker than one might assume. The start and finish were in Nettuno on the Mediterranean coast, south of Rome.

The race in Italy was half as long as RAS and was held earlier. It would be a good test for my new bike, for a new seating position, for my nutrition concept and also for the use of improved auxiliary lights on the follow car. Ultra-cycling is constant tinkering. Even if the training still has to be the focus in order to get me in top form, from a certain level, I also need to work on improving my methods and technique to be able to reach my full potential. The early 24-hour races of my career, such as the 24 Hours of Kelheim, where I won with two carefree teenage family members as crew, was a happy exception.

Although the competition in Italy was about preparing for RAAM, I still wanted to win it.

We calculated that it would be possible to complete this technically easy route in about 19 hours or less. On a time trial bike, I started last in the field, found my rhythm, and on the very first climbs—which came after 75 miles (120 kilometers)—I passed all of my competitors, that is, except for David Misch. Misch was a training colleague and a friend, and this year, also a participant in the Race Across America. He had been the first racer to leave the start. Much to his chagrin, the Viennese racer had a mechanical issue and lost time. I caught up to him about a quarter of the way through the race. He had slowed due to a broken spoke and a resulting wobbly wheel.

Misch was in the "unsupported" category and was racing without a crew. He had to provide for himself. Despite this huge disadvantage, he was one of the few who could challenge me and make the race interesting. When I heard he was in trouble due to a broken spoke and needed technical support, I sent my follow car with a spare wheel so he could continue the race. Such a favor is fair play for me and should be self-evident. I prefer to win races on the road by riding stronger, not because my competitor had an equipment problem. By sending his crew to help me after my follow car broke down, Robic had behaved equally fair in Slovenia, when it was me on his tail. So we helped Misch, at the risk of losing a lot of time myself should I have an issue and need my crew. And later, I did need my crew for myself and David had to cope on his own (which he did impressively in spite of his gastrointestinal problems, which arose when he ran out of water and, out of necessity, had drank from a stream).

The first time racing on the Specialized "Shiv" time trial bike.

In the week before the Race Around Italy, David and I not only shared a room but also our disappointment about the bad food in the hotel, a circumstance that is barely imaginable in Italy. We finally cooked using a gas stove on the balcony.

David Misch and I are connected by a long-term training partnership that has evolved over time into a deep friendship.

During a joint training trip, which also served as our route reconnaissance, David hid some packages of liquid food at a rest area so as to not to have to carry all that weight with him from the start. It was not a lot of weight, but in ultra-cycling, every gram counts!

After training together, my comrade was still working on his bike. Now, I'm not a genius mechanic, but I can handle a wrench. Misch, on the other hand, not so much. Let's put it this way: if he worked at a bike shop, he would not be the mechanic, he'd be the guy that the mechanic sends out to get coffee and sandwiches. When he mounted a water bottle cage, he was confused as to why he couldn't put a bottle in it. The mistake was soon found: he had mounted the cage upside down! We laughed for hours at this luckless, inconsequential mistake. It's probably just this trait that connects David and me; we do not take ourselves too seriously.

In the race, David Misch used his cache of liquid food and also amused some party guests when he ordered two hot dogs at a sausage stand in the middle of the night before continuing on. He finished second in the Race Around Italy, by 3 hours and 22 minutes behind me, and his performance cannot be overstated. Other racers with multi-person crews had finished behind him, including Omar di Felice, who for years has been one of the most well-known ultra-cyclists in Italy.

Night fell after the turn in Chieti at the halfway point of the race, but I kept on attacking. At the pass behind the city of Avezzano, on the border of the Abruzzo and Lazio regions, there was an impressive meteorological show, with lightning and thunder on one side, and starry, calm skies on the other.

I was well cared for by my team and realized that a target time of under 18 hours was feasible. The thought of achieving this unimaginable time spurred me on. Even on the downhills I cranked hard and took the technically easy corners at full speed. In the flat sections, I held my performance at over 280 watts and 25 miles (40 kilometers) per hour. It was a very long finish sprint to the port of Nettuno. At 3:30 in the morning, after 17 hours and 44 minutes, and an average speed of 22 miles (35.5 kilometers) per hour, we had made it.

All our goals and expectations had been fulfilled in Italy. At the same time, my performance sent a message to Reto Schoch, the RAAM 2012 winner, that I was a force to be reckoned with in RAAM 2013.

In retrospect, this upcoming duel with the Swiss was also the deciding factor that allowed me to muster an incredible amount of energy towards the end of the race. I did not just want to send a message; I wanted to intimidate Schoch—on the one hand

The finish-line arch had not yet been set up when we arrived at the port of Nettuno.

with performance, and on the other hand with the fact that I was one of the first ultra-cyclists to compete in a complete race on a time-trial bike. Before the race, I was silent about it.

I had not posted photos of the time-trial bike on social media—I wanted to have a surprise effect. I have to thank Specialized for encouraging me to take this step. Initially, I was against the use of the time-trial bike. I was concerned that its low position could cause back problems because for many years there has been the ultra-cycling motto, "comfort above everything." But after the Race Across Italy, I was sure that this weapon would be of enormous benefit and I would doubtless use it on RAAM.

The *"Braveheart"* film setting provides a brilliant atmosphere

"Madness, all the dead sheep here..." I said to my surprised crew.

My crew did not become distressed when I'd have one of these hallucination moments, although they sometimes weren't exactly sure about what to do about them. "Madness! Unbelievable!" they answered from the car.

What else should they have said?

I did not know where I was, what I was doing, why a man I knew ran up the slope next to me, and why I could hardly follow him on the bike. Eventually, I realized that it was my photographer, Lex, but not before he ran barefoot through thick brushwood and injured his legs on the thorns. In those moments when I was all alone and saw the asphalt instead of the thicket, I thought fleetingly that perhaps it had not been such a good idea to include this race in my racing calendar. These thoughts made me smile and the next few miles grew easier and easier.

In 2013, The Race Across Italy, Race Across America, and Race Around Austria on a four-rider team were already behind me. The fact that we wanted to participate in the Race Around Ireland was due to our sheer thirst for adventure. "Let us participate in an exotic race! One with lots of sheep, a lot of rain, a lot of forest and traffic on the left," I said to my crew. "That's even more exotic than RAAM!" I said to motivate them. We smiled at each other.

The closer the start date was, the more demotivated I became, eventually I reached a point where I would have liked to cancel the project. "Why torture me again? Had not I achieved enough this year? Dry Austria is certainly more beautiful than wet Ireland!" I finally explained to my people. But they did not release me from what I had committed them to. The decision was made and couldn't be reversed.

The last days before the start were three rainy days, and the word from the locals was not encouraging, "Last summer it really rained every day." Not what you want to hear before you go on a 1,367-mile (2,200-kilometer) cycling event with 73,000 feet (22,000 meters) of climbing, that is always along the wet and foggy coast! The goal was to win the race, stay under four days and perfect my sleep strategies.

The start of the multi-day race is at Trim-Castle, northwest of Dublin, which served as the setting for Mel Gibson's 1995 film *Braveheart*. The route leads north, into the Great Britain region of Northern Ireland, and west along the Atlantic, and south and east to the finishing Navan (now the finish has relocated to Moynalty). Ireland was much as I had expected: beautiful landscapes and many sheep, with quaint villages and many sheep, with impressive castle ruins and again many sheep, and, of course, rustic roads. Because it was mid-September, it was wet and windy. There were many sheep, and at times, many that I saw were dead.

I rode on narrow roads, lined with ten-foot-tall ferns and plants, and felt like Alice in Wonderland.

At night, I could not ride at the speed I would have liked, because the asphalt was bad, and steep passages with 15 percent inclines and 90–degree turns in the downhill sections were common.

Déjà-vu can also be found in Ireland. Two years earlier, I was on a training ride in preparation for RAAM. From Flagstaff, Arizona the road drops down toward Monument Valley, where there are no bends and it's easy to navigate. My RAAM photographer, Harald "Harry" Tauderer, had been behind me with a car, but we had agreed that he would go shopping in Flagstaff and catch up with me later. I had a tailwind and was pedaling up to 37 miles (60 kilometers) an hour on the mostly downhill route from Flagstaff to Tuba City. "When will he finally arrive? What is taking him so long? Why is he not here already? When will he arrive and bring me something to drink?" I asked myself after riding alone for two hours. I was getting more nervous with each passing minute. One hour went by, and then another. There had been no cell phone reception there, so each of us had done what he thought necessary. I had stopped and waited at the side of the road for a while, and then continued to ride on, after Harry did not pass me. I began to wonder if the car had broken down. When Harry still didn't arrive, I thought maybe he had overlooked me and was already ahead of me. But Harry was behind me, and after apparently being unable to catch up with me, he had turned around and worried that I might have crashed or been driven off the road. He asked gas station clerks if a cyclist had come by.

"Nope," the clerks told him, "No bicyclist." Each of us had been worried about the other, and after all, I was out there alone, without ID or money to even buy a drink. I was exhausted and finally waited at a gas station in Tuba City—the same one that is Time Station #10 in RAAM—hoping that nothing had happened to Harry and that he would find me. It was already dusk when he finally raced up the rise to Tuba City and we greeted each other with relief.

In Ireland, I also lost my team. We were going through a small town, I honestly do not remember where, when the car was stuck in a traffic jam due to some big local event that had clearly attracted a lot of people. "I'll ride ahead, you'll catch up with me later," I explained to my crew.

At the next intersection, I had forgotten about the route description, which I wanted to keep in mind, and I did not know where I was and where I should go. Also, I had only a single bottle and no cellphone with me—a classic rookie mistake. After wandering for 45 minutes and wondering if this road, or that lane on the right or left side was the right route, I panicked. A feeling of powerlessness and helplessness came over me.

The locals I asked for help had never heard of the race. Only one could remember an announcement on the radio but knew nothing about the route. A silver streak of hope opened on the horizon when I saw another crew's follow car. But the four-man team did not fare better than me, quite the opposite. They had lost their current rider. The four of them moved on hectically before I could ask them directions.

> **I was no longer in control of the situation. How could I ever find my team again?**

It is surprising in these situations, how stress and fatigue block one's ability to think analytically. I could have gotten out of my predicament immediately by displaying the GPS route on my bike computer, which was installed for just those purposes. But this idea simply did not come to mind because I always ride without navigation in everyday life, so it is not anchored in my subconscious.

To put it bluntly, I would still be stuck in this Irish village had I not tried to stop passing car drivers to borrow a phone. When a nice Irishman stopped and put his cell phone in my hand, it occurred to me that I did not know who to call. Of course, I did

83

not have the telephone numbers of my crew members or those of the race director in my head! There are exactly two phone numbers that I know by heart: that of my best friend Rene and that of my partner Sabine. I called home in Graz and told Sabine my dilemma, asking her to call my team and explain to them where I was at the fork of this and that road.

I am always happy when I see people I like and trust. But I have never been as happy as in those moments when my crew found me in Ireland. That we managed to win Race Around Ireland was the perfect way to complete this adventure. But it could have been different, very different.

In the results list of the Race Around Ireland 2013, is a person who is worth a closer look. The Italian, Valerio Zamboni, made his living by selling private aircrafts before he became sales manager for Bombardier. He lives in Monaco and indulges himself daily in his passion for cycling. Zamboni is now 65 (in 2019) and now rides in the age group "sixty plus." Because he does many races, he has also won the Ultra Cycling World Cup several times. He lives for ultra-cycling, and if the competition is not too deep, then he triumphs in the general class, such as the Race Around Ireland 2011. In 2017, he went to the Montichiari Velodrome in Brescia, Italy where he pedaled for just under 40 hours to set six indoor velodrome records in his age category. The 63-ye-

ar-old now holds the record for 100 miles (4:37:40.106, average 21.61 mph / 34.78 kph), 200 miles (9:35:41.746, average 20.84 mph / 33.55 kph), 6 Hours (127.502 miles, average 21.25 mph / 34.20 kph), 12 Hours (247.998 miles, average 20.67 mph / 33.26 kph), 24 Hours (414.895 miles, average 17.29 mph / 27.82 kph), and finally 1000 kilometers (39:53:01.74, average 15.58 mph / 25.07 kph). "This was one of the most insane things I've done in all my life," he said after.

Zamboni and I have known each other for years. Our friendship was solidified when I once spent my holidays with Sabine in Liguria and he invited us to dinner with his wife and him. There we sat in one of Monte Carlo's most exclusive restaurants, talking about our sport with pizza and wine, exchanging funny anecdotes and RAAM experiences. Valerio is a man from two worlds: On the one hand, he is the youthful cyclist, who follows his crazy ideas, who does not take himself too seriously and can enjoy his own shortcomings. On the other hand, his training is extremely consistent and extensive, and he participates in almost all possible long distance races.

When I once gave him the well-intentioned hint that he should reduce his competition calendar to focus on individual competitions with all his might and improve his time there, he answered: "I know that I actually do too many events, rest very little and can't ride so fast. But you know, I know my strengths and weaknesses. I will never win a fast and strong race—I'm not young enough anymore. I can't compete with racers like you. But I'm tough and always make it to the finish line, and for the Ultra Cycling World Cup, the number of successful finishes counts more than individual top results. The only thing I can win is this year's ranking and that's what I like to fight for." On the other hand, Valerio is a businessman who is apparently successful in his job with typical Italian charm, while not talking about money. When he is not sitting on

the bike, you'll see him with a briefcase in tailor-made suits. Sometimes, there are also overlaps in his two activities, such as the aforementioned Race Around Ireland 2011. My film production team, groox, which accompanied him for the filming of the DVD, *It's All About...Ultra-Cycling*, told me that in the midst of the race he had to get off the bike to answer an important call. He walked to the follow car and disappeared for a quarter of an hour. While getting back on the saddle, he reported that he had just sold a plane to a major customer, but now would have to continue as soon as possible—after all, he wanted to finish the RAI victorious.

Valerio Zamboni might seem like the type of entrepreneur who usually plays golf, tennis, squash or possibly polo, but he does not. The former pilot is not only looking for his limits, but also for the competition with others.

This is an aspect that I find so fascinating about this sport; I get to know a great many people, the most extraordinary personalities from all professions. Valerio sells planes.

Valerio Zamboni and me before the start of RAI

Other colleagues are lecturers at the university, social workers, or bicycle couriers.

What do Valerio Zamboni and I have in common? More than you would think at first glance. Zamboni has his wife by his side. Alessandra is unconditionally committed to what her husband does. The same applies to me with my partner, Sabine. And that is enormously important, because if partners do not share and support each other's passion or profession, harmonious living together will not be possible in the long term.

Ultra-Cycling attracts people from all disciplines. Perhaps this is exactly what makes this sport a bit more unique than others because it is made up of a conglomeration of different personalities. We all love our sport and therefore our way of life.

At RAAM 2009 I suffered one of my toughest setbacks.

VI

"DID NOT FINISH"

ULTRA-CYCLING IMPONDERABLES

It's the highs and lows in a career that make an athlete's life interesting, even though it's clearly more fun to talk about successes and triumphs.

As unpleasant as those negative experiences are in the moment, my defeats and setbacks are just as important because I know that they have shaped me, and made me the person that I am today. Any failure is a chance to improve, and a lesson to take with you. The reality of this, however, is that you face the learning process, wound your pride, and admit your weaknesses and mistakes. Those who blame others for their own failure, blame mistakes on their crew, or believe themselves to be infallible, will gain experience but will not learn from it.

You can always learn the most when you have to work through defeats. Because then, weak points are shown ruthlessly and clearly. Successes give you affirmations and strokes for your own ego, but few chances to evolve. To strive for a DNF (Did Not Finish) is still not a good idea. But, you should not shy away from a challenge just because failure is possible. The underlying risk must not be the reason for not pursuing a dream.

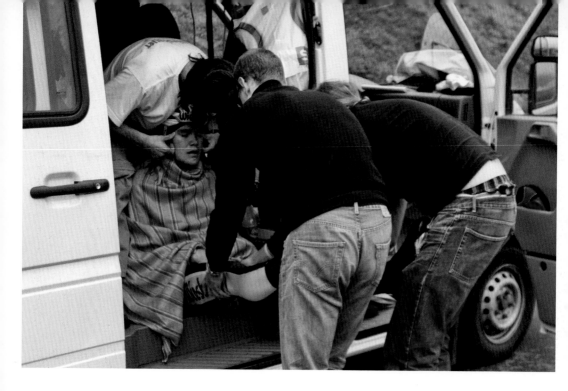

A DNF is for a sportsman, no matter the level, a maximum penalty. My first DNF was at the Glocknerman in 2008, when due to illness, had to give up in the race that I had won the year before.

It happened so fast: in 2007 I felt invincible, yet twelve months later I realized that I too was only human, and therefore, vulnerable.

It was a season of sickness for me. It started in January; I had only been home for a few days after a five-week training camp in South Africa, with my friend and webmaster Günter Weixlbaumer, when I became ill and was diagnosed with pneumonia. But I soon recovered, and did not attach much importance to what happened. Due to over-motivation and minimal rest time, I slipped into over-training and fell ill again. I wanted to defend my title from that previous year at Glocknerman 2008, just two weeks after winning the twelve-hour Kraftwerktrophy, which was held just two weeks after Race Around Slovenia. This schedule had been too intense. The small periods of weakness in the days before the start eventually developed into a feverish cold. A break of several weeks in the second half of the year was the result.

I promised myself that 2009 would be better, but my hope was not fulfilled. 2009 was a disaster on all fronts. It started with the fact that although my sponsor Wiesbauer continued to be loyal to me, their financial support had to be massively reduced due to the economic crisis. It may sound unbelievable, but in the year of my first RAAM participation, my little home community of Kraubath was my main economic sponsor.

At Glocknerman 2008, I had to give up because of fever.

I learned as a child that saving my money was the key to getting anything important to me, so I used my own savings and what sponsorship funds I had, to put together a team for my American crossing. Viktor Weinrauch was my doctor, while Rainer Hochgatterer looked after Gerhard Gulewicz, who at that time was one of the best. Gulewicz had his strongest time within my weakest years and was quite justified in not only dreaming of a RAAM victory, but also in pursuing it. I, on the other hand, was a freshman, a so-called rookie. But I did not want to come in with big talk. No one likes a boastful rookie. So I spoke of hoping to finish among the top five finishers, while secretly hoping for more—a place on the podium.

The number 377 was assigned to me by the RAAM organizers, but another number is more relevant for me: 1982 is not only my year of birth but also the year of the first RAAM. So, were we created for each other?

Since RAAM, like all other ultra-cycling races, is an individual time trial, I was one of the first rookies to roll out from the start—about an hour before Jure Robic. Shortly after he passed me, he had to stop for a shoe change on the roadside, which gave me joy and euphoria, because I could pass him back. RAAM was only a few hours old, and though I was not really first in the ranking because of the earlier start, I rode through the desert on the border from California to Arizona, in front of the sport's biggest champion. The sun was setting, the temperature was pleasant, and the sky was bathed in bright orange. From small caves in the desert sand, one heard insects chirping, it smelled of parched grasses, my spokes whistled evenly in the easing wind.

RAAM 2009: Shortly before reaching Monument Valley when I was still fit

All went well as we rolled to the east, despite the rather bumpy asphalt. My crew handed me bottles, I enjoyed the freshly brewed Bedouin tea and my vanilla-flavored liquid food.

Yes, we seemed to be made for each other; RAAM, me, and my crew.

Although all seemed to be going well for me, soon my crew and I were stopped by a hugely angry, nervous official. Let me state that I appreciate (most of) RAAM's officials. These volunteers have a tough job and most sincerely want to help keep the race safe and fair, just as the racers do. But they're human and some seem to take the job for the wrong reasons—these few seem too enamored with having some authority and lean too far into the "tough cop" approach of officiating.

This guy was clearly upset about our amber flasher lights, that the rules require to alert motorists approaching from the rear that there is a slow-moving vehicle ahead.

The RAAM organization wants the flashers to only be visible from the rear so as not to confuse or annoy motorists approaching from the front of a follow car. My crew had put tape over the front of the lights, and this modification had passed technical inspection back in Oceanside before the start. But apparently, the official thought different, which seemed to confirm the opinion of a few on my crew that some officials are more stringent with RAAM debutants.

Our tape was too thin, he claimed, and we would have to reapply it. He first briefed us on our misconduct for a quarter of an hour, and then snarled that on top of the delay he's subjected us to at the roadside, he'd also assessed a 15-minute penalty that we'd have to wait out in the "penalty box" at the final time station at Mt. Airy. Just then, Jure Robic rode past us again. I do not know if he secretly grinned and muttered the word "rookie" or if he even had me on his radar as a serious competitor at all.

Anyway, I pushed my anger aside and regained my rhythm. For a long time, I took third place behind the Slovenian and Swiss racer Dani Wyss. I overtook Wyss when he slowed down at the end of the first night due to problems with his nutrition. He developed stomach issues due to the desert heat and eventually vomited on the side of the road.

From the second day, I began to suffer, slowly but surely, but enjoyed the wondrous sunrise in Monument Valley and then the stunning scenery at the beginning of the Rocky Mountains. While the pedal kicks were slow and cumbersome, I knew that I was pushing into a new dimension of long-term stress for me. I accepted that there would be physical hardships and was not surprised by these aches or those pains. However, I also noticed that my body changed. My face and legs were a little puffed up, "This happens to many RAAM racers," I thought to myself, recalling images of RAAM veterans who had also struggled with this phenomenon.

The ascent to the La Manga Pass—the first of three passes in the Rocky Mountains at over 9,800 feet (3,000 meters) above sea level—was not too difficult, much like the two following it. These climbs have constant six to seven percent grades, which really is not so steep. The difficulty of these Rocky Mountain climbs comes from the high altitude; the air is thin, and the temperature is usually low. Plus, when I get to the mountains, I already have more than two days non-stop on the bike.

Placebo's "Black Eyed" droned in a continuous loop from the follow car's speakers. Although the lyrics had nothing to do with my own life, I still shed tears of joy as these lines rang through the speakers. I created my own mood, which could hardly be better. I was in RAAM, and was in second place behind my idol! I was not feeling well physically, but mentally I was on cloud nine.

RAAM 2009: Massive problems in The Rockies, DNF in Kansas

Weaknesses come and go in RAAM, and while Wyss recovered from his issues, my own caught me. When I suffered over the third pass of the Rockies at no more than three kilometers per hour and spewed mucus, again and again, I could hardly breathe. "My body is not working anymore," I told myself, and panic and anxiety spread.

"When we get back to the valley, when you get more oxygen, it will get better," I was told. That was not the case.

> My team doctor prescribed me antibiotics, but at the next sleep break, he diagnosed bronchitis.

We did not think about giving up yet, the strategy was that I should roll on at an easy pace. When we arrived in Kansas, I was favored by a tailwind and covered a few hundred kilometers with minimal effort. Nevertheless, this phase did not serve as a rest, because in the heat of the day my condition escalated. My mucus expectoration became bloody, the bronchitis worsened, I got a fever, and the outside temperature of almost 104 Fahrenheit (40 Celsius) at 70 percent humidity (it was one of the hottest July months ever in Kansas), were too much for my body.

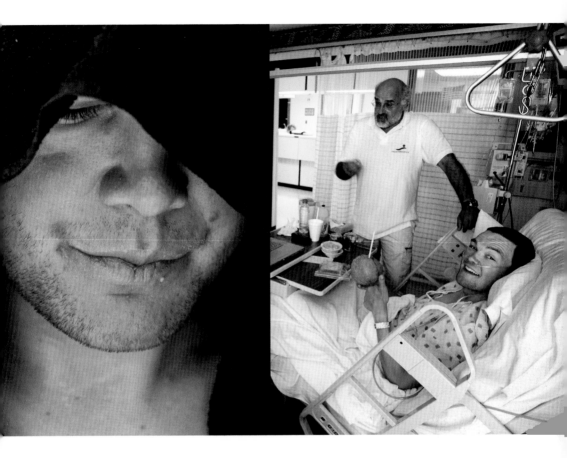

My team was looking for a motel. A 24-hour break was announced. We no longer raced for a top-ranking position. Instead, we let the race go and formulated a new goal: to just recover and finish the race. We did not want to quit the race at that moment and refused to DNF. We had a big cushion for the next cut-off at the Mississippi River, so we could easily pause for one day. But in the end, my condition did not improve. We were forced to go to a hospital because bacteria had accumulated in the damaged lung, which led to pneumonia, and I'd suffered heat stroke in the last hours on the bike.

One on my left, the other on my right, Albert, my physiotherapist, and Viktor, my doctor, supported me like a battered boxer who can hardly stand on his feet, in desperate need of medical attention. Every step I took felt like pedaling during an interval workout. My face and legs were bloated, my butt was littered with bloody spots, and now, where muscles had been seen at the start, the waistband of cycling shorts dug deep into my skin, creating an undefined body mass. In the stifling air, the dust from surrounding cornfields made my breathing difficult.

I felt like I was dying.

The Pratt Regional Medical Center is about halfway across the course. I had made it there with a lung capacity that had dropped to one-third of normal. I was given anti-biotics and cortisone for three days and I recovered. The conclusion was neverthe-less sobering: After 1,471 miles (2,367 kilometers), my first RAAM was over—with a DNF.

While my rookie RAAM ended in a DNF, nevertheless, at least I still got to see the finish line that year. We had to go to Washington, DC to return the cars to the rental company, and catch our return flights to Vienna. Annapolis is only a small detour from Washington, and unfortunately, we had more than enough time.

I wanted to be completely with me and my dreams under the RAAM finish banner. So I sent my crew away so that I could let my tears of anger and disappointment flow. It was moments like this that hurt, and yet they are so important to my relationship with the Race Across America. "I'll be back next year," I told myself, " And I won't ride here in a car, I'll ride here on my bike." In any case, I already knew what the finish looked like and was able to recall these mental pictures over the following months.

For two years, I was further reminded of RAAM 2009 by a standing order for a bank transfer to the Pratt Hospital. My three-day treatment had cost $10,000 (€8,700). Not only did I have to recover physically and mentally, but I also had to recover finan-cially. I could not cover this sum in one fell swoop, so I had to pay it off in installments. No one ever said that funding RAAM is easy.

Another racer did not reach the finish, although his motivations were completely different from mine. Dani Wyss and Jure Robic battled for days in a fight to the finish. At many time stations, the two were separated by mere minutes. The lead changed with each sleep break. It seemed the race would come down to the tightest finish of all time. Then, 80 kilometers from the finish line, at Mt. Airy Time Station #52, which is called the "penalty box" for a good reason (any time penalties accumulated during the race have to be served here).

Robic had arrived at Mt. Airy just a few hundred meters ahead of Wyss, which was not nearly enough to overcome the 60 minutes he'd amassed in penalties. His first was a 15-minute penalty for "inappropriate behavior at the start." Moments before being called to the start ramp to begin his race, he'd stopped and peed on a beachfront garden plot, in full view of a police officer who wanted to arrest him. Fortunately for Robic, the chief of police, city officials, and the RAAM owner and race director were there. When the officer saw them all shaking their heads "no," she relented, and Robic was allowed to start, instead of being hauled off. Another 15 minutes was assessed when he passed another rider on a freeway—the rules state that on the freeway sections of RAAM, the passing of another racer must be done by using the off-ramps and on-ramps. His biggest penalty of 30-minutes came when his crew realized that they and their rider were off-course, and so put Robic into the follow car and drove directly back to the route. They'd talked with an official, and knew that this decision would mean a 30-minute penalty, but also recognized that this penalty was actually less than the time they would spend in following the rules and going all the way back to the point at which they'd made their wrong turn.

Robic protested unsuccessfully. In his opinion, the penalties were unfair, and he chose to give up the race. Out of anger towards the officials and the race director, he dropped out and took a DNF. That, too, was a character trait of his. If he did not perform as he wished, he became nervous and impulsive. He was obviously unable to control his temperament. Wyss, on the other hand, delivered the race of his life in his second RAAM victory, making him the only one to beat Robic at the zenith of his career. Second place went to Gerhard Gulewicz, third place to Marko Baloh. Eleven of the 21 ultra-cyclists in the Under Age 50 classification finished, with Robic listed as the last of ten athletes who DNF'ed.

> **Although I had to give up the race early because of severe pneumonia, the positive experiences of my first RAAM inspired me. I had seen how fast and how well I could ride, and that I could maintain the enthusiasm for the sport despite extreme conditions. And I was only 26 years old.**

I recovered at home in Austria and consulted with sports medicine specialists several times to avoid subsequent damage. A second place finish at the 24 Hours of Le Mans provided a reasonably conciliatory end to the season, but my sights were already set on the next year.

I am not a person who insists on getting what I want regardless of the circumstances. I realized relatively quickly, that from a financial perspective, participation in the Race Across America would not happen the following season. Instead of being frustrated and depressed, I took a different direction and focused on RAS, Glocknerman, and Race Around Austria. RAA would especially be a test for the American crossing in 2011.

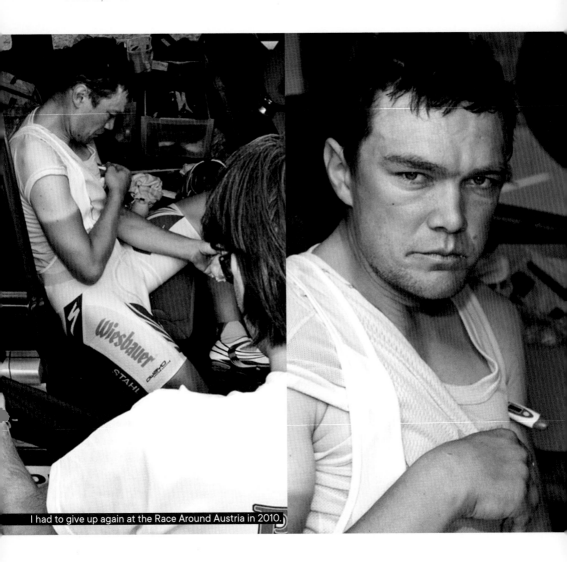

I had to give up again at the Race Around Austria in 2010.

"Shit, I spit blood," I radioed my crew.
"Please, what?"
"Blood. I have blood in my spit. My white glove is already very bloody."

It was the fourth day of the Race Around Austria. I was on the Silvretta High Alpine Road, and it was there that I first feared that I might not get to the finish in St. Georgen. It had all started quite well. As planned, we had started with a moderate pace, which meant that some top riders had passed me. In Styria, the eventual winner Edi Fuchs was an hour ahead of me, but this impressed me little. I was waiting to attack on the second, difficult half. After 33 hours, I took my first sleep break. At this time, the Fuchs/Strasser duel had already flared up at the front of the race. The lead changed several times. Only at the end of the third day, could my rival settle for a while again.

This happened because I had slipped into a physical crisis on the Grossglockner High Alpine Road. I suffered from stomach cramps and diarrhea and had to take an unplanned break. After leaving the Hochtor (the highest mountain road in the Austrian Alps), my people had to support me from both sides as they walked me to the toilet, before they put me in our car for a 50-minute break in the sleeping bag.

I survived the Gerlos pass and the twenty percent grades to Kühtai, but in the Paznaun Valley, I felt pain in my lungs.

I did not have a team doctor with me on this race, but Rainer Hochgatterer was available to us day and night. Over the phone, he gave my crew some tips and dictated the names of doping-free medications, and they drove to Ischgl to get them. My crew kept me awake and in a good mood with puzzles and games, such as "Hangman." Despite the sleep deprivation, I was doing amazingly well mentally.

Then I spat blood.

I gasped. I got nervous. I got frantic.

My body was getting worse by the minute. My first thought was that I should keep this bloody spit a secret—I didn't want to make my crew nervous. But then it was clear to me that I had to address it openly. Hoping that the condition of my lungs would improve itself was not realistic. To show what I coughed up, I collected the slime on my glove, and showed it with trembling hands to the open side window of the follow car.

At that moment, all of the problems and fears from the previous year's RAAM, which I had hoped to have behind me, came back again.

In these moments, I could not help but question everything. The dream of being able to make a living in sports had now become a nightmare and a psychological burden. I did not complete my studies, my job was ultra-cycling. Did I have a physical defect that preven-

> I became unable to increase my pace, the pressure in the lungs grew bigger, and I had to spit again and again. I was unsure. The problem came out of the blue and it frightened me.

ted me from performing at high altitudes? This was the case for RAAM in 2009 and also for RAA in 2010. My trust in my biggest asset—my body and my health—was put in doubt. How could I succeed if my lungs regularly failed me? What should I tell in my lectures and seminars if I have been getting DNFs over and over again?

I was tormented by the Hochtannberg and Fernpass mountain passes, where I was finally examined by another racer's doctor, Thomas Hölzl. He was about a day back, on his way to Vorarlberg, while I was already heading for Tyrol. Although we did not ride on the same road, the route brought us close together, and for Dr. Michael Stö-bich, a colleague of Rainer Hochgatterer, it was easy to come over to us. You can see how the fair play idea was regarded in this race. I would again like to thank Hölzl for temporarily loaning me his doctor.

Stöbich's consultation did not last more than five minutes. He stopped me, diagnosed pulmonary edema, and recommended that I stop the race immediately.

Even if I was frustrated about another DNF, I tried to see the positive side of my racing season. After all, I had won the Glocknerman and finished second in the Race Around Slovenia. Too bad I was unlucky at the season finale. Even without illness, it would have been very difficult to beat Edi Fuchs. He won with a fabulous time of four days, four hours, 36 minutes, and came close to the 100-hour mark, which the race management had predicted a probable time for the winner.

But my doubts remained. Did I have the body to succeed in RAAM?

In retrospect, it is clear that Rainer Hochgatterer has played a major role in ensuring that my career took a favorable course. He told me, "I'd say you should try RAAM again in 2011. I'm writing you the training plans for this goal, and if you want I'm on your team." His support gave me courage and hope again. "Have faith! I know that we can bring you to the finish healthy!" he reassured me. Trust and faith were the most important ideals for me in the last months of 2010.

Probably because of some good words that Wolfgang Fasching had put in for me, my sponsor Wiesbauer remained loyal to me. For those responsible there, it would have been easy to end their support of me. How hard must it have been for them to continue a sponsorship with a racer who DNF'ed two years in a row at the most important race? Wiesbauer could have easily put their euros behind another Austrian ultra-cyclist—there were many to choose from.

I am firmly convinced that you meet the right people at the right time, or that you are at least doing the right things. On New Year's Eve, I happened to get into a conversation with a businessman who was enthusiastic about my ambitions and my approach to the sport. He offered me a little financial support. In the end, that sponsorship did not happen, but even the fact that he WANTED to support me, gave me positive vibes. After a few years, that company gave me the chance to talk in front of their business partners and staff about motivational topics. So that sponsorship did, in effect, happen a few years later in form of an engagement as a speaker. Although it only occurred to me later, I had found something crucial for me that evening: other people trusted me and my ability to become big in this sport. My sponsors were faithful to me, and my acquaintances shared their enthusiasm for me and my sport. My family and my partner Sabine believed in me and strengthened me. So why should I continue to doubt myself if others did not? I started to regain confidence in myself and focused on my goals for the future. And one of those goals was to return to the US and the Race Across America.

It was September 15, 2015, when I returned to Graz from an Italian camping holiday with Sabine. We had been in Orbetello in Tuscany, and had enjoyed the weather and the beach. A few days, I even rode my bike to view the landscape from the saddle.

After we had unloaded our things at about five o'clock in the afternoon, I decided to stretch my legs and swung myself into the saddle. The ride took less than an hour. When I was riding a light downhill section at almost 31 miles (50 kilometers) per hour—still within the residential speed limit—I rode off a driveway, when from out of nowhere, a car hit me from the right in my pedal. I crashed, but was lucky in misfortune—a second, and half a meter earlier, and I'd have flown over the hood.

> My right knee hurt badly; the kneecap was broken. And my right shoulder was dislocated once again.

"Once again" is relative. I could say that in my sporting career, I have been largely spared from accidents. Or, I could say that I had a fragile shoulder, which I dislocated around fifty times between 2005 and 2015. With a wink, I could say that my unsteady shoulder was due to a podium finish in Fohnsdorf in 2005. As a reward, I went to surf and paddle in the west of France. In the Atlantic, my shoulder had popped out for the first time, and I had felt every bump when I had been taken to the hospital in the ambulance. I was tense and gasping while three medics pushed and forced my shoulder back into place.

Half a year later, I had been in the hospital again, this time in during a backcountry ski trip, which I had undertaken as training at the 9,649 feet (2,941 meter) high Hochkönig in the Salzburger Land. I had fallen on the first downhill and my shoulder popped out. It dawned on me that I had no insurance for alpine accidents, so calling the rescue helicopter wasn't an option. I had to grit my teeth as my two friends dragged me back to the car. Hufi, who had been riding his snowboard and carrying my backpack down to the valley, took me to the emergency room.

From this point on, the popping out and pushing my shoulder back in (mostly on a door jamb), was almost an everyday thing for me. Sometimes, I was lucky and it only happened every three months, in the worst case, every three weeks. Picking up bags, cleaning the bike, sleeping, swimming, beach volleyball or mountaineering were now "risky sports" that I avoided. I just sat on the bike. If I lifted my arm to slip into the sleeve of a jacket, like the RAAM or RAA 2013, then it could also come to an incident during cycling with my "articulatio humeri," my shoulder joint. But, in the presence of a physiotherapist, such a dislocation was quickly remedied.

No advantage without disadvantage, and no disadvantage without advantage. The accident in 2015 hurt my right shoulder so badly that surgery was inevitable. The operation in the UKH Eggenberg was excellent, as well as the subsequent therapy under Christian "Chri" Loitzl, who not only looked after me at four RAAM's and in Australia, but also found time between treatments to treat minor ailments. Since then, my shoulder has been stable again and fully capable of movement and load. And, I cannot say that I have missed pressing my body against a door frame since then.

Yet another accident is worth mentioning: On July 1, 2017, I was in Upper Austria, where my sponsor Fever-Tree had organized a victory party for the successful Strasser crew. Not two weeks before, I had clinched my fourth RAAM victory, the atmosphere was relaxed and carefree. For the afternoon, an easy ride with some business partners and bike friends was planned.

I did several months of stabilization and rehab training at the hospital in Graz.

There would be a party that evening. Instead, I spent that evening in the hospital because, during our ride, we were knocked down by a motorist. We suddenly saw a too-fast delivery van in the middle of the road, coming right at us. The road was narrow, and to avoid a head-on crash, we had to ride far right into the shoulder gravel. Still, there was not enough room and I flew, together with others, over a fence into the embankment.

It was the first fractured collarbone of my life, and I thought, in pain, how astonishing it is that Wolfgang Fasching had finished RAAM in 1998 with such an injury and had been second on the podium.

When I was visited by my crew the morning after the operation, I had a plate with eight screws in my body and was somewhat hungover because of the anesthesia—but there were others in the room with hangovers as well, though theirs were because of the party. My team certainly had more fun the night before than I did.

RAAM 2012: Sunrise in Monument Valley

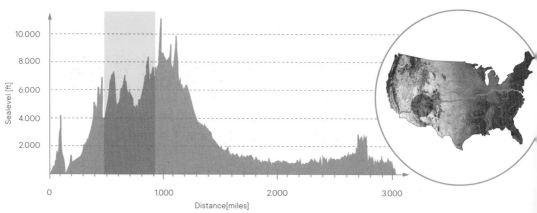

VII
"WHEN'S BEDTIME AGAIN?"
RAAM, TIME STATIONS 8–16

In RAAM 2014 I rode through Tuba City while it was still daylight.

To race the Race Across America fast, you need: the right strategy, knowledge of the climatic and thermal conditions, luck with the weather and the state of your own body, and to be in the right place at the right time, among other things. Flagstaff is such a strategically important point of the race to the east. "We have to be there before it gets dark," Rainer Hochgatterer told me in a 2011 tactics briefing, "then we'll enjoy a tailwind on the following descent. The wind goes to sleep during the night." That meant being in Flagstaff thirty to thirty-three hours after the start. One time in 2014, though, I was even faster, with an hourly average of 20.5 miles (33 kilometers) per hour for twenty-seven hours—which wasn't bad either.

In 2011, I was behind Marko Baloh when I came through Flagstaff, a city of nearly seventy thousand inhabitants. I'd had but one power nap; my first full sleep break was scheduled for Monument Valley. Marko, on the other hand, had pushed through and pursued the classic strategy that Wolfgang Fasching and Jure Robic had used before him—riding straight through the first 36 hours.

So I was fresher and more energized than he was when it came to the showdown at Monument Valley that night.

It was pitch dark. Nature had laid to rest. There were no chirping crickets or howling coyotes. My bike buzzed evenly, the car engine droned steadily, and the voices of my crew in my headset conveyed composure and safety.

Far in the distance two lights appeared, vanished briefly, and appeared again. It was the hazard lights of another vehicle—Marko Baloh's follow car!

An adrenalin rush coursed through my body and all my thoughts turned to the two lights ahead that were mesmerizing me. "I'll have him in a minute," I thought to myself. But on a kilometer-long, seemingly endless straight, nothing happens quickly. Even though I pushed myself a little harder than our plan (there's nothing like seeing another rider ahead to help me to pick up my pace), it still took about half an hour until I had actually caught up with him.

"Listen to me!" My team boss, Rainer told me. "If you pass him, then crank at 250 watts instead of 180 or 200 for five minutes. Work to rush past Marko and disappear as quickly as possible out of his sight." For a moment I was perplexed. How could I do what he wanted? I'd been on the bike for 36 hours, so I could not just dial up my performance. I looked at Rainer incredulously, but before I could answer, my brain blotted out the question marks, and I nodded to him, driven by the euphoria of the moment.

As I rode past Marko, I raised my right hand and formed the peace sign. "Hi Marko!" I called to him. Between Marko Baloh and me, then, as today, we are competitors as well as friends. We combine sport, fairness, and camaraderie. But in RAAM 2011, I also

In front of me, rode the favorite of the race. And immediately I had him!

played psych games. I wanted to show him that I was in a hurry and had no time for small talk, not even to wait for his answer.

"I did not think I could fulfill your request," I later said to Rainer. But the duel with the Slovenian—which was decided in my favor within minutes—proved once again how

After overtaking him, I tried to shake off Marko Baloh and pull away.

important the mind is in sports. It's amazing how good I feel when I pass someone. The opposite also applies of course. I always feel poorly when someone else passes me and I cannot follow.

In 2011 I was carefree and at ease. At that year's Race Across America, I had no pressure from media, sponsors, or crew members. Everyone knew that I was strong and that I had what it took to get on the podium. But was I strong enough? Would I be able to keep my level of performance not just for a day or two, but for a longer distance? In 2009, I quit for health reasons and failed to attend in 2010 due to financial constraints. Now I was back in the race, but not really on a watch-list. Media attention focused on Marko, and RAAM fixture Gulewicz. It's different today; victories also changed the priorities of the journalists. Expectations and pressures are now incredibly high, and one success after the next is taken for granted. It makes me all the more happy that I still have friends who do not really know what I do professionally.

"Would you have time for a trip together this June?" they ask me.
"No, I'm sorry, I'm in the USA."
"Ah yes, I forgot. The bike thing again, right?"

When I passed Marko Baloh, none of us could have guessed that this was the pivotal moment of RAAM 2011. Retrospectively, those five minutes brought me the victory, but the foundation for success had been laid much earlier. As in all the years after that, Rainer provided me with training plans, and placed emphasis on comparatively shorter but more intensive training sessions. These workouts can be more painful than you think. It's easier to train eight hours in the endurance zone than for one hour at the personal max threshold. Rainer's thought is that less training time and more intensity brings better fitness, more recovery, and a stronger immune system. It had already been evident years before that I had trained too much and had rested too little. At the time, I had a lot of performance increases with training on an empty stomach, but fell ill more often. Thirty hours of exercise a week with simultaneous carbohydrate reduction had weakened my immune system. Although I remain loyal to the protein-based Paleo principle, I also pay attention to the intake of sufficient carbohydrates, but I do without milk and cereal products as much as possible. I still do some training session without breakfast and with empty glycogen stores, but not to the extreme of my early years—now I do it only up to twice a week and begin to eat after a few hours.

Because I was doing well physically and because I was mentally motivated, my crew decided that we would get through the second night without a break. While Marko Baloh paused for two hours after Monument Valley at the Mexican Hat Time Station, we pushed on ahead.
"When do I finally take a break?" I barked sourly at my crew.

Rainer responded, "You know, Jure Robic was the only one who made it to Montezuma Creek without a sleep break." His words motivated me to push on, to do the same as the great Jure Robic.

That information was motivation enough for me. Spurred on by these words I held out until 6 o'clock in the morning. Then my first one-hour break came.

Thanks to our racing strategies, I had further increased the gap on Marko Baloh. I would not see him again until the finish in Annapolis.

RAAM 2017: The most famous vantage point of Monument Valley; the point where Forrest stopped running in the movie *Forrest Gump*. Forrest turned around here, but I keep going.

RAAM 2011: A sleep break near Montezuma Creek

Monument Valley is one of the most fascinating tracts of land that the Race Across America passes through. The red rock mesas are natural spectacles that have appeared in many movies. *Once Upon a Time in the West, Easy Rider, Missouri, Forrest Gump*, and many other greats, all have epic scenes shot in Monument Valley. Every time I rode through Monument Valley at dawn, and the sky brightened to the right of me between the rocks, I was impressed by the size and beauty of nature. It was like standing on a lonely mountain peak in the The Alps, surrounded only by perfect calm and natural light. In Monument Valley, there was always only me, my crew, and the dawning of a new day. I greatly appreciated the fact that I had picnicked between the rocks during my acclimatization training in 2011, together with photographer Harald "Harry" Tauderer. We went through the Navajo Indian Reservation and followed the route to Wolf Creek Pass.

> **Beautiful sunrises; sad Native Americans. These are the two sides of Monument Valley.**

The Navajos and their living conditions are the flip side of the Monument Valley coin. The impacts of of a long and complicated history do not go unnoticed as we pass through. The indigenous people have suffered a lot of injustices in the United States, that has left many deadlocked in their existence as they try and hold on to their way of life and culture. Each year, the RAAM organizers instruct us to drive with respect through the reservation and refrain from playing loud music from the follow car. We like to abide by these requests, but unfortunately, they don't do anything to change the condition of what we see.

The sleep break I took in Montezuma Creek in 2011 was replaced in the following years by a power nap. Fiddling with the right break strategy is as old as the Race Across America itself, and never ends, because there are always different riders, different needs, and different attitudes.

When American racer Jonathan Boyer competed in RAAM in 1985, he was a professional cyclist at the zenith of his ability, having raced in the Tour de France five times between 1981 and 1987. He boldly said that he would win RAAM because he was the best athlete. He announced that his tactic would be fast riding and long sleep. He made no friends with this announcement. Boyer compatriot Michael Secrest responded to this challenge with a different idiosyncratic tactic: he rode the first eighty hours without a break, but then suffered a major setback when he slowed down while in the lead. Nevertheless, Boyer would not have won had he not adopted classic RAAM tactics of limited sleep and riding through the nights.

A year later, another racer from the United States, Pete Penseyres, won and set a course record that stood until 2013. In 1987, Secrest took the win, followed a year later by Franz Spilauer, the first RAAM winner from Austria. They all looked for a balance between riding time and resting time after it had become clear that riding straight through was just as unsuccessful as getting a long night's sleep.

> The RAAM sleep tactic is almost a science: To get no sleep at all is not possible, but sleeping too much is also not good since you'll never get back the time lost while having a break. What is the best balance?

Wolfgang Fasching and Jure Robic came to the conclusion that the first 36 hours could be ridden before the first sleep, and then a one-hour break per night had to be enough. Sleeping, according to the common opinion at that time, would be a sign of weakness. Sixty minutes at a stretch would have to suffice.

Meanwhile, the dogma of the 36 break-free hours crumbles. More and more people are working with power naps, which can be flexibly scheduled. In 2011, my crew tried all the tricks to delay sleep and overcome my fatigue. A sure instinct was needed. On the one hand, I was not allowed to fall half-dead off the bike, on the other hand, my people were not allowed to give in every time I demanded another break. If we had responded only to my level of fatigue, I would have been able to sleep five times a day. In 2018, on the other hand, I had the fewest problems with fatigue. I was experienced, fought hard, and kept awake. It was worse for me shortly after RAAM, on a 3-hour relaxed recovery ride home after visiting my parents. After just 45 minutes on the bike, I was plagued by micro-sleep for ten minutes while stopped in a parking lot, one foot on the ground, one on the pedal, and seriously thought of getting twenty minutes of sleep right there on the grass.

Between Monument Valley and the Rocky Mountains, is Durango, a major RAAM Time Station. To reach it, I had to climb over Hesperus Hill to more than 8,200 feet (2,500 meters) above sea level—the first time at high altitude in this RAAM. At the end of the descent, I reached the former gold mining town, which has far more historical significance than many other places in the US. Durango is also home to Race Across The West, the smaller sister of Race Across America. The finish is in a city park. After the descent into Durango, the competitors ride the main road into the village and then turn right to come to a stop under a banner on a sports field. There's very little in the way of glitz or glamour at the RAW finish—cycling doesn't attract many fans in The US, ultra-cycling even less so. So as the finish emcee welcomes and congratulates a RAW finisher over the sound system, he's usually only addressing the racer, his crew, and perhaps a few people who'd come to the park to toss a Frisbee or kick a ball around.

I keep a list of time stations that I like and those that I don't. The section from Durango to Pagosa Springs, which I tackle when I'm already very tired, is definitely among those that I don't like. The two places in Colorado are only connected by a single road; there is no other highway or practical alternative routes. The route to Pagosa Springs flows over many small ascents and descents and is really quite scenic, but all traffic is at the mercy of the "sacred cows of the highway"—the trucks. The Leapfrog Support still applies, and so I ride without a secure escort vehicle protecting me from behind. The thought of a truck passing too close (or worse) is always in the back of my mind.

Receiving support from my crew is often difficult in this section because the traffic makes it hard for them to do Leapfrog Support. They cannot always get past me so easily or find a place to stop and do a hand-off. In addition, as a cyclist, at traffic lights, I'm able to stay to the right on the road and pass all of the stopped motorists while

Just before Cortez: Near Hovenweep National Park

my companions are stuck behind traffic. Which many times lead to delays in their roadside support of me. But even if the crew would be allowed to drive next to me for one minute, four times per hour, as they can later in the race, they'd probably only be able to do this two or three times during this 56-mile (90-kilometer) stretch of road.

"I'm overdue for my next power nap," I told Rainer.
"Soon, soon," he answered.

He kept his word. When we reached Pagosa Springs, I would rest and recharge for the challenge of the Rocky Mountains. The RV was waiting in a quiet parking lot and in the last few miles to get there, I slowed down and dropped my already low pulse a little further. In the RV, I closed my eyes and thought back to Marko Baloh. Five weeks earlier, he had won the Race Around Slovenia and intercepted me. "Where is he now? Will he catch up with me?" I mused. He had come to RAAM 2011 with his wife and their three children. While Irma worked in the support crew, the little ones were allowed to experience the adventure from the RV. "Marko is a good-natured family man, but can he really push his limits with his loved ones on board? There is still much of the race to go. The coming days will show," I decided.

I was tense, trying to reassure myself with a few sentences that I had learned in autogenic training: "There is currently nothing to do, time to relax. I'm completely calm and..." then I fell asleep.

RAA 2015: The Grossglockner High Alpine Road offers a wonderful panorama in the morning sun.

VIII
"JUST GREAT TO WIN HERE!"
THE RACE AROUND AUSTRIA

"What if we were in a relay race at Race Around Austria?" I asked David Misch on a training ride a few days after I won RAAM 2013 and he finished in sixth place as Rookie of the Year. "And who should be on this team?" Misch asked.
"Well, you and me definitely," I laughed.

The rest of our team was made up of two other RAAM 2013 finishers; Franz Wintersberger, winner of the age 50–59 category, and Gerald "Geri" Bauer, winner of the Jure Robic Award for the fastest time in the final stage over the Appalachians.
There are puzzles that are so simple in design that they slip into the right position, almost just by looking at them; four Austrians with recent RAAM success, four people who knew and understood each other, four ultra-cyclists who wanted to attack Race Around Austria (RAA), were those puzzle pieces. We were able to rely on the support of the organizers of the Race Around Austria, we had all known them for some time, and our team also brought additional attention to the event. Gerald Bauer took care of organizational matters and logistics, so we were also well taken care of in this regard.

The media wrote about a "dream team," and yes, when the first, sixth, ninth-place finisher, and the winner of the age 50–59 category are united in a team, it's a dream!

For our team name we chose "RAAM Racing Powered by INN's Holz," in recognition of our sponsor, a health and recreation-oriented Austrian hotel.

For me, RAA 2013 was a change from the solo races that I am known for. We wanted to split the quartet, each shift would take four hours, and the two riders would alternate every forty minutes within that time. It was a good plan—and ultimately a successful one.

But, I had gained six kilograms since the end of the Race Across America, in the second half of June to the start of RAA in early August. David had sat on a road bike a mere three times during that same period. And the other two were probably more concerned with rest and regeneration than with active competition preparation. We were a damaged dream team. Our spirit of adventure and team morale was great, but our physical condition in comparison to our top form was at best, modest to mediocre.

> **If we had been a luxury car, our engine would have sputtered and desperately needed an oil change.**

Nevertheless, we were at RAA, the longest ultra-cycling race in Europe, and the one with the most atmosphere and pageantry at the start/finish venue. The organizers really put on quite a show, which makes it very rewarding for the racers who come to take on the extremely difficult and mountainous course.

Despite our less than perfect condition, we were determined to deliver a good race.

The route should not be underestimated—on the contrary. "What harm could come from having a beer the night before the start?" we thought. So David and I set off to indulge in a little pre-race relaxation and to enjoy the flair of the upcoming start in St. Georgen im Attergau, whose center was bathed in a green and yellow sea of flags.

Let me make it short: our plan failed. One beer became two, then three, and four, and at some point we stopped counting. By the time we got back to our very old-school lodging (the place was many years overdue for an overhaul) in a distressed neighborhood outside the village center, the pressure in our bladders had grown so great that we found ourselves desperately looking for the toilet we thought was down an unlit corridor. Though actually, we really didn't remember exactly where it was. In the end, my buddy peed from the balcony and I took the sink.

RAA 2013: Rider exchange in the relay team: David Misch takes over.

I rarely smoke and I am not proud of it. It only happens when late-night celebrations throw professional behavior overboard in favor of youthful stupidity. The eve of RAA 2013 was one of those moments. I left my room and first searched our rental car for the objects of desire. In the end, I found one, when I finally remembered that the innkeeper was a smoker.

As soon as the first crisis situation was put aside, the next one immediately turned up: "Where are cigarettes? I need cigarettes!

Do not ask how we must have looked the next day. Thankfully, the start was scheduled for five o'clock in the evening, which gave David and me a bit of time to regenerate after our night's outing. I had behaved like the worst weekend cyclist, and in the short term, a bad conscience plagued me. "I'll leave the team hanging," I thought to myself. Geri was to ride from the start. Forty minutes after him, it was to be my first turn. But I felt like a battered boxer, desperately trying to stay on his wobbly feet and survive another round. Again, a few hours later, everything was pure sunshine. RAA has shown us its best side. At the start/finish in St. Georgen, the mood was good for days on end. Numerous cycling enthusiasts along the route celebrated the riders, and summery weather intensified the positive mood of the racers, organizers, and spectators. The RAAM Racing team made some wrong turns and we lost our way a total of three times, but due to the fast pace that the four of us could deliver, we were already in the lead by the halfway mark of the race.

We were able to continuously expand our lead to the finish, and even set a new course record of two days, eighteen hours, forty-seven minutes. Anyone who had said, "Logically, it will end like this," was right. Nevertheless, the Race Around Austria remains one of the toughest ultra-cycling races in the world, whether alone or on a team. First of all, it has to be finished! We benefited from our basic fitness and

RAA 2013: Victory in the 4-person-team

long-distance experience, but also knew that serious, targeted preparation, better route knowledge and professional "carbo-loading" (and not our liquid-carb method from the night before) would be much faster. Meanwhile, we managed to break the course record, much to the delight of some of our biggest fans—the St. Georgen Blaskapelle, the local village orchestra with whom we've had many beers. These guys, they can drink, and they encouraged us to join in and we had a lot of fun with them. Two years later, another team broke our 4-person record, but this did not diminish the bond created over the many beer glasses emptied by our team and the band.

Incidentally, the Race Around Austria has been around since 2009, and the idea for it was born in Wolfgang Fasching's follow car during a RAAM. At that time, Michael Nussbaumer and Rainer Hochgatterer pondered why there was no ultra-cycling race in Austria and what would have to be done to create one. Manfred Guthardt acted as RAA'S midwife because he had cycled the route along the Austrian borders in 1988. His route was about 1615 miles (2,600 kilometers). He didn't ride non-stop, but rode long sections each day so it took him nine days to do a lap of my country. Twenty years later Guthardt's tour was reported on in Radwelt magazine and piqued my interest. The editor had posed the question of whether current ultra-cycling, using

Training ride around Austria 2008: successful nonstop tour despite rustic technology

modern equipment, methods, and ultra-cycling knowledge, could complete the route faster than Guthardt. This idea fit my schedule, actually. In the fall of 2008, I'd wanted to ride the "Le Tour Ultime"—non-stop, ultra-cycling version of the Tour de France—but this race was canceled that season when too few racers entered. So instead my "Nonstop Around Austria" became a personal endurance test for RAAM, which I wanted to do a year later. I wanted to check how I would fare after three or four days on the bike, how my head and buttocks would react to such a strain. I wanted to gain experience on my equipment, seating position, and nutrition. It would also be a test for my crew.

"Hello! How are you? Where are you?" Wolfgang Fasching said when he called me on the last night of the tour, when pain and fatigue had both already reached epic levels. "There is still much of the route ahead of you. But you can do it. Have courage, and soon you will have done it."

His call and his words pleased me and encouraged me. I cycled the entire route of the future Race Around Austria, convincing the organizers that the 1,491-mile (2,400-kilometer) route with the profile of 114,829 feet (35,000 meters) would be feasible. Incidentally, Gerhard Gulewicz had the same idea, but he was unable to complete the circumnavigation of Austria in October due to wintry weather conditions on the Grossglockner. Yet somehow, he still received more attention from the media, which I did not feel was fair.

> The RAA route that I rode still included a few minor roads that were closer to the state border but were in poor condition, which is why some changes were made for the final RAA route before Michael Nussbaumer decided in 2009 to hold the first RAA.

The RAA organizers repeatedly call their race a "European counterpart" or a "little brother" of RAAM. The race duration is about half as long, it's a RAAM qualifier, and can legitimately be considered as an ideal preparation race for RAAM. RAAM participants who have successfully completed RAA in their run-up have been able to put in outstanding performances in America. In my opinion, RAA is a valuable highlight of the ultra-cycling racing calendar and not just the springboard for the "World's Toughest Bicycle Race."

In my opinion, RAA is not physically easier than RAAM. The RAA route is tough to beat in terms of difficulty. Nowhere in RAAM are there climbs as steep as in RAA, nor the long ascents such as those on Grossglockner, Kühtai, or Faschina, which have double-digit percentage increase and bring knee joints and musculature to the limit. I've had my worst musculoskeletal ailments and inflamed thigh muscle attachments in RAA. My ass and the nerves in my hands, however, suffer more during that famous race in the United States. Of course, the RAAM is longer and has more altitude, but there are also many more sections where you can roll and relax a bit.

I see great differences in sleep management between the two races, which is majorly important. The Race Around Austria is just long enough that doing it without sleep isn't feasible, but it's short enough that one can do it on just a few power naps. In 2015, for example, I managed to do it with a total of one hour of sleep in just less than four days, divided into three short breaks. Nevertheless, the sleep deprivation does not reach the level of a RAAM, and that is essential for the technically difficult downhills.

> To put it in a nutshell: The Race Across America is mentally tougher than the Race Around Austria, but physically, these two challenges are at a similar level.

Also, the meteorological conditions are more unpredictable at RAA than at RAAM. From the biggest sweltering summer heat to snow storms on the alpine passes, everything is possible in Austria in August.

There are some races that took me several tries to win. That was the case for the 24 Hurs of Fohnsdorf as well as for the Race Around Slovenia. I also did not win the Race Around Austria in my first attempt in 2010, in fact, I DNF'ed. It wasn't until 2014 that I won, and then only with immense problems. We were only just over 140 miles from the finish line when race director Michael Nussbaumer called my crew to ask how I was doing and when he should expect us to finish. He told us about the atmosphere there, of the thousands of visitors to the St. Georgen Market Festival who were looking forward to my arrival. He also mentioned, by the way, NADA—the National Anti-Doping Agency—was waiting for the winner. Initially, I found this information to be quite inspiring, but then it hit me like lightning: it was about the doping control, which I had to undergo at the finish! I have been tested many times over the course of my career: All RAAM's, RAA, the King of the Lake Time Trial in 2017, and for my 24-hour track record. Many races test the winners, and usually randomly choose some of the other riders to test as well. In those last 100 kilometers of RAA, when I heard that the NADA controllers were waiting for me, my enthusiasm and pedaling became less powerful. For outsiders, it may have made it appeared that I did not want to continue.

"Guys, I'm scared of the finish line. I'm afraid I may be riding into my own ruin," I said to my crew members.
"Why? How?"
"Well, what if something is wrong? Didn't I take a caffeine tablet that we bought in America? Could I test positive?" One thought after another rushed through my brain, panic spread; I experienced sweating, hot flashes, dizziness. I got off the bike.

Caffeine is a perfectly legitimate and legal means of fighting fatigue—everyone knows it and almost everyone drinks coffee. I do love coffee, and it would be nice to have some during a race, but brewing coffee in the follow car isn't practical, and coffee can be hard on the stomach. So, for me and many other racers, caffeine tablets, which contains the same 100 milligrams of caffeine as an espresso, is the alternative. At RAAM, my crew had bought such caffeine tablets at a gas station for their own use. Some of them were left over that we did not want to throw away. Usually, I buy these tabs in Austria at a pharmacy, where there can be no contamination.

I thought in panic, "What if I've inadvertently taken contaminated caffeine? What if these gas station pills meant for the American truck drivers had added stimulants? What if I'm actually positive? What if my whole life, and everything that I have achieved so far, is taken from me? What if I am publicly ridiculed? How should I argue credibly?" I'd heard all of the weak explanations from athletes who had been convicted of doping. All of them—from sabotaged toothpaste to contaminated sweets, which someone's grandmother had supposedly brought from her vacation in South America, and countless other excuses. Was I at the end of my career?

RAA 2014: Hours of uncertainty

"Guys, what are we doing?!"
My team took my concerns seriously, researched which tablets they were and phoned Rainer Hochgatterer. He assured them that all was well. "You're clean," my crew told me.
"For sure?" I wanted to know.
"For sure."

I do not understand how others, in more prominent and lucrative sports, consciously dope and then hide that fact. How athletes who have knowingly doped can keep a calm conscience and sleep well. Or how they can cheat on themselves for a top position in the classics, accept the fame, honor, prize money, and sponsorships, knowing it is all a lie and they didn't earn it. I also live on my sport, and even if I earn bread crumbs compared to the stars of other disciplines, doping is not an option. Yet, outsiders could also argue that that doping would also increase my performance.

There is no prize money in ultra-cycling, which many consider unfair. But I think that's a positive thing, because that's one of the reasons why this sport stays clean, which is reinforced by the fact that there have never been positive doping test results. Isn't it true that everywhere in the world, where there is a lot of money—be it sports, politics or business—people are trying to gain an unfair advantage with every imaginable trick? If you want to make a living from ultra-cycling, you first and foremost, you need a story to tell. The sporting success alone brings no revenue. I like to compare it to mountaineering; no one gets a check handed over when he climbs a famous peak, but there is the possibility to make a profit through books or lectures. The prerequisite for this, however, is that you're able to report authentically and rousingly about your experiences and inspire others. Often, a perfect champion is not as interesting as someone who has a special life journey behind him. Using the example of RAAM, I think of Jure Robic, who, as the best in his field, hardly earned any revenue from marketing. On the other hand, for example, the German physician Michael Nehls managed to publish a book about his 2010 RAAM and his special strategy, which sold well, even though to be honest, in purely sporting terms his performance was mediocre. The placement in the competition is therefore only part of what determines earning potential and in principle, a completely different field of activity than marketing.

The purely physical performance is surprisingly low at the RAAM (see appendix); I did my fastest RAAM with a 164-watt average power. In training, my base tempo is between 200 and 275 watts. My functional threshold power (FTP) is just under 400 watts. Theoretically, in the race, I am riding in my recovery zone, for which no performance-enhancing substances are needed. The limiting factor is the calorie balance; the body can't metabolize an infinite amount of food. Its maximum limit is about 15,000 calories per day. For higher performance, a much higher supply would be necessary, which is not possible. There are no regeneration phases at RAAM. If you turn your inner engine over longer periods into the "red zone," you're entering into life-threatening areas. Team dynamics, the treatment of sleep deprivation, and mental strength are factors that are equally important, and not things that can be dealt with by swallowing a pill.

In other sports, it is obvious that the athletes under the pressure of success, and with the prospect of making big money, resort to performance-enhancing drugs, but regenerate after short and high-intensity strains. Tom Simpson, who suffered a tragic death in 1967 at the age of thirty on the Mont Ventoux ascent in the Tour de France, is a prominent example. Stimulants led to dehydration and eventually cardiac arrest. Would a long-distance cyclist, who expects a wooden board as "prize money," risk his life for this? Certainly not, I hope.

Only through the encouragement of my crew was it possible for me to reach the finish of RAA

I know that those moments in August 2014 fried my nerves. I blamed myself for not accurately controlling what I put in my body, and I seriously thought of giving up RAA to evade doping control. I'm an honest sportsman. I do not dope. It does not occur to me to take an unfair advantage. Nevertheless, there remained a thought: "What if I made myself punishable by thoughtlessness, out of negligence?"

My crew and I agreed that I would take a break 50 kilometers before the finish. After that, I completed the race, where I was celebrated by a few thousand spectators. It took me three days, fifteen hours, fifty-six minutes to fulfill my own goal of setting a course record. I was grateful for all the ultra-cycling fans and sports enthusiasts who celebrated with me at the start and finish. But even more friends and fans touched me at the edge of the route, in bad weather, in the middle of the night, waiting for me with their encouragement and banners of support. Goosebumps ran down my spine.

But then it got serious. "Christoph Strasser, please come to doping control!" A friendly, but definitely businesslike NADA official told me. I gave the required urine sample—and I can't say that I did that kindly. The next few nights, I often suffered from insomnia. Not even on my vacation with Sabine could I really switch off and enjoy my success.

> **A few weeks later came the result of the doping control test and I could breathe again: negative.**

If this episode about a possible doping offense was the first and last horror moment of RAA 2014, then you could shrug your shoulders and say, "Well, what the hell, a funny anecdote and nothing more." Are you kidding me? Are you serious when you say that!? I can't overstate the success of this Race Around Austria.

I had already decided before the Race Across America that I wanted to start in front of my home crowd. Before the season highlight in the US, I had no other races on the calendar, and to have a season consisting only of RAAM would have been too little for me. Those who do not pursue any further goals after RAAM often fall into a mental hole of listlessness and depression. So after a short break, I wanted to prepare for the next competition.

But RAAM is always in your bones. Whether RAA is now tackled on a team of four or as a soloist, I just had to rely on myself and my body so I could handle both loads. Moreover, I also wanted to clearly undercut the four-day mark at RAA.

This time there was no beer the night before. This time I was wide awake at 10:28 am on the 13th of August. I had to be, because we were not favored by the weather. The very first day leading from Upper Austria to Burgenland was a test of endurance. It rained continuously. With the wet, hilly roads, I made slow and cautious progress even on the downhills. Nevertheless, I stuck to my tactics: start fast, develop a lead, and manage that lead in the second half of the race. We needed several short breaks so that I could change clothes and get dry pants and jerseys, but I did not let this affect my strategy. I did 497 miles (800 kilometers) in the first twenty-four hours without sleeping.

After the Soboth in Carinthia, 599 miles (964 kilometers) into the race, my left knee began to hurt, and after crossing Lesachtal I could barely move it. In Lienz, 764 miles (1,230 kilometers) into the race, I was standing at a gas station and could not get off the bike because of the pain. It was freezing cold and the muscles in the left leg were inflamed due to the previous strain and the constant cold and wetness. My scheduled break of twenty minutes became sixty while I was treated my physiotherapist, Christoph Kohlbauer. He did this so well that I was able to continue relatively well with (allowed) analgesics. Later, he admitted that he had not believed the knee would reach the finish.

RAA 2014: Rain on the first day of the race

This finish, this RAA, was harder than most of the RAAM's I have competed in. There was a blizzard on the Grossglockner High Alpine Road, rain in the Salzburger Land, constant rain in the Inn Valley, heavy rain, wind and temperatures of just over freezing in the Kühtai and on the Silvretta. According to meteorological statistics, it was one of the rainiest and coldest August months of all time.

After leaving the mountainous western part of Austria, the weather finally changed, and it became comfortably warm and dry. At this time, we had the steep mountainous climbs of Vorarlberg behind us, and were about twenty hours from reaching St. Georgen. These were the best hours of the race for me. My knee was feeling good again, the roads were flat, and my pace was high. I received a phone call from my friend and training partner Severin Zotter, who was racing the Tortour (Race Around Switzerland) at that same time, and he was on pace to take the victory there. We motivated each other and wished each other the best. We learned a little later that he won the race, and I pedaled even more powerfully. From Saalfelden to St. Georgen there are a hundred kilometers, and my first pursuer was twice that distance behind me. The RAA was as good as done. Or not? Suddenly chills and sweats caught me at the same time. "Guys, I am afraid of the finish line. I'm afraid I may be riding into my own ruin."

Snowstorm at the Hochtor, a dangerous descent

Twelve months later everything was different. I had not won RAAM. I had failed, and my health had failed on my way to my supposed fourth triumph. Instead, the win went to Severin Zotter. That was the main reason why I competed at the RAA, because I wanted to take up the challenge and end the season with a positive result, so as not to worry too much about the RAAM failure. No one ever forced me to race at RAA just two months after the DNF; nobody would have resented me for recovering and attacking again next year. But one sentence had firmly burned into my brain: "Come back stronger!" There was another difference between the Race Around Austria 2014 and 2015: if it had been only wet and cold in the one year, it was just hot and humid in the other. August 2015 was one of the warmest in history.

With all that, the top priority was to pay attention to my health. I had prepared myself for RAA at an altitude of 6,500 feet (2,000 meters), where each night I slept in a small mountain hut on the Rettenbach Glacier, and by day I worked as a bike guide at the Ötztal Cycling Weeks Festival. During the race, to avoid imminent water retention in the body, my weight was checked every few hours, and not only did I get the obligatory garden sprayer showers for refreshment, but also increased amounts of salt and magnesi-

um in addition to the planned calorie intakes via my liquid food. The heat caught me, like all other participants, on the first day. I suffered from tropical temperatures and decided to take it easy and reduced my speed. I was third after Patric Grüner and Pierre Bischoff, but after about four hours riding time, I overtook Bischoff, as he had stopped at the roadside. A little later, Grüner was sitting wearily in a folding chair under an improvised sunshade as I pedaled past him. At the time, I did not feel like I was traveling very fast and my performance data verified that impression. Although I could not say I was fine, I saw that my main rivals for the RAA victory seemed to be even worse off. My "precautionary tactics" instead of "brute force tactics" seemed the right strategy.

Under the mild night temperatures, I was able to challenge my body more and the next day my team cooled me with ice water. Part of the way up the Soboth, my friend Severin Zotter, the current RAAM winner who was out on a training ride, accompanied me for the allotted ten minutes that the rules allow a racer to accompany.

On the Soboth, I was two hours behind my course record of the previous year, and the hardest part of RAA was still ahead. And what a spectacle! Because the RAA organizers had organized buses, over a hundred fans gathered at the pass on the Grossglockner High Alpine Road, the highest point of the race, where I rode through a tunnel of people. I had seen such scenes on television broadcasts of the Tour de France and the Giro d'Italia, but I did not think that I would ever experience this goosebump feeling as an ultra-cyclist.

I was fortunate and did not have any of the lung problems that had occurred in the recent past. My lead over Patric Grüner grew. Compared to 2014, my 2015 pace was slower in the first half of the race, then into the second half, I went fast enough to equal the previous year's average speed. And then, in the final miles, I was fast enough to increase that average and set a new course record.

Three days, fourteen hours, forty-five minutes after takeoff, with only one hour's sleep, I came out victorious.

I came back stronger. I was proud. I rarely use that word—pride. It is not necessarily positive for me; many people develop too much pride, and that can lead to an oversized ego and overconfidence. But I was proud of myself because I chose to race, face the fear of another failure, and make no excuses for myself.

I could write again about the tough and steep climbing, the harsh weather conditions, and the mental and physical challenges, when in 2016, I won the Race Around Austria (in three days, twelve hours, forty-one minutes), again in front of Patric Grüner. But more important to me, is to address other aspects of the RAA.

In a nutshell: winning here is simply great.

I think RAA was the perfect answer to not finishing RAAM. In that year it became clear to me that a sports failure can happen to everyone, and that a finish may never be taken for granted. After RAAM, I wanted to come back stronger and learned the necessary lessons together with my team.

During the Race Around Austria, a 5-day-long festival takes place in St. Georgen en Attergau, with a great supporting program, which focuses on cycling but not only on that. You set off, you have 1,367 of the hardest miles (2,200 kilometers) in front of you, and you have, not only your crew behind you, but in each village, at each key point, there are also fans cheering, and cheering for you—with posters, banners, and signs. The inhabitants of St. Georgen, those who have their houses ten or twenty kilometers from the finish, stand in the street and some of them even light bonfires. Those who have not experienced these emotions themselves cannot imagine how inspiring and how motivating this roadside attention is.

In 2016, RAA was my comeback race after surgery due to an accident. I was in the best possible shape one year after my previous competition, and not only wanted to win, but also to check that my injuries had been completely cured and that I was prepared for future tasks. The weather was catastrophically cold; the Glockner High Alpine Road was once again closed. The racetrack director decided to redirect the participants over the shorter Felbertauern, as there was the danger of black ice on the original course, making the downhill too dangerous. The only athlete who did not follow this order was the Italian, Angela Perin. No one on her team spoke German or English—only loud, forceful Italian. Perin suffered over switchbacks in the direction of Glockner, mastered this section, and won anyway, as the only female participant to reach the finish that year. I congratulated her, but thought to myself that a team should be set up for international races, in which at least one person speaks English. On my team, we do not travel to the US to compete in RAAM without having someone who can understand and speak English.

But back to St. Georgen. I won by seven hours over Grüner, but I did not just ride over a finish line. At RAA, the last meters lead through a marquee, where thousands of people gather and celebrate the finishers. It goes up a ramp—and you have arrived. I got off the bike, stood on a podium, looked into the crowd, and was struck by thousands cheering. My team and I let our emotions flow.

One day later the award ceremony took place. While the Austrian anthem was played and the flag was raised, tears of joy came to my eyes.

It was an indescribable moment. After that, in contrast to RAAM, in which I am physically too exhausted after eight days, it was time to celebrate. In that too, we put in a strong effort. We celebrated until Monday morning, and then hung over but happy, we were roused way too early from our beds.

RAA winner or not, checkout time is 12 o'clock.

EDITOR'S NOTE:

After not taking part in 2017, Christoph Strasser returned to Race Around Austria in 2018. That year was a special one: For the first time in its history, the Austrian Cycling Federation acknowledged Ultra-Cycling as an official discipline in their race calendar and called the Race Around Austria Challenge (the shorter version of RAA) the official Austrian Championships in Ultra-Cycling. This was a huge achievement for this sport in Austria since previously the Cycling Federation only accepted road-racing, track, MTB, cross country, BMX, paracycling, and indoor cycling ball.

Christoph Strasser became the first Austrian Ultra-Cycling Champion in 2018 by virtue of his first place in RAA Challenge. The 560–kilometer (348–mile) route around the state of Upper Austria featured 21,325 feet (6500 meters) of climbing. By pushing a normalized power of 282 watts he completed the race in 15 hours and 54 minutes at an average speed of 21.984 mph (35.38 kph).

RAAM 2015: Severin Zotter overtakes me on the climb to Cuchara Pass

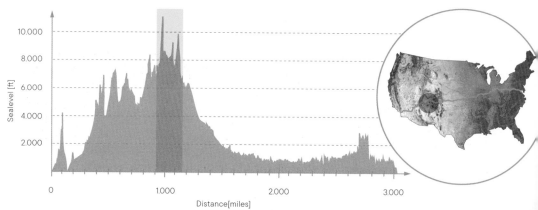

IX
"NOTHING TO WIN, BUT EVERYTHING TO LOSE"

RAAM, TIME STATIONS 16–20

I held on to the support car and gasped for air. One, two, three deep breaths to overcome the efforts of a short conversation we'd just had.

Severin Zotter had just caught up with me on the climb to Cuchara Pass and had tapped on my shoulder.
"How are you?" He asked.
"Not perfect, but not so bad," I answered. "Just go on, I do not want to stop you."
Severin is one of the best climbers on the ultra-cycling scene, and I was just not in a good mood.
"In Kansas, you'll catch me again anyway," he said, trying to cheer me up. He stepped harder on the pedals and was gone. His crew also had nice and appreciative words for me. It was a duel of fairness and mutual respect.

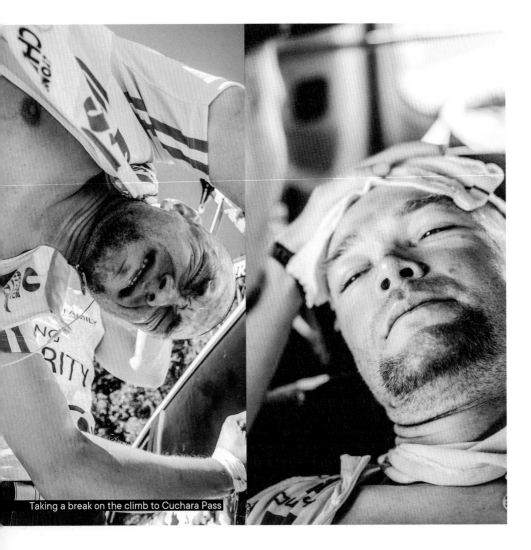

Taking a break on the climb to Cuchara Pass

I had pulled myself together, tried to stay strong, and wanted to send no sign of weakness to my sharpest opponent, not show him how much I was suffering. But after he was out of sight, I could not help it, I had to stop and take a deep breath. I could hardly breathe.

At this time station, in 2015, I lost nearly four hours to my competitor, training partner, and friend. Four hours from one time station to the next. That's half an eternity.

In this RAAM, I had decided to make it my goal to become the first rider to win three years in a row. For the first time, Rainer Hochgatterer was not there, but the largely new crew, led by Michael Kogler, my crew chief, and Arnold Schulz, my doctor, was well prepared for RAAM. Perhaps in retrospect, the situation in the new team could

be described as follows: We were strong and well-rehearsed when we had no problems. If it did not go smoothly, then the crew lacked the experience to meet the challenges that arose. It also added that we—and especially me—lacked humility, and we didn't have enough respect for the race. After two record wins at the Race Across America in series, it seemed that I'd forgotten that I would have to fight to get through first.

Anyway, I was standing by the car, hoping that my health would improve and not worsen. 2015 was one of the hottest RAAM's in years, and the tremendous temperatures had bothered me from the start. You can drink too little—that's bad, but you can also drink too much—that's even worse. Budgeting your water intake with a continuous physical effort in the heat is a complicated thing. The assumption that you have to drink more, the hotter it is, is wrong. This only applies to events that last a few hours, but not in ultra-cycling. The body

Cooling down my head with ice

cannot possibly use more than one liter of liquid per hour over the course of a day. Plain water is the worst thing you can drink. Much better are mineral and salty electrolyte drinks. If the water budget tilts, then there are fluid deposits in the body, and these can be the breeding ground for a lung infection or pulmonary edema.

Since the second day, I've had hydration problems. My face was puffed up and my weight was on the rise. I looked like the Michelin Man—except that I did not smile.

One of the reasons I had so much trouble in the heat was bad acclimatization. In the week before the start, it had been quite cool; there had even been a rainy day in Borrego Springs, which was very unusual. Due to the mild, almost pleasant temperatures, I could not adapt and get through the physical stresses of the race. I also had problems with food, and suffered from diarrhea as a result.

When I tackled the Rocky Mountains after the power nap near Pagosa Springs, Time Station 16, the first duels with Severin were already behind me. He had started very fast and I had needed 466 miles (750 kilometers) to catch up with him after my problems in the desert. We pushed each other and used the fifteen minutes allowed by the regulations to ride side-by-side and exchange a few words before I could pull away.

Crossing the Rockies is always a bit of a concern for me because I know this is the most critical point in the race. The danger of getting sick is greatest here, and even one of the best, Jure Robic, DNF'ed on Wolf Creek Pass in 2006.

In the Rocky Mountains, the Race Across America route passes through three Colorado passes: Wolf Creek Pass (10,856 feet, 3,309 meters); La Veta Pass (9,412 feet/2,869 meters); and Cuchara Pass (9,937 feet/3,029 meters). Wolf Creek Pass not only reaches the highest point of RAAM, but is also the most difficult of the three, with a maximum gradient of 6.8 percent. The rise is not very steep; the eight hundred meters are distributed over fourteen kilometers, but the slope begins at the height at which you would stand at the summit of RAA's Grossglockner High Alpine Road. However, RAAM's mountain roads do not have any serpentines, as we are used to in Austria, but are three-lane and resemble highways with a few, elongated curves. In contrast to the Race Around Austria (RAA), on the simple de-

RAAM 2015: Shortly before reaching Wolf Creek Pass

scents of RAAM, it is difficult to stay focused and concentrated. The Austrian down-hills are technically challenging, and keep you wide awake and aware.

In the years before, we had done much better at putting the first 1000 miles quickly behind us. We had always managed to reach the Wolf Creek Pass in mild temperatu-res—some years even before nightfall. I'd also managed to reach the two other high mountains in the night, putting me in the lowlands at dawn to take the first long sleep break. But 2015 was different. It was midnight when I reached the summit of Wolf Creek Pass, and it was freezing cold. I weakened physically. I suffered mentally. Again and again, I fought with micro-sleep. These hardships demanded more from me than any previous race. My body called for a break, but we did not want to take one at such a high altitude. Good regeneration is possible only at lower altitudes.

And there was also bad luck. We had a flat tire on the motorhome, which made an early sleep break at 8,200 feet (2,500 meters) above sea level necessary. My crew was aware that my condition was not the best, and although Arnold realized the se-verity of the situation, while some of my crew did not really believe that I was suffe-ring much, they thought that I was only experiencing the usual fatigue, and that I was only trying to take more breaks.

I barely recovered in that break, and then had to dig deep over the second pass. Suddenly, I was shocked to find that I was in a meadow next to my bike. I'd actually gone to sleep while riding uphill and had crashed. From that point onwards, I was in red alert. I knew that I was in serious trouble. For the first time, I had to tackle Cuchara Pass in the midday heat. It was unbearably hot at 86 Fahrenheit (30 Celsius) at 9,938

RAAM 2015: Crash on the climb to La Veta Pass

Our mutual decision to report a "DNF"

feet (3000 meters). Like a drowning man, I gasped and began to look around, again and again, anxiously waiting to see Severin behind me.

"In Kansas, you'll catch up to me anyway." His words echoed in my mind as I sat next to my bike like a steaming pile of misery at the pass for half an hour or so. When Arnold did a medical check on me and listened to my lungs with a stethoscope, we knew that I had to get to lower altitude as quickly as possible. Pulmonary edema can only get better under 4,900 feet (1,500 meters). But in my unstable condition, the downhills were extremely dangerous and the risk of falling was enormous. The team doctor decided that we would continue—there was no choice other than giving up the race. Once we got to a lower altitude, the team pushed for another sleep break for my health's sake. We lost more hours on Severin, but the basic tenor was: let him go, forget about wanting to lead the race, get well!

RAAM 2014: Christian as cowboy on Wolf Creek Pass

Our team in a great mood: "Jawui!"

Unfortunately, I only temporarily got better. One day later, we had to quit the race in Kansas for good.

As I battled the passes of the Rocky Mountains, all the sentiments and experiences I'd had here in past RAAM's came to me in a rush. In 2009, when the route was farther south, I held second place here, as a rookie, just behind my idol, Jure Robic, before I had to later DNF. In 2012, I struggled to keep up with Reto Schoch, and a year later, I was trying to hold my lead against him across these mountains to Kansas. That was the year of forest fires, and I wore a surgical mask for the smoke. And just twelve months earlier, in 2014, I had a strong performance right here and dominated the race. I arrived at Wolf Creek Pass in the afternoon, earlier than ever before, and then enjoyed a tailwind on the high plateau of Alamosa.

"If the wind comes from behind, we will drive about a hundred meters behind you," said Johnny, one of my first cycling mentors and three-time crew member from 2013 to 2015, "Because then you'll feel the wind as well. On the other hand, we will be right behind you when there are headwinds." Johnny is a perfectionist, a thinker, and a detail-loving and competent mechanic. His special abilities have always enriched our team.

I thought back to all the emotional moments on Wolf Creek Pass, where the air is noticeably thin. Every time I reached the summit, my people were already there, dressed up, running in costumes next to me and making me laugh. There was always a party mood at this highest point of RAAM. After getting me dressed for the windy and cold descent, we got into a circle and I made a little speech. "So far, we have done well, things are running brilliantly, and we are working well, but the most difficult sections are ahead! We cannot win RAAM in the Rockies," I once said, "but we can very well lose. Today we are at the highest point of the race, but not the most important. This one will come to us all in a few days, in Annapolis. And if we work hard, we'll be there as winners and then we will have fun!"

"Jawui!" we all shouted, and on we went. ("Jawui" is Austrian for "Oh yeah!" It is nearly a trademark for me, as my crew and supporters always use the hashtag #jawui.)

My thoughts returned to the present. Now someone with whom I had formed a training partnership for the past three years was kicking my ass. "Sevi," formerly a civil servant like me, worked as a social worker at Caritas and worked as a bicycle messenger for Veloblitz in Graz. As early as 2003, when I was still trying my hand at mountain biking on the Fohnsdorf circuit, Sevi was already active in the then biggest 24-hour race in Austria. He finished third in the Silberreiher Trophy behind Jure Robic and Johann Mädl. In the years after that, he was on teams and also went solo in various endurance races, but had no ambition to work his way up to the front of the pack of elite racers.

When our cycling colleague Alexander Gepp, a RAAM-Finisher in 2005, got married in 2010, the polterabend (traditional German day-before-a-wedding gathering) consisted of a bike ride.

"This pace, it's a bit slow," I said with a smirk.
"Yes, accelerating would be fun," Severin replied.

"In any case! Have you ever thought of racing a little longer?"

"Yes, yes. But that's a lot of work and I do not know how to tackle it."

"If you like, I can help you. I already have some experience."

From some conversations and shared trips, a friendship was formed. I was happy to give him advice and specific tips for training, planning and racing strategies. I enjoyed helping Sevi and seeing him getting better, improving in training, and in competitions like RAS and RATA, until he could even win the Glocknerman and the Tortour in Switzerland.

Before Sevi left with his girlfriend Angela for a multi-week bike trip to Asia in 2012, I gave him a question to ponder on his journey: Where was his next path? After his resounding successes in European races, did he want to now take on RAAM? He used the time, ordered his thoughts, and was clear about his goal: He would do RAAM in 2015.

In the spring of 2015, while he was preparing for RAAM, I was still training for my 24–hour world record attempt in Berlin, which I tackled three months before RAAM. At our joint training camp in Croatia, where we shared accommodations and spent five to eight hours a day training, I promised him: "I'll continue to give you tips and help you, but only if you give your very best at RAAM and do your best to compete with me, one-on-one." I sincerely wanted him to race as good as possible and try to win, and not be happy with second place behind me.

It's pure speculation, but given my predicament in 2015, without a Severin Zotter, I might have tried to slow down much earlier to be able to finish, at least. Apart from Sevi, no other serious opponent was in sight. "Nobody can really race at their own pace," Rainer once told me. Anyone who believes that succumbs to imagination or desire, because each racer, to a certain extent, sets his pace based on the pace of their competitors. Unconsciously, Zotter's strong appearance stressed me. I had known in advance how strong he was; I wanted to go with him, and suddenly realized that I could not. For too long I pushed myself, trying to stay in the race for first place. But there comes a point where the body can no longer recover while riding.

My cooperating and training with Severin Zotter gave me hope that there would be someone that could race me at my level. Reto Schoch had given up ultra-cycling after only two RAAM's. Gerhard Gulewicz had passed his prime and had several years of consecutive DNF's. Marko Baloh was only a factor in races of two days or less. And Jure Robic was sorely missed. Many others also did their best, but never made it to the top, like Mark Pattinson, a slow starter who gets faster and faster as the finish gets closer. But at the Race Across America, you have to be strong from the first to the last mile.

When I was training with Zotter, during our interval training sessions I became aware of what good shape he was in. As I pedaled through my ergometer sessions alone, I was fully aware, that I must not let myself go. No easy going while training, no lazy days allowed. If you're not the best cyclist you've ever been, he'll worry you. Still, I was sure I could handle my friend, who I thought would be my rival for only the first few days of RAAM. I wished to be on the podium with him—me first, him second.

> **Severin had my full support, even as I watched him grow into a really serious adversary.**

We will never find out if I would have been able to beat him if I had stayed healthy. Sevi had my full support in generating his training plans, but he had organized all the other aspects, which also belong to a RAAM success, on his own. He had put together a team that harmonized wonderfully. He had found the necessary funds, and most importantly, he had the head for years of training and the coolness of being a rookie.

It honors my friend and training partner, and me too, that he sees it a little differently in retrospect. "What you have done for me over the years has been outstanding on all levels," he wrote shortly before RAAM 2018. "It was not just about the training plans, but also about your motivation during my European races, and the help at the organizational level. The positive emotions in our many discussions in preparation for RAAM were perhaps the most important part of our collaboration. I've always had the feeling that you honestly take thoughtful time in your feedback for all the issues I've brought, and you carefully addressed my many doubts."

I've always been aware of how much I helped him to race RAAM. But that email told me how grateful he is, even 3 years later. Was my supporting him a sign of genuine friendship or of great arrogance? Everyone can answer that question for themselves, and some of my crew also blamed me after the race. For me, it was simply one friend helping the other, but it was also more than that. We understand each other really well, so I wanted to fulfill my offer to the final degree. There is a second, more egoistic, approach: I wanted to see for myself how I functioned as a coach and whether that was an activity that I could imagine for my future.

> **I am very empathetic to others and I like to work in the background for their goals.**

Finish of RAAM 2015: I am congratulating Severin Zotter for his great win.

After my team had reported my DNF to the organizers, we took one rest day so that Arnold could attend to my health needs. The crew appreciated this, and made good use of this time out of the "pressure cooker" that was the follow car. Afterwards, we continued east in our three cars to Annapolis, where we had accommodations booked. Shortly after the halfway mark of RAAM, we eventually caught Sevi—but not in the way that we wanted. We all would have preferred it with me on the bike, and my crew in the support cars. No, when we finally caught up to him, all of us were in the cars, including me. We overtook our compatriot and all lined up roadside as the aspiring RAAM winner rode past. "Now Zotter wins RAAM," one of my crew said, his voice full of surprise and disappointment

The Race Across America is more expensive if you DNF. You and your crew do not drive through The US but sleep in motels. It costs. But this also brings opportunity to dissolve tensions, such as the ones that formed in our unfortunate 2015 adventure. After leaving the race, I realized that there was a deep chill among some of the team members and they did not even talk to each other anymore. That hit me emotionally because I wanted everyone to have a good time.

Eight days and eight hours after RAAM started, Sevi had reached Annapolis. His performance was great, and his team had mastered all the difficulties. I could have partied with them and said that this was my first success as a coach, but it would have been

RAAM 2017: My crew and I are celebrating the crossing of Cuchara Pass without any health issues.

a small consolation, if that. In fact, for me to see him cheering was very hard for me. I was sincerely very happy for my friend, and waited at the finish to be among the first of his well-wishers, and yet, I would have liked it all to have been very different.

If you finish faster than you have planned, you also face logistical challenges. Team Zotter spent the night with us in the house we'd rented in Annapolis because they did not expect to be that fast. Two days later, the successful competitors returned the favor by inviting us to a BBQ party. We talked about victory and defeat, and on a recent occasion, about how quickly one's own disappointments can be put into perspective; on the penultimate day of RAAM, Danish ultra-cyclist Anders Tesgaard, was riding at night in West Virginia and was struck by a motorist traveling at a speed of over 60 miles (100 kilometers) per hour.

Anders suffered severe injuries and fell into a coma, and remained in a coma until his death in February of 2018. What makes this all the more sad, is that it could have been avoided. According to his crew, just prior to this tragedy, the crew had told Tesgaard that they needed to stop to fill the follow car's gas tank, and that although it was night, rather than lose a few minutes waiting for this gas stop, he disregarded the rules and chose to go on without a follow car. I would never, ever consider leaving my follow car at night, especially on the winding roads of the Appalachians, where the locals know the road's every dip and curve and drive nearly as fast at night as they do by day.

RAAM racers Brett Malin and Bob Breedlove died in 2003 and 2005 from collisions with cars on the course. In RAAM's nearly four decades, these three are the only casualties—which is a remarkably low number given the length of the race and the dangers of the roads.

Three weeks later, we met again in Graz, where the mayor and the city council had wanted to honor Severin Zotter, plus me and Franz Preihs—the three hometown men who had raced RAAM that year. When asked how he was doing, and what he wanted to do next, he was torn, "I'm still thinking, maybe I'll give lectures, or I'll stay in my job as a social worker. Riding? I don't know, perhaps I'll continue, or perhaps I'll quit racing and start a family." I tried to encourage him to continue on his chosen path as an ultra-cyclist, but also to choose the path that his heart said was right for him. I would have been happy for him as a friend if, after his long and hard journey and his deserved RAAM victory, he could reap the rewards of his efforts more sustainably. Lecture requests, sponsor interest, and financial benefits are only there when you continue your career after successes. As a competitor, I should have hoped that I would never have to go against him again, but we were, and still are, friends, and a lost RAAM does not change that. Besides, I'm good in defeat; I'm certainly not a bad loser. But Severin decided to move on with life, unfortunately. Again, ultra-cycling has lost a great athlete. But hope lives on: Sevi does not entirely rule out a comeback.

When I thought of my next RAAM, I had to swallow. How would I fare in the Rocky Mountains? If I had physical problems again, would the weather be more comfortable for a nonstop ride, would our water sprayers, which we developed to keep my body cool, do their job? But we soon found these questions unnecessary after we had studied the Route Book for 2017. Between Time Station 8 and 9, an additional 105 miles (170 kilometers) and 9,900 feet (3,000 meters) in altitude had been added to the race, meaning that the challenges of the Rocky Mountains would have to be mastered differently than before. I would not reach Wolf Creek Pass in the afternoon, even at ideal speed, but at midnight, at freezing temperature, and the subsequent descent would be ridden at below freezing.

Two years ago I had thought too little about things such as lung problems, ailments on the bike, and of cars. I was convinced that of course I would finish. My mental attitude has now changed permanently. It is never self-evident that you get through RAAM, even if you have trained well and are the favorite. With a great deal of respect, I set about overcoming the three RAAM passes. This time I had no problems. I stopped at Cuchara Pass, not to catch my breath, but to celebrate a special moment. For a few minutes, together with my team, I celebrated having escaped my personal "Sword of Damocles". That year especially, I put great emphasis on a good performance in the Rockies in the direct race preparation, and had spent time at 8.200 feet (2,500 meters) two weeks before the start. I had traveled with Jürgen in the motorhome to ride the main mountains passes, to acclimatize me, and help my body feel comfortable at altitude. It cost me time and money, but the extra effort paid off.

From Cuchara Pass, I pedaled downhill to the Great Plains, looking forward to the scheduled one-hour sleep break. As I washed, I had to think back to Severin Zotter, who three months after his triumph, had asked me if I would continue to support him.

In my mind's eye, I saw him climb away from me at Cuchara Pass. My mind told me that each one of us should now go his own way, and that I had kept my promise. So I told him no, that I would not help him with his training plans anymore. Of course, we are still friends. But as far as training, it is best that he does his thing, and that I do mine.

Shortly after I remembered that moment, my eyes closed.

My coach Max Kinzlbauer and me after arriving in California

X

"WÖDMASTA IN THE WEITRADLFOAN"

(WORLD CHAMPION IN ULTRA-CYCLING)
24-HOUR TIME TRIAL WORLD CHAMPIONSHIPS, BORREGO SPRINGS

"Hey Max, here is a spontaneous idea! Don't you have the time and desire to go on a 5-day trip to California next week? It would be because of the 24h-Worlds in ultra-cycling!?"

My text message to Markus "Max" Kinzlbauer was succinct and his answer was the same: "Hi Straps. I always like to fly to the home of beef jerky (This is a running joke with Max, he loves American beef jerky and eats it constantly when we're there). I just have to check a few dates, I'll let you know."

After a few more e-mails, and both of us modifying our schedules and calendars, I found my 1-man crew for my "Plan B" and was overjoyed. After my illness and the cancellation of the 24-hour world record attempt on the track, which had been planned for mid-October, I did not want to leave my mixed year 2016 just hanging there. As my cold subsided and usual fitness returned, the 24-Hour World Time Trial

World Championship in Borrego Springs became a worthwhile destination. Organized by the same people as the Race Across America, Borrego Springs is a place I always like to come back to. I got one of the last starting slots just before registration was closing.

The destination of our trip is approximately 80 miles (130 kilometers) from Oceanside, the starting point of RAAM. The small town lives on tourism and astronomy. Borrego Springs was California's first "International Dark Sky Community," which means that there are no traffic lights and no street lights at night so as not to diminish the view of the starry sky. And really, there is so little going on in Borrego Springs that a traffic light would just be silly. Borrego Springs has an area of about 70 square miles (112 square kilometers), so in terms of area it's roughly ¼ the size of San Diego, but has only about 4000 residents compared to San Diego's 1.3 million people.

In principle, I consider myself a deliberate planner, a strategist who weighs pros and cons and embarks on undertakings only when I am prepared that there is a high chance of success.

Sometimes, however, I get more excited over those unforeseen, quickly planned and implemented actions, and I enjoy them more, too. My seasonal cornerstones, like RAAM or the 24-hour world records, are fixed dates that need to be confirmed long before. Not just because of physical preparation, but also for logistical reasons: my team must be assembled, schedules coordinated, flights booked, accommodations and cars rented. The sudden decision to race in Borrego Springs as my season finale woke my ailing cycling enthusiasm. The last times that I spontaneously entered small events were many years ago. So I really got excited about sort of returning to my simpler early career. There wasn't much thought or tactics behind it, there was no big announcement, no expectations, no interview requests or preliminary reports in the media. I could just concentrate on cycling and ending my year on a high note.

Two weeks of training on the ergometer followed, because in this training phase, the temperatures in Austria are getting lower and the weather gets less pleasant. So, I usually train in my basement gym, my "pain cave."

Despite the short-term decision, and although this World Championship hadn't been on my agenda at all, for the short term, I increased my training to between six and eight hours a day. I booked a flight that got me to the US as efficiently as possible, and did the organizing by writing e-mails and making phone calls while sitting and pedaling on the exercise bike. My equipment was subjected to a quick check, my preparation, my one crew member, and our strategy left nothing to be desired.

I wanted to compete to win, and I knew that I would not be the only one on the starting line with this plan. To name just one competitor: Marko Baloh. Again and again, Marko. Another interesting name was found on the start and result list: Jamshed Jehangir entered the age group "20 to 29 years." He won his category and he was third in the overall standings. The American is one of many who can put themselves in the spotlight once or twice, but isn't a full-time ultra-cyclist. This can be for many reasons, starting with professional living conditions, personal motivation, and financial opportunities. Although there are only a few long-established riders such as Baloh and myself, I am pleased that many young guns are interested in ultra-cycling, but I still wish there were more.

> With new faces, the sport is revived—and they also motivate me. Long ago I learned that new competitors should not be underestimated.

If you look at the organizational effort of other events, for example, the European 24-Hour Championship race or the Race Around Austria which have great public interest, then you might expect that this race in the US, the cradle of commercialism, would also be very high profile. But it is just the opposite. Borrego Springs does not have the population to attract crowds. The advertising for the 24-Hour World Time Trial Championship was limited to online campaigns (yet it still sold out).

When I first arrived, I was a bit confused about the sparseness of the venue's support area: there was the finish arch (the same inflatable one they use for RAAM), some temporary fencing that formed the start/finish chute, a tent for the timing staff, and not much else, no permanent toilets or infrastructure. It definitely wasn't a Formula 1 pit marquee. And then there was the fact that the 18-mile route is without lights or rails on the curves, but then I really enjoyed the pure atmosphere and the peaceful spirit of the race, which is unique! You have the feeling of being on your own and that there is nothing but you and your bike. It was a new experience for me to rely solely on my bike's headlight at night. Usually, I have the lights from my follow car, but these were not allowed at the World Championships. I learned to like that this event was without frills, and that it made the racers focus on the race and not the hype.

The road itself was wide, I was able to ride through every curve at full speed and because the 18-mile (30-kilometer) circuit did not exceed 100 meters in altitude, the slight rises did not grow into noticeable hills until the end of the race. But there was sand at the roadside and if you over-braked, you could have somersaulted off the road when the wheel drifted from the rough asphalt. I do not even want to talk about fan zones or spectators. At about the middle of the lap, there was a stop-sign where a steward waved the racers through, or if a car approached, signaled the racers to stop.

The sky full of stars at Anza Borrego State Park is overwhelming, but the competitors' behavior is not.

At sunset on the 4th of November, at 6 pm, the starting signal was given. It was my birthday and I promised to give myself the best gift: a world championship title.

The race developed in a way that was the best possible for me, but also provided some adrenaline rushes of anger and annoyance right at the beginning. I was able to take the lead and together with three others, we put down some fast laps. I was well ahead of Marko Baloh, and also the Spaniard, Julian Sanz Garcia, who usually can keep up in the first hours of a long distance race, but then tends to fall back. The fourth rider was US-resident Frenchman, Evens Stievenart, who gave me a headache.

The 24-Hour World Championship was an individual time trial, which meant no drafting—we had to keep ten yards away from another rider, except while passing. Stievenart put in a strong performance, sat down temporarily with a few hundred yards ahead of the rest of us, but then fell back into the chase group and ignored the no-drafting rule. Baloh and I kept to the specified distances, but Garcia and Stievenart were always right on our rear wheels. Since the officials had already issued a warning against all four of us top riders, I was indignant.

"Get out of my draft! If you keep this up, we will all be disqualified," I told Stievenart. He barked back that he was racing his race and that I should focus on my own. We exchanged a few more angry words and then kept apart. Stievenart ended the competition in 30th place with severe knee pain that required longer breaks. After returning to Austria, we exchanged some friendly messages, restored peace, and I really got to like Evens and his attitude toward sports.

In any case, at Borrego Springs, the Frenchman, who has had some impressive performances at other races, such as the 24 Hours of LeMans, did not deliver much more

than some temporary excitement. After five hours, I was still in a group of four, but since my legs felt good and I did not want to engage in any discussions with the officials, I decided to gamble a bit and push the pace. Within two laps of the 18-mile course, I'd put such a big hole between myself and my competitors that I could no longer see their lights behind me on the long straights. Then I reduced the

I believed that I had become a bit like Jure Robic: consistent and tough when I'm in a race, but accessible and in need of harmony before and after.

pace again because I couldn't hold it any longer. I had made an impression on my competitors, but now I had to pay attention to my rhythm again.

It was a pitch-dark night under a starry sky with only my favorite music and the sound of my wheels to keep me company. The temperature, which rose during the day to over 86 degrees Fahrenheit (30 degrees Celsius), was 20 degrees lower at night and thus pleasantly fresh. Taking my feeds in the pit lane was challenging. Since it was not brightly lit, I had to yell out to Max as I approached and find him by his reflective vest. As he sprinted beside me, he'd hand me a water bottle, which I put into the cage, and he'd also give me a bottle of Ensure, which I'd drain all at once. Max would also tell me the current intermediate information, informed me about my calorie balance and always had a few motivational words for me.

Max's job was not easy; sometimes I came into the support area with other riders and it wasn't always easy for us to find each other, take care of my needs, and get going without a major loss of time. During the time I was on the course, he had to prepare drinks, update the food log, gather information, assess my situation, and keep my fan base up to date on Facebook and my website.

At the halfway point of the race, I had covered 289 miles (465 kilometers) and saw that reaching the 900-kilometer mark within 24 hours, which I had just missed in Berlin-Tempelhof the year before, was within reach.

I would be the second rider—after Marko Baloh, who had reached 903 kilometers on the track—to ever do this.

But the meteorological conditions were against it. As the laps piled on, I slowed down in the Southern California heat. If I had cranked at 280 watts during the night, then it was probably a third less between hour 17 and hour 23. The willpower to achieve a magical record had given way to the urge to survive until the next bottle of water. But after all, I was not the only one who suffered, which left my lead unchallenged.

My hotel in Borrego Springs was on the route and I rode past it 29 times during the race. An idea solidified more and more in my brain: How about a quick stop-in for a cooling dip in the pool? I rode past for a second time, then a third time, but then, the urge prevailed and I stopped. I didn't want to dive in in my sweaty cycling gear, but at least I did cool my head down.

My spirits were newly awakened. As stipulated by the rules, the racers were diverted onto a shorter, approximately 4-mile-long (6.5 kilometers) lap during the last two hours. I was able to increase my lead even more. I wanted to finish the 24-Hour World Championship with style—without looking at the clock, without looking at the standings, but only pushing with all of my remaining power—going "all in" with whatever I had left in my legs. At that point, only a serious crash or physical problems would have

cost me victory. Still, the time to put my feet up had not yet come. I pushed myself all the way to the finish. I owed this to the organizers, to myself, to my one-man crew, and to all those who supported me and had been watching me over the previous 24 hours.

I finished my last lap mere minutes before the end of the 24 hours. The 900-kilometer mark was narrowly missed. Ultimately, 550.53 miles (886 kilometers) were next to my name, ten kilometers less than about 20 months earlier in Berlin, but still a record for the 24-Hour World Time Trial Championships—no one had ever achieved more miles on the Borrego Springs course.

One day after my 34th birthday, I had the satisfaction of having successfully implemented "Plan B," and with great pleasure and joy.
"Now you are Wödmasta in the Weitradlfoan," Max told me, as we ordered the largest hamburger in our favorite typically American bar & grill in Borrego Springs.
I grinned as I bit into my burger.

EDITOR'S NOTE:
Christoph Strasser returned to Borrego Springs in October of 2018 with a goal of not just winning the 24-Hour competition in the 6-12-24 Hour World Time Trial Championships, but to also reach the 900-kilometer mark that he'd come so close in 2016.

Strasser pushed himself to a slightly faster pace than in 2016, and he and his race assistant did everything they could to minimize his time in the pits. On most laps, he didn't stop at all, and merely tossed out his empty bottles and was handed fresh ones. It wasn't until the heat of the day that he began taking very short stops as his assistant cooled him down by pouring water on him. Their efforts paid off; Strasser's final tally was a new record of 913.463 kilometers (567.6 miles) for a startling overall average speed of 24 mph (38.624 kph).

My start of the 24-hour world record attempt at Berlin's Tempelhof Park

XI

"WORLD RECORDS HERE, WORLD RECORDS THERE"

BERLIN 2015 AND GRENCHEN 2017

IN THE HAMSTER WHEEL OF BERLIN

"It's probably more appropriate that we stop the record attempt."
"That cannot be done! You can't do that!"
"But you can see how many people are in the park and how dangerous it is!"

The people who, without my knowledge, discussed one of the hardest, most success-ful, and significant 24-hour ventures, were the Berlin Tempelhof security officers, and the representatives of my bike sponsor, Specialized. I do not know how long this con-versation lasted, nor do I know what arguments there were for and against canceling or allowing the record attempt, but I am still glad that I had not been informed. Finally, Specialized's people prevailed and I was able to continue with my record attempt.

I fought a really long time with myself until 2014, when I finally decided to attack the 24-hour road world record. My hesitance may have been because the owner of the record was named Jure Robic, who had ridden 840 kilometers, and I had simply not dared to outdo this achievement. Perhaps it was also in my subconscious, out of respect, that I did not want to take this entry in the "book of records" away from someone who was no longer alive. In any case, I needed a few RAAM victories to be confident enough to trust myself to have it in my legs to improve my idol's record.

My search for a suitable course was helped by Specialized, my California-based equipment supplier, whose European representatives were scheduled to have a booth at the Berliner Fahrradschau, a big bike expo. Along with this fair, there was also to be some cycling races—one of them in the Berlin-Tempelhof amusement park. So it made good sense to make the record attempt there. Jan Bruns, Specialized's event manager, proved to be my most important supporter and advocate in the months of preparation. He organized the permits and infrastructure, was responsible for funding the extensive campaign, and encouraged me at times when, due to the stress and the hurdles put in our way by the people in charge of the park, I was already struggling with thoughts of rejection.

The first time I visited the route at the former airport, I was skeptical. Strong wind seemed to be normal there, the road surface was only half good, and the course was not closed, but only secured. That meant that I had to reckon with recreational athletes and walkers from time and again. Initially, we'd wanted to make our route on the original runway. But the park official didn't approve this, or our request to allow a follow vehicle to accompany me on the runway, so we had to instead plan our route on the outer perimeter road.

However, there were other problems with the route choice: the lap of the Tempelhof was only 3.7 miles (6 kilometers) long, which is why—according to regulations of the Ultra Marathon Cycling Association (UMCA) (The name has since been changed to WUCA, the World Ultra Cycling Association)—the record would fall into the category "Outdoor Track." In order to get this attempt into the "Road" category, we needed a road loop that had a lap length of at least 5 miles (8 kilometers). I wanted to avoid the category of outdoor track since Marko Baloh's record was 553 miles (890 kilometers), set on a very fast 400-meter track. I would not expect to beat that on a course with such tight corners as those on this historic airport's perimeter road.

The final course was officially 11.8 kilometers long and had two turns which could be taken quickly, but not at full speed. Four officials were ordered to accompany, supervise, and record every aspect of my ride, and the record attempt was registered with the UMCA.

Even though RAAM was the big goal for this season, I had meticulously prepared for the world record attempt. At the beginning of the training in November, I had already lowered my seat position on the bike by five centimeters, in order to offer the windless attack surface, even though back pain could occur more easily. My clothing sponsor, owayo, sent me a special time trial suit made of thermo material to defy cold temperatures, yet still, offer aerodynamic advantages. The biggest advancement was on the tires. Working with Specialized's tire developers, we worked out the differences between different models, comparing times and performance data. I decided on the "Turbo Cotton" tires, which were 24 millimeters wide on the front, and 26mm wide on the back. These tires were up to two kilometers an hour faster than with my usual training tires.

I had installed a crank with power2max power measurement on my new bike, and had tested it in advance during training. The bike was in optimal condition when Lex rolled it to the park, while I was able to relax in the minivan we used as a follow vehicle. After a few minutes, Lex arrived at the start/finish area and reported in a panic that the crank was loose.

> From a technological point of view, we had also done everything to be prepared to attack the world record mark of Jure Robic.

"There are Specialized mechanics at the expo, they'll make it right," I reassured myself.

However, they did not have the proper tool on hand because they were actually responsible only for the mountain bikes being offered for demo. After rousing their colleagues on the west coast of the US out of bed via Skype, they knew that the crank could be fixed with car tools, that Lex picked up in front of our hotel with a hearty sprint in my private car. I was immensely grateful that I didn't have to hear these details, but instead lay ashamed in the backseat of the car and could wait for the all-clear, which seemed to take an eternity. Camera crews from RTL and SKY, the two leading TV stations in Germany, had come to film the start, and having to stop them was a bit embarrassing.

A bolt in the crank was supposed to be installed with Loctite; not knowing this, I instead greased the threads as I've normally done. Due to my lack of mechanical skill, the record attempt would almost have failed before it even started.

The start had been delayed by about half an hour, but when it finally started, I was cheered by several hundred onlookers. My nervousness had given way to relief. I was just happy that I could start, and was now ready to earn my salary for my many months of preparation. At the beginning it was fantastic—I could go with my targeted 270 watts, and for hours was keeping a constant pace of over 25 miles (40 kilometers) per hour.

Due to the nice spring weather, many people visited this park during my attempt.

It was a sunny Friday afternoon in March, perhaps the first really warm day that Ber-
liners saw that year. They flocked to the parks and the banks of the Spree and Havel.
Running, barbequing, playing football, flying kites, just strolling—the Tempelhof was
buzzing with activity. And right in the middle of it, I did my laps on my time trial bike.
There should have been posters at the three main entrances to draw attention to
the world cycling record attempt, and it had also been planned that security guards
would talk to the park visitors. But none of this had happened because the responsible coordinator fell ill and was absent. Some pedestrians were terribly upset with
me, one even threw rocks at me, and there was a woman, who while swinging her bag
onto her back with an outstretched arm, nearly hit me with the bag, which surely
would have put me on the ground.

Considering these incidents, the phrase, "You see how dangerous it is!" made sense.
But, ninety percent of the people who watched me on my journey were extremely
positive and cheered me on. A hundred meters in front of me, Jan and his colleagues
rode on e-bikes to draw the park visitors' attention to me, and to clear the route in a
friendly manner. This goal was further aided by my three-person crew, who also used
the speakers mounted on the car's roof to loudly tell all that I was riding for a world
record.

Toward evening it became quiet. At 19 o'clock they closed the gates and we had the
Tempelhof to ourselves. A memorable sunset was the last highlight of the day before
night fell. I enjoyed the atmosphere, and for the first time, I felt really good on the
course, and with my performance. Physically, I was still quite fit except for a slight

162

During the night the park is closed to visitors. I enjoyed the silence.

pain in the lumbar spine. The first four hours had been a tightrope walk and hard to beat in stress, because I had to leave the racing line over and over again to avoid collisions. But by the end of the day, I was finally able to devote myself to my rhythm. It was clear that I had to wear warmer clothes for the next few hours and thus lose the aerodynamic advantages of my usual kit. That's why I waited as long as possible to change. Only when the thermometer was already approaching the freezing point, did I stop and pull on leg warmers and put on a jacket. This was one of two stops I would make of 120 seconds each, plus five pee stops, each lasting half a minute.

Due to the close-fitting time trial helmet, I couldn't have radio communication with my crew—there was no space to install my headset, which I have relied on for every race since 2012. I'm a communicative character, and I need dialogue in the hard, tiring phases to stay awake and focused, and to combat the monotony of pedaling mile after mile. The regulations stipulated that the car was allowed to drive next to me, but only a single minute per quarter of an hour. That was not enough to tear me out of my loneliness and isolation, because I could barely hear a word through the closed helmet and wind when someone shouted something out of the car. One is tempted to believe that since I can do without sleep for days, staying awake for just one night wouldn't be a challenge. But it was grueling, and being alone gnawed at me. Several times I was close to microsleeping. The cold consumed my strength, and I could not keep up with the planned pace. This circumstances demoralized me.

In retrospect, that night at the Tempelhof is one of the toughest in my career. It was a night that would never end, a night in which I briefly asked the question, "What if I

cannot do it? Is it worth it? Will I weaken unnecessarily just before RAAM and risk the most important race of the year?"

There was no flow, no ease, and no joy in Berlin. It was a pure fight lasting for hours—against the clock and against my head, which could not stop brooding. As my mind went into a negative spiral, my legs still continued to crank, and I automatically moved forward at a respectable pace.

It got light but barely warmer, and because Saturday's weather wasn't as nice as Friday's, there were far fewer park visitors. I was aware that the record would be mine if I rode on at my comfortable pace. But by then, I would not have been satisfied with that—I wanted to do a great job, I wanted to exploit my full potential, and could only be satisfied with myself if I put down what I considered to be the "perfect 24 hours." My own goal was, in fact, not tied to the record, but to the maximum kilometers possible. All of this was only now becoming clear to me, now that rational thought was abating and the emotions were taking over. I was mentally battered and dissatisfied with myself in the final hours of my journey, and a close-to-the-target goal would not satiate my fighting spirit. The nine hundred kilometers I wanted to cover were no longer realistic. But the old record was almost certain. So why this effort? While

I quarreled with the situation, it started to rain, and the cold was now reinforced by moisture.

I had screwed up during those hours.

It was not until the spectators at the edge of the course increased in number and cheered me that I found my old strength. "Give everything again" was my motto. Now it was time to stop thinking, to stop indulging in my own dissatisfaction at not surpassing the 900-kilometer sound barrier, which no one on the bike yet had managed to do. After 72 laps, I had matched Jure Robic's record, yet I still had one hour and 23 minutes to raise the bar even more.

In the last hour, I was about as fast as I was in the first one, and was touched that so many people had come out to cheer for me despite the cold, the wet, and the wind. Of course, I understood nothing, but their presence and the body language said more than a thousand words.

After 76.5 laps the time was up.

Kougi gave a countdown over the loudspeaker, which gave me extra power for a final sprint. The spot where I was after 24 hours was marked by a UMCA official, and then evaluated by the distance surveyor.

I had covered 896.173 kilometers and missed my dream destination by a ridiculous 3,827 meters (just over 2 miles).

> I realized that now I could write history. And that's what I wanted to do, because maybe this opportunity was only once in my life. Suddenly, I was once again in full possession of my strength and rode as if my life depended on it.

In the start and finish area, a small podium was prepared, on which I let my joy run free. With my brother, who surprisingly had traveled from Austria with long-time friends from Switzerland, and with many fans, I celebrated the new record. I got the obligatory champagne shower, was then wrapped in all the blankets that could be found, and after 24 hours of liquid food, I once again enjoyed something solid: a hot goulash. As cold as I was, it was so beautiful.

At that moment, setting a new world record was more important to me than missing the 900-kilometer barrier.

I had reached my goal and realized once again that I could not get through 24 hours straight on the bike without some bad moments. Nonetheless, the performance in

Done! 896 kilometers in 24 hours

Berlin was gold for my self-confidence. I had contested RAA in record time, RAAM as well, and I had improved the 24-hour world record by over 31 miles (50 kilometers). I worked hard to take my ultra-cycling to a new level.

What I definitely did not take to a new level was my ability as a mechanic. When I lifted the bike out of the trunk at home in Graz, I noticed that the seat post had slipped down by two centimeters during the record run—that is what had caused my back pain! The screw had not been tightened enough. I could not help but laugh out loud, and promised to leave my equipment preparation to the professionals in the future.

My success in Berlin impacted the months that followed. I took many appointments, gave lectures and was often in a quandary (as some companies asked more than ex-

pected). Should I prefer to train, or make additional money through an appearance? I was well trained and in shape, I was looking forward to the upcoming Race Across America, but some of my decisions to monetize my sporting excellence were the first signs of new priorities. When I deliberately thought of the balancing act that I had to carry out between sports and business, I told myself that I was humbly grounded in the facts. What I cannot really say for sure today, is whether or not I might have gotten a bit too cocky, too over-confident, and started to think successful racing was a given, or assuming that I could get away with shortening a training session here and there and maybe, still win by giving only 99.5%, instead of 100%. But is it reprehensible to want to make a small profit after sporting achievements, if you are active in a marginal sport in which there is no prize money?

But could I allow myself this loss of power? Was not Severin Zotter in very, very good shape this year?

"G'SCHISSEN UND RICHTIG G'SCHISSEN" IN GRENCHEN
"SHITTY AND REALLY SHITTY" IN GRENCHEN

"Please stop and get out of the car."

Michael Kogler, Sabine and I had expected nothing less when we wanted to enter Switzerland with a fully packed CS30 minivan. Our car, packed with wheels, spare parts, equipment and sponsorship gifts, was an open invitation to customs officials to take a closer look.

"What is this?" the officer asked.
"A three-kilogram sausage from Wiesbauer, my sponsor. It's a raffle prize" I responded, quite dryly.
"And this?"
"Those are Cabanossi snacks." (Something like American Slim Jims™.)

For all the high-tech gadgets in the car, including the display mannequins and the jerseys that we sell in my online store, the customs officer had no interest. But the meat products aroused his suspicion.

"You have to declare that, right?"
"But that's just something to eat for our trip over the long weekend. We're going to a cycling race."
"This is import of food, it has to be declared."

My cousin and crew chief Michael "Kougi" Kogler, who had been driving at the time, was allowed to handle the bureaucratic part, because although the car and its contents belonged to me, the driver was responsible for it.

After about ten minutes, Kougi came out of the customs building and said, "It will not be that bad, they treat it like a speeding ticket."

Well, anyone who has ever received a speeding citation in Switzerland knows that these are by no means comparable to our penalties.

Should I complain, engage in a longer discussion, and risk that the Swiss officer might find other declarable items? I stayed back. We'd considered selling some of the items from our online shop there, but found that the customs regulations were very complicated, and so decided against this idea. But we still had some jerseys and mannequins for display, and we told any interested people how they could order from our online shop. But we had not read the regulations about food items.

We finally paid three hundred euros in import fees for nine kilograms of sausage—just over $300 US. I hope that anyone who got a bite of our sausage really appreciated and enjoyed it.

We would have spent many times that to see the the 24-hour world record attempt on the velodrome in Vienna go as we had hoped. As early as 2016, when I first toyed with the idea of challenging the 903 kilometers of Marko Baloh, we, with the help of the Austrian Cycling Federation (ÖRV), approached the city of Vienna (operator of the Dusika Stadium Velodrome) about renting it for the record attempt.

The experience that I had with them is typical of the civil service in Austria. Imagine that the people who work at your local department of motor vehicles were the ones running the velodrome, and you'll understand how it was. My telephone calls did not lead to any result. Requested return calls never came, and e-mails were not answered. I did not want special treatment; I just wanted a business contact. When, after months of pressing, I finally got a price list that took my breath away. Every little thing was subject to exorbitant fees. The finish line band with the necessary adhesive material was 251.10 euros, each plastic armchair (dozens were to be placed in the infield during the attempt) would have been five euros, the light in the hall would have cost three hundred euros an hour. On top of the rental fee, I would have had to pay an additional fee for special software for the timing system, because modern operating systems were no longer compatible with it. I'd also have to pay the wages of a dedicated technician who had the ability to operate this time-honored equipment. Looking through the multi-page estimate, I got the impression that the city of Vienna wanted to renovate the Ferry Dusika Stadium with my financial contributions. When I first read the estimate, I truly wondered if they were joking with me. But no, unfortunately, they were 100% serious.

But we let it be. As much as I'd have loved to set a world record in Austria with the great support of a local audience, it was very clear that I had to look for other options. Montichiari near Milan—where Marko Baloh set his record in 2010—would have sufficed, as would the Velodrome Grenchen in Western Switzerland. The town with about 18,000 inhabitants is located west of Zurich and north of Bern. The organizers of the velodrome (in part due to an integrated hotel with a restaurant, shops, courses on how to ride a velodrome, races, and brisk activity year round) responded to the request by return mail. The basic tenet was: "We from the Tissot Velodrome, the Swiss National Stadium of cycling, would be pleased if you complete your record attempt with us and guarantee our absolute support." The rent including all ancillary and operating costs was much cheaper than in Vienna, never mind that Grenchen is one of the fastest and most modern cycling tracks in the world. That's why Jens Voigt and other professionals set their hour world records here.

I did not expect any special treatment in Vienna. I come from a marginal sport, which has only become more famous in the last ten years. So I'm used to organizing a lot myself and coping with the financial burdens with the help of my sponsors. However, the attention and courtesy from Switzerland did me good, and the decision to ride there was quickly made.

I set the date of October 14, 2016, for my record attempt. The preparations, again with Specialized as an organizer on hand, were already in progress. Wheels were provided for test rides, a space was reserved in front of the velodrome as a bike-expo and test-ride area. DJs, music, and entertainment were scheduled. It was almost done. But then, after a strong single-time trial at King of the Lake at the end of September, I got an infection. It was probably a viral infection, and I had to deal with a cough and runny nose. Most of the medicines that are used normally for severe colds (e.g. aspirin complex) are on the doping list, so athletes need to resort to rather weak medicines. Could I get fit with herbal tea and saltwater nasal spray within two weeks?

There was much more at stake than just a failed world record attempt. My sponsors invested a lot to set up the event site—the world record attempt was embedded in a big event. Should I take this completely incalculable risk and try it? Or should I cancel the world record attempt?

For two weeks I quarreled with myself, but then I was proud of having had the coolness—despite pressure from sponsors and the media—to delay the attempt. Of course, that was an immensely difficult decision! Too much time, effort, and preparation had fallen victim to a banal cold. I reproached myself for a long time and asked myself if I had acted recklessly and could I have prevented getting sick. But in the end, I had no other choice because without one hundred percent fitness it would have been much more irresponsible to tackle such a venture. I am also just an ordinary person who gets sick every now and then. There is no professional training that can prevent that.

The understanding of all my sponsors was great. Even the velodrome management gave me an all-clear: we had one year to complete the world record attempt at no additional cost. That was yet another moment when I was glad to have chosen Grenchen.

364 days later we were at the Swiss border and paid for the most expensive Wiesbauer sausages of our lives.

In Grenchen, it was Kougi that failed in the tests before the big day. One last time, we practiced our technique at transferring the bottle with the least possible loss of time. He had to start running half a lap before the handoff, and then sprint for a few yards beside me. I was flying—around 25 miles (40 kilometers) per hour—so a sporty performance was required. Kougi strained a leg muscle in training and we had to quickly find a solution to this unpleasant situation. Luckily, we had Lukas, who had come along as a journalist for bikeboard.at, and Jan of Specialized. They were registered together, along with Sabine, as members of my support crew. The many obstacles and hurdles of preparation were now finally overcome, after word of Kougi's injury reached me, there was no more negative news. I was ready.

When I stretched out my legs in the hotel room bed, a few minutes before I started, I closed my eyes and reviewed the previous few weeks. When I thought about the next 24 hours, I knew it would be very hard. I thought through the processes in detail. In my imagination, I rode the ideal line on the 250-meter long Siberian oak track, and the two tight 180-degree curves with 46-degree banking.

In my hotel room in the last minutes before the start

In my last of a total of eight training sessions in Vienna, which had served as the final test ride, I was able to achieve an average of 26 miles (42 kilometers) per hour for six hours, for which I had to pedal at an output of 250 watts. That ride was scheduled on a Friday morning and the hall warden had not been informed about it. At 8 o'clock in the morning, we had to disturb some gentlemen by telephone before we were finally allowed on the track—one and a half hours late. Vienna, oh Vienna!

Although the cooperation with the Dusika Stadium was sometimes difficult, I am grateful that I could use the track for training purposes.

This dress rehearsal had made me confident. The implementation of the nutritional plan went smoothly, I held the seat position without back problems, and was mentally strong and focused. The ride would be monotonous, but this time, unlike the Berlin record, I could use an earbud on one side of the helmet and a Terrano headset on the other ear (which took a little creative handiwork to install), allowing me to have music AND 2-way communication with my crew. Afterwards, I played more or less realistic mind games, but finally set myself clear goals. The fact that I had achieved an average power of 254 watts in Berlin, in difficult weather conditions, was a positive indication for me that I'd be able to keep the performance on the track equally high.

My minimum goal was Baloh's record, but in reality, I wanted more. If I could hold forty kilometers per hour for the entire time, that would be 960 kilometers. My dream was even the absolutely incredible mark of 1000 kilometers, for which I would have to hold 25.81 miles (41.67 kilometers) per hour, which to me, after the six-hour test, seemed possible.

Marko Baloh and his wife Irma were two of three officials of the Ultra Marathon Cycling Association, which monitored and would recognize my record attempt. Another prominent name of this jury was Anna Mei. The Italian had set world records over twelve and twenty-four hours, and over a thousand kilometers.

The fact that Marko agreed to accompany this world record attempt as an official, shows once again how friendly and benevolent it is in ultra-cycling. He could have refused. Many consider attacking one's own record as an affront, or rather want to watch one from afar, but are not themselves part of the action. To set a new record, and be able to personally congratulate on camera the one whose record was broken, is not something that usually happens.

The reality after the start was sobering. The circuit in Berlin had offered me darkness and brightness, sunshine and rain, crowds and loneliness, flow and fight. The hamster cage in Grenchen offered me no fun factor, no flow, no variety.

I radioed to my crew: "In RAAM, RAA, and everywhere else, there is a variety of all kinds. Here it is really nauseous. I just waver between g'schissen and really g'schissen—shitty and really shitty." This was of my own doing; no one had made me do this. "Dude, Strasser, what were you thinking?" I asked myself. And I answered, "It's your own fault, you have no choice now, you have to endure it." It would have been disappointing to all my supporters, and just embarrassing, to break off the record attempt. To endure would be agony, but it was, as strange as it may sound, the lesser evil.

My cramped sitting position felt catastrophic after a few hours. In this untypical ae-ro-dynamic-optimized position, it was difficult for me to eat the scheduled liquid food. There were stomach problems and indigestion; I had to fight constantly against nausea, although I have tolerated the liquid food well for years.

I felt my stomach struggle with a slight dizziness. And due to the centrifugal force generated in the banked curves, it was only possible to get out of the saddle for a few seconds—so getting any relief in my upper body was hardly feasible.

Each lap I dissected into four sections: Seven seconds of the highest concentration in the curve, holding the ideal line to avoid losing unnecessary meters caused by a line that is too high, but also so as not to fall when I drifted inwards; Four seconds on the straights, a quick glance at the scoreboard and then immediately focus on the next corner; And then, hold my line for seven seconds before I again tackled the four seconds of the straights, and briefly, without twisting my head, risking a glance out of the corner of my eye to my crew, ideally even with a thumb up. Meanwhile, my thoughts circled around my aching back, the question of how to continue to take fluid, and how to overcome the crippling fatigue. I did not come to any conclusions in these thoughts, since the next curve again demanded my full attention. I didn't even want to indulge in thinking about problems, but to bring myself into such a flow state that I would be totally absorbed in action, in movement. It was a bit like meditation.

What I've learned so well over the past few years is turning off the pondering, choo-sing things, and then pulling through. I have to recognize the deeper meaning in ad-vance, and can think about my motives for weeks and months, but during the action, there is no question about the "why?" anymore. There is only do. And pedal. And hold a tight line on the curve.

I thought a maximum of an hour ahead. I tried to keep the watts stable for the next hour, feel the sitting position, and to listen to the body, sliding regularly from left to right on the saddle, in order not to have the seating contact area (and adjacent or-gans) fall asleep. During the event, I decided that this track world record attempt was the worst thing I've ever done and that I would never return to the track again. I had reached a point where I just wanted to survive the whole thing in order to complete a big chapter.

I switched to a lighter gear; the higher cadence was a change. Fortunately, for this record, the UMCA says that a rider is free to use a road wheel with a freehub and the ability to shift gears. Real track wheels have a fixed ratio with a rigid hub, so coasting is not possible. Technically, a standard direct-drive track bike has advantages, as less energy is lost over the friction of the chain. The disadvantage is that if brain-fade

sets in—for example, if you forget to pedal—you'll fall, because the pedal lifts the rider from the bike like an ejection seat. Out of fear of such a moment, I chose to use a road wheel and gears. In this way, I could also relax a leg and roll, except I never actually did this. I did not let my legs hang for a second. I cranked continuously, as coasting in the corner would have meant less grip and therefore a fall.

Hours later, because of the calorie deficit, my performance was down, but my team reacted great, adapted the food, and got the situation under control, even though we had little radio contact. Many spectators in the velodrome meant many phones. Their frequencies disturbed our radio network, which is why the communication with my team only worked sporadically. On the other hand, many spectators, and their many shouts of encouragement, also put me in a good mood, though I only partly heard their cheers due to the time trial helmet. Really, I could hardly perceive anything acoustically and visually, except the creaking parquet floor, which was flying under my wheels.

I started at 1 pm, and during the night I was unable to pedal the wattage I demanded; I only got 218 instead of the predicted 250. I forced myself to stay focused and was locked in my thought prison. I had no choice. There was no escape. Incidentally, this was not only true for me, but also for my support crew.

Part of my crew was continuously working for 35 hours (including the preparation time). They supported me and did their best to keep me in a good mood, and to keep me focused and at peak performance, especially at night, when it was quiet in the hall.

After 22 hours I made my first and only pee break, although I had actually scheduled four. Previously, I simply had not felt the need to relieve myself, which was probably due to reduced fluid intake and ongoing nausea. The break had done me good. I was able to recover a little and felt fresher. Emotionally, the two minutes standstill was a highlight of the world record attempt, as I saw the determination and the confidence in the eyes of my crew. I took but a few glances to rekindle my inner fire. Bob, who was on my team for the first time at RAAM 2017, had joined us during the night. He patted my shoulder and encouraged me. Sabine hugged me briefly. She does not often come to the races, and that's why I wanted to give everything that day. How nice is it to have loved ones around!

57 minutes before the deadline I had matched Marko Baloh's record.

With the relief of having successfully mastered the initial challenge, my wattage rose again. I saw the whole thing now as a privilege, was grateful for the support, and now saw it as my duty to fight again for each lap. I wanted to show my full commitment to the hundreds of people who had come to the velodrome. The moderators pushed the mood to a climax, loud music played, and hearing the countdown created a tremendous atmosphere that allowed me to sprint over the last few minutes.

Pure joy and relief after surviving my 24-hour ordeal

In the end, it was 585.252 miles (941.873 kilometers). After 3,767 laps and 7,534 left turns, the torment came to an end. Rarely has my relief been so great at finishing an event. I did two more laps of honor, in which I no longer had to keep the uncomfortable aerodynamic position. I cheered and celebrated with the audience, feeling the pressure of the past 24 hours and the months of preparation dwindle away from me. I was getting slower, and when I thought of going to the support zone, I slipped off the last corner due to lack of speed and crashed. Nothing happened to me; I arrived with a crooked handlebar and a little abrasion on my hip in the exit area. But I realized how fast the whole thing could have gone wrong, and just how present the danger of falling on the track was in every curve.

To Marko Baloh, who handed me the certificate, I said, "Those were the most brutal 24 hours I've ever experienced." He laughed, knowing what I had been through, and congratulated me. Later, he told me that in many RAAM finishes, there had been no other 24 hours that would have been nearly as hard as those on the track.

The dream to break the 1000-kilometer mark remained a dream. With all the problems I had overcome, I was more than satisfied with my record. "When are you going to attack the 1000 kilometers?" I was asked.
"It certainly could have gone better, but it could have also been a lot worse. Now I'll let someone else try."

Marko Baloh, the former record holder, hands over the certificate to me - a generous action

I think there are goals in life that you can always pick up again. It is good and important to always strive for improvements and optimizations. But in certain cases, I find it presumptuous to chase after a dream that may not be realistic. In retrospect, I have to admit that I had formulated my goals in the ignorance of the actual severity of what it is to ride the velodrome. I was probably a bit cocky. I am now humble; my naivety was probably helpful in advance. As for another attempt, I currently have no desire.

Incidentally, the nine kilograms of Wiesbauer sausages were not completely consumed in Grenchen. And so Sabine, Kougi, and especially me, tried to eat the last on our way to the border of Austria—not that the Swiss customs would impose an exit penalty for food.

Long straight roads and flat terrain, there is not much to see in Kansas

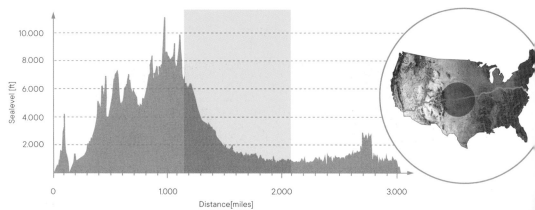

Sealevel [ft]

10.000

8.000

6.000

4.000

2.000

0   1.000   2.000   3.000

Distance[miles]

XII
STINKING, STORMING, BELOVED KANSAS

RAAM, TIME STATIONS 20–35

Aerodynamic testing in Specialized's "WinTunnel" in Morgan Hill, California

"How about if you came to us and we do some tests in the wind tunnel?" Sebastian, from my bike sponsor Specialized, asked me in the run-up to the Race Across America 2014. I was absolutely thrilled with the idea. My team and I had been working on improvements for some time by then. Those improvements were hard to find; the year before, I became the first rider in RAAM's history to finish in less than eight days, so the bar was already set enormously high.

Specialized is headquartered in Morgan Hill, California, south of San Francisco. The town is a satellite city for high-tech companies in Silicon Valley. There are a striking number of cyclists, an extensive network of cycle paths, nice cafes, Mexican restaurants, and, a wind tunnel. Such devices are hi-tech, rare, and therefore expensive. If I had wanted to rent it for use, it would have cost me somewhere in the middle five-digits in euros. For an ultra-cyclist, a wind tunnel is practically priceless.

Two weeks before the start of the Race Across America, I spent a full day at Morgan Hill with Lex Karelly, and could scientifically test which aerodynamic effects I would have in an upright, as opposed to a curved, sitting position, and how big the actual advantages are between different frames, wheels, helmets, and equipment.

For example, based on the tests, I was shown that a water bottle carried behind the saddle produces less air resistance than one mounted on the bike frame in the usual position. That's why I started RAAM 2014 carrying my bottles in this way, but we returned to using a water-bottle cage on the fourth race day. It was not a problem for me to reach for the bottle behind the seat, but it was tricky to put it back after drinking. The longer RAAM lasted, the riskier it became, and I didn't want to take the gamble of falling while battling against the wind on the time-trial bike.

Also, I learned in the Specialized "WinTunnel", how important it was not to cover the helmet vents with sponsor logos. If the air flowing in from the front does not find a way to exit the helmet, then resistance builds up. More drag meant, clearly, a slower ride in this test, because the wind had more attack surface and slowed me more, although I pedaled with the same power.

Owayo has been my clothing supplier since 2008, and since 2013, they've made custom jerseys for me specially designed for the weather I endure while crossing the United States. These left nothing to be desired. The so-called "desert jerseys" were made of very thin fabric, but when it was hot or when I was sweating, I opened them anyway, but that was before I'd learned how much this was slowing me down. In the Specialized wind tunnel, a cruel truth came to light: An open jersey generates so much air resistance that all other aerodynamic advantages are negated. That was the last thing I wanted—after all, I had invested in an expensive wheel that was going to pay off. I wanted to race RAAM, win it, and with my aerodynamic modifications, trim another two or three hours from my current course record. In practice, that meant the jersey had to stay closed, even if it got uncomfortably warm. We went even further into detail, and sewed the two outer jersey pockets shut so that the wind on the sewn-on waistband would find no attack surface. Only the middle compartment was left unsewn to leave a place for my mobile phone or GPS tracker.

After we had tested sufficiently, and been supplied with a wealth of important data, Specialized's staff invited me to attend an in-house bike ride. "It would be cool!" I thought. I expected this would be a challenging ride, and I definitely wanted to do another round, and chat with the people from Specialized, so I agreed. I thought to myself: "They are great guys, we will have fun, but it will be very easy for me since I am in the best shape of my life after months of training." There was fun alright, but for them, not for me. The ride turned into a race for these cycling experts and engineers, all of whom were really fit and extremely fast. Due to a flat and a subsequent tube change, I lost so much time that I had to ride as hard as I could to catch back up to the forty-rider group. After that, this RAAM winner was done. Completely exhausted, I sat back in the car and slept the long way south to Borrego Springs, while Lex drove.

The long straights of Colorado, Kansas, and Missouri, between Time Stations 20 (Trinidad, CO) and 34 (Washington, MO), are described by many RAAM riders as "monotonous and boring." Wolfgang Fasching speaks in his lectures about the fact that the highlight of an entire day is a small left-right turn before hundreds of barren kilometers that go straight ahead. Kansas, in particular, is often described as a "sheer horror." Dividing this state into two halves, the completely boring and straight-line actually begin in Colorado, after the descent from the mountains, and end at the RAAM halfway point. In the second part of the state, also known as the "United States Granary," flat elevations and slightly undulating terrain are added to make the mental aspect a little easier again.

Everyone has their own perception and their own physique. Fasching is smaller and lighter than me; the mountains are more to his liking than mine. On the other hand, I feel good in the plains. Maybe that's also why—and on principle—I want to show strength where everyone else moans. Just saying that I love Kansas makes many competitors cringe, which gives me a mental advantage.

Another reason why I really like Kansas: Leapfrog Support is over. From then on, the crew may be with me in the car around the clock. So, it is those last miles in Colorado that are often the hardest in the race, because I have to ride on my own, and after three days the fatigue gnaws at my concentration. Music over the speakers, conversations about the race, and funny quizzes or joke questions (some more funny than others), breathe new energy into me.

> Now RAAM really starts again. The team and I are together again and do not have to deal with the day separately.

From RAAM 2013 to RAAM 2014, my aim was to defend my title, and I spent months doing nothing but training—my whole life was focused on this goal. I did not underestimate any of my competitors, but at the same time, I was deeply prepared for it to be a long race against the clock if it were to run as smoothly as the previous year.

The race started as expected and was almost too easy. The first two days were hot, but much more pleasant than in other years. In addition, a tailwind helped me through the desert and allowed me an incredibly high average of 22.3 miles (36 kilometers) per hour in the first 394 miles (635 kilometers) to Congress. I did not really have to keep my speed in check to conserve my energy as in some years. In other words, I didn't need to measure out my power, since it was cooler than usual. So I was riding full throttle with an average of 245 watts until Congress. These kinds of numbers are not possible if it is too hot.

At Time Station 6 in Congress, Arizona, I was already three hours ahead of runner-up Gerhard Gulewicz. I had mild lung problems in The Rockies, but they did not get any worse and went away in Kansas. After 61 hours, the first sleep break was on the schedule—until then, I had only enjoyed two power naps of a quarter of an hour each.

I imagined Swiss racer Reto Schoch, my great competitor of the past, sitting at home watching the live ticker on the official RAAM website. I imagined he would witness how I would have stayed under eight days again. Whether he actually did this or not, did not matter to me. In the Midwestern plains, I wan-

> Once the desert is over, and the first mountains are crossed, and you've managed to still be on the road without any health issues, only then you can carefully begin thinking about finishing the Race Across America and start watching the competition's positions in the race. To do so before is just foolish.

ted to get one day ahead of my first pursuer, and all the information my team and I received gave us wings. By 2014, no rider had ever completed the first nine hundred miles at an average speed of over 20 miles (32.2 kilometers) per hour. Never before had a rider completed 949 miles (1,528 kilometers) in the first 48 hours. There was already talk of a new record, but I wanted to know nothing of this yet. "We stick to our strategy," team boss Rainer Hochgatterer told me, "we're racing from Time Station to Time Station!" I nodded in agreement.

Once again, it turned out that RAAM can't be ridden and won with a slow start and a fast finish. Anyone who believes that they can succeed with this strategy succumbs to wishful thinking. In practice, it shows that being in the lead is highly motivating. I felt mentally strong and enjoyed the feeling of having everything under control. The leader of the race brings questions to the minds of the guys behind him. What is he doing differently than us? When and how long will he take a break next time? Where else could he have a period of weakness? Body and mind also get tired, one way or the other, whether a racer has started fast or slow. After four days nobody can ride as fast as at the beginning, as a tired brain always wants to give in to the need for sleep, and can no longer fully emit signals to the muscles. Under sleep deprivation, perception, thinking, and reactions all become slower. Starting fast and slowing down is thus more effective at RAAM than starting slowly and still slowing down.

I passed the halfway point between Pratt and Maize at a time when Gerhard Gulewicz was about four hundred kilometers behind. At Time Station 28, in El Dorado, Kansas, Gulewicz once again ended his race. This time due to health problems, the most serious of these were his neck muscles. He had developed "Shermer's Neck," a condition in which the neck muscles become exhausted and the rider cannot lift his head on his own. In the advanced stage, the head hangs down, a rider has a li-

RAAM 2017: My team and I celebrate over reaching the halfway-point

mited field of vision, and so riding in traffic becomes very dangerous. Patric Grüner was another victim of this malady in RAM 2017, which he ended prematurely due to Shermer's Neck. A case of Shermer's Neck is a serious matter, and one of the most common causes of a DNF in ultra-cycling. But smart and determined racers can arm themselves against it, with special strength training before the race, with massages during the race, or even by using a neck support. Wolfgang Fasching, for example, used a neck support in 2007, and although he was afflicted from the halfway point, he toughed it out and took second place behind Jure Robic, less than four hours behind.

The eponym of "Shermer's Neck" is a co-founder and five-time participant in RAAM, Michael Shermer. He finished third in the first race in 1982, and suffered a year later from the neck pain named after him.

There's nothing spectacular to see where the race reaches the halfway distance. No time station, no supporting program from the organizers, no cheering fans. If it were not marked in the route book, most teams would not find this point. Traditionally, the first crew to reach the halfway point places a mark on the road. In my case, my team members wrote with chalk on the asphalt, "Halfway Point."

We also took a short break at the halfway point during our first RAAM's and had a mini-party with Cokes and costumes for the crew, which boosted the mood and the atmosphere of the team. My crew cheered for me before they continued on with new momentum. But things changed in 2014. We were so time-fixated, focused solely on our speed, that we threw away our halfway mark traditions (which by the way, we reached in the middle of the night). Any stop that was not absolutely necessary had been canceled, save for my people doing "the wave" as I rode past them.

Sometimes, text messages come from the race director after we've passed the halfway point. Often these texts are about weather warnings. Sometimes, we ourselves witness how the sky is closing and the natural spectacle of the weather begins. In all

my RAAM participations, only once have I made it dry through Kansas—in 2018. In 2011, a murderous wind and rain tormented me; In 2012 there was a tornado warning; In 2013 there was a storm and a cloudburst; In 2014 there was an extreme tailwind, coupled with rain that swept across the road at 50 kilometers per hour, which left me in danger of falling over broken branches or other obstacles; In 2017, the wind blew so hard that it almost tore my bike out of my hands during a short stop.

With a big lead over the pursuers, my record race in 2014 was one against the clock. But outstanding achievements succeed only if there is a deeper meaning in the big picture. My deeper sense of RAAM 2014 was of attachment to the team; that we should all be a part of a triumphal journey. My personal concern was, therefore, to give my best at every stage of the race. In a non-stop ride, this is not always easy, and sometimes, even damn difficult. In Colorado, I had benefited from favorable weather. In Kansas, the crosswinds hampered my progress. At speeds of up to 50 miles (80 kilometers) per hour, the gusts almost blew me off the bike. The wind noise made communication with the team almost impossible. I could not drink either, the wind was so fierce, I had to hold my aero bars with both hands, and couldn't risk using one hand for drinking.

"The weather is the same for every participant!" That is true for many sporting events, but not for RAAM. A hundred miles behind me could be the worst thunderstorm, or also the sun could be shining. The way the racers get spread out, every racer could experience weather unique from everyone else.

And as if these problems weren't enough, the trucks on the highways whirled up so much dust that I had to ride with a face mask nearly all the time. Having this wet cloth in front of the mouth filters dust from the air. But it wasn't just the dust that made it necessary. In Kansas there are cattle farms, which shouldn't bother me, I grew up on a farm, so I know stable smell. However, I'm not talking about the 20 or so cows my grandparents had in their pasture. In the Midwest, there were thousands of cattle standing by the side of the road, producing a stench that was hard to bear. The smell

Signs of American patriotism can be seen everywhere

of ammonia and yellow dust clouds brought me to the brink of vomiting and strained my lungs. To make it bearable, we resorted to spraying the dust mask with peppermint oil to cover the smell.

Good moods were rare that year in Kansas, which is usually my favorite section of RAAM, but it had been my maxim before 2014 to take responsibility for my own actions and condition. When a sour mood struck at the Race Across America, it helped me to be alone and completely within myself for a short time. "Do not moan to the others," I told myself during a short few minutes, when my crew had left me riding by myself, "Handle the situation yourself!"

When breaks are planned and organized to the last detail, the crew is all the more important. While I slept, my knees were treated, my team got the equipment and cars up to speed, and after a one-hour break, I was put back on the bike. Previously, the doctor had listened to my lungs and analyzed my blood levels. My mechanics had serviced the bike, checked the air pressure in the tires, oiled the chain, and loaded the GPS files. They then also attend to my personal quirks. Knowing that I do not want to feel anything sticky, they cleaned the water bottles and the inside and outside of the bottle cage. If anything was sticky, it would get on my fingers and then onto the handlebar tape.

I need to keep my concentration when trucks pass me while I'm fighting crosswinds

RAAM has a number of special prizes that are awarded for the fastest times through selected time stations. In 2014, I won the "King of the Mountains," being the fastest over the three most mountainous sections, and also the "King of the Prairies," for being the fastest over three of the flattest sections. It was simply my year!

In Missouri, I made particularly good progress on the time trial bike. Only the honking cars and truck drivers who were driving past made me nervous. US semi-trailer trucks are often equipped with special equipment—metal tips protruding from the rims. An already close distance of twenty, thirty centimeters to the monsters of the highway can, therefore, be too little.

The RAAM Route Book clearly states the basic rules for road traffic: It is important not to obstruct traffic flow. The trucks enjoy a high status in the USA. At RAAM 2014, we were warned by an official because we had not let a truck pass us on a one-lane, one-kilometer-long construction site. There was simply no space available, if the truck had overtaken me, then I would have flown into the guardrails. At that time, my follow car was shielding me, but that particular racing steward would have preferred to see the car avoid the truck by whatever means necessary, and have it pass through, however dangerous it may have been. The fact that I had covered the entire section in two minutes, and that in reality, the truck lost very little time, seemed to be no argument against a life-threatening maneuver.

Sunsets in Kansas are a true natural spectacle

As I rode through Kansas, I was pretty sure I could stay under eight days again. The finish time of 7 days, 15 hours, 56 minutes was far below our initial expectations, and only became apparent during the course of the race. On the fifth day, we reached the Effingham, Illinois Time Station, which is at a high school. My crew was excited because the Route Book said there were food and showers (something they all appreciate after five days on the road), but they were disappointed when we arrived and found that this station wasn't open yet. When we arrived at City Dock, it was apparent that the finish line arch and stage in the finish area had only just been completed. The organizers were happy about the new record, but at the same time, they seemed a bit frazzled and overwhelmed.

Due to the constantly changing route, the end time has relative importance, the average speed, however, is an absolute. So far, I have been on the "average speed podium" three times. In 2014 I achieved an average speed of 16.42 miles (26.43 kilometers) per hour, in 2018, it was 15.93 miles (25.65 kilometers) per hour, and in 2013,

I went 15.57 miles (25.07 kilometers) per hour. But even in the early days of the Race Across America, there were racers who were incredibly fast, considering that there was little in the way of optimized aerodynamic equipment, no lightweight carbon wheels, and no helmet-mounted radios. In 1986, Pete Penseyres (USA) achieved an average speed of 15.39 miles (24.78 kilometers) per hour. This record held until I broke it in 2013. This speed puts him currently in fourth place—ahead of Dani Wyss' 15.27 miles (24.59 kilometers) per hour from 2009, and my 15.22 miles (24.51 kilometers) per hour from 2017.

With a travel time of just under five days, we reached the Mississippi. Crossing the fourth longest river in the world is a landmark moment in the Race Across America.

"Two-thirds of the race is done," I told myself, as I got into the RV for my next power nap. But at the same time, I knew that the hardest sections to the finish were still ahead of me. I pondered that RAAM, which had already started days ago, actually starts again every hour. Then I fell asleep.

XIII
"NOW EVERYTHING IS GONE!"
CHILDHOOD AND YOUTH

My mum Helga was 18, my dad Herbert was 20, when I was born on the night of November 4, 1982 in the hospital in Leoben, Austria. So I'm a Scorpio. Sophisticated, profound, emotional—these are some of the traits attributed to this zodiac sign. At least according to astrology charts.

However, I can't understand the belief that the characteristics of people are associated with the stars. I am sure that qualities develop through education, life experiences, and challenges faced; not because they are written down in one astrology book or another. People who are dissatisfied with themselves, but also do not want to work on themselves, like to misuse these personality traits, which have supposedly been bestowed on us by the stars, as an excuse, pretext or apology.

Mom and Dad did not live together at the time of my birth, they were a couple, but still too young to marry. Even though I was not a planned child, the whole family was happy when my mom had the certainty of the doctor that a "surprise child," as she lovingly called me, was on the way.

My mother grew up with her siblings on her parents' farm and worked after graduation as a saleswoman in a farmer's shop in Leoben. My father was a trained locksmith foreman in plant engineering. In addition to his actual profession, he's a very gifted

Our dog "Sultan," my faithful companion and playmate

and industrious building craftsman. He's built room additions, replaced roofs, and repaired and renovated cars and furniture. His regular work took him away for four or five days, to two weeks at a stretch, but every time he came back—from Russia, the former Czechoslovakia, Southern Germany or other places in Austria—he always had a small gift for me. He hid the surprises somewhere in our home, which for me was a huge joy. Searching for the gift, and the anticipation of finding it, were just as great as finding it and playing with gift itself. Often, I got a little Lego set, or a three-dimensional wooden puzzle that would train my patience as well as my skill. When I went shopping with Mama, I was allowed to choose these simple little puzzles that fascinate me to this day. It can be so fun to watch friends struggling with a pyramid of just two parts, taking minutes to solve the seemingly simple riddle.

I spent my first four years on my grandparents' farm and was allowed to help however I could. There is nothing more exciting for a little child! I was not overprotected, which gave me some freedom, and I was not taught or even punished for every little thing.

I had a close connection with Susi and Andreas, my mom's youngest siblings. Being only a few years older than me, they are like a sister and brother to me. We played in the barn, worked on the dung heap, fed the young piglets and chicks, dug in the sandbox, and built small houses of twigs and loam in the forest. In short: I was allowed to do everything, as long as I did not hurt myself or wander off. Of course, both happened anyway. One time I ran after my mother, who had just left for work by car. I was three years old and imagined being able to see my mom after the next turn, then

Aunt Susi and Uncle Andreas were like sister and brother to me

the next turn, then the turn after that. My companion was our Saint Bernard named Sultan, who was as tall as me, and ran everywhere I did. An hour later, Uncle Hermann caught up with me by tractor shortly before the village, after the search for me at the farm had been unsuccessful.

My self-planned trip led to no other dramas—everything had gone well. Looking back, I remember only a single slap. I was three years old when I entered the farmhouse with dirty shoes and made a nasty mess of the freshly cleaned kitchen floor. My great-grandmother Aloisa—whose credo was: "Be diligent, work a lot, do not complain!"—was then over 90 years old, but she was still strong enough to deliver a solid slap, and hard enough that afterward I heard drumming in my ear. What was going on? Why did I get smacked? When I saw what I had done, I hung my head and apologized.

When I was five years old, my parents got married. I still remember the wedding and the subsequent party. I curiously stood in front of the Wurlitzer as it spit out song after song, to which the guests danced.

My parents and I moved to an apartment in my grandparents' home in Kraubath. The small town with about a thousand inhabitants was only a few winding kilometers away from the farm on the mountain. I was fortunate enough to have both of my grandmothers and grandfathers, who lovingly looked after me. We enjoyed the hikes to the nearby mountains and forest. In our new home, my father soon set up his own workshop in the basement. I liked to be his "little helper," and before long, he let me do my own small projects, like the wooden hockey goals that I built (which were then maltreated by my friends and I when we played with hockey sticks and tennis balls in the yard).

And yet, I wonder why I am a bad bike mechanic and why assembling a new bike does not bring me much joy. It is probably because I like to work in my spare time, but I see the racing bike only as a working tool. Hobby runners probably love their running shoes more than marathon pros. It is because my parents did their part that have I become a patient, detail-oriented person.

I inherited my love of sport from my father. My dad liked to ride a mountain bike or run. He lifted weights that he had welded himself. But he only did sports for himself and he never took part in competitions. When I went to kindergarten and elementary school, I played ice hockey and soccer, and learned that skiing and cycling could take me, with my best friends, into nature where we built camps and shelters. Video games (Super Mario was very popular at that time) did not appeal to me. I'd play with my friends' consoles, but was not ready to invest my own pocket money in this pastime. My parents were eco-conscious and made sure that unnecessary lighting in the house was turned off and that the heating was used intelligently. I saved my money because I wanted to buy something at some point—although I did not know when and what exactly. Mostly, I waited until my next birthday or Christmas, because hopefully my wishes for these events would come true. I've always been patient enough to wait for the things I want. If I did not have enough money, I accepted that I just could not afford it, and saved my pocket money so I could buy whatever it was later on. Even later, at school, I never borrowed money from classmates to buy candy or snacks at the school counter.

> **Puzzles shaped me, and still shape me. After all, is not every bike race, every venture, life itself, one big puzzle?**

A little while later, when I had a hot dog for 18 shillings in Leoben, I burst into tears, even though minutes before I had proudly ordered my favorite snack and paid for it with my savings. Whenever I went to Leoben with my grandmother to pick up Mom after work, Grandma invited me to the sausage stall and I was allowed to choose a snack. But this time, I wanted to order myself and I felt like someone who fulfilled a great dream.

"What's going on now?" Grandma asked in surprise.

"Now everything is gone!" I sobbed in horror, "the money and also the hot dog." Thoughtful and a little defiant, I decided never to spend money again for things that would not please me in the long run.

When I think back to this story, I have to laugh, because today eating is one of the nicest activities for me, and I really love to spend a lot of money on good, high quality food. Does this have something to do with this childhood experience? I do not think so. This is probably more about the huge hunger that always plagues me after the training sessions, and the happiness of, after a long bike ride, being allowed to treat myself to a huge portion with a clear conscience.

In elementary school, I was a good student, learned in a classroom with 14 other kids, and did well in all subjects. I still like to remember the nice teachers and my school friends, especially my best friend Alfred, who was two years older. For years we spent every afternoon together. But he continued his secondary school education, as did eighty percent of my other classmates, while I moved to another school.

The high school I went to was located in Knittelfeld, 9 miles (15 kilometers) away, and unfortunately I lost more and more contact with Alfred because of this distance.

Friendships have always been important to me, and I have always had many good friends with whom to spend my time sharing beautiful experiences. There was nothing sadder for me than situations where I had to choose between two friends. I could not visit them at the same time and I was often sad because I had to cancel on one of them. I would have liked to stay home crying because I could not

To want to disappoint no one is a trait that developed in my childhood and youth, and to which I am still faithful to in my need for harmony today.

bear to see one of my friends feel that he was not important enough for me. It was not until Mama encouraged me to visit one of my buddies that I was able to enjoy the day, and a beautiful afternoon game. New friends developed through the change of school. My best friend at home in Kraubath was Tao, and the best mate in school at Knittelfeld was Peter.

That's me when I was 2 years old

If I receive praise and recognition from others, then I would like to show my appreciation and answer all e-mails and messages individually. But in this time of social media, it's almost impossible to live up to that standard, and instead I often just extend general thanks to the community. Only when Sabine reminds me that I have already made many people happy, and given them an exciting and inspiring time through my appearances, or through my mastery of RAAM, or through my lectures, can I enjoy the encouragement without despairing that I cannot personally thank everyone for their support.

During my school days, our small family grew. My siblings, Philipp and Julia, are ten and eleven years younger than me.

As a caring big brother, I helped my parents as well as I could and had great joy with my two siblings. From changing nappies and feeding, to playing with Legos or having ball games or shopping together—I liked everything that had to do with those two. On the one hand, I loved my brother and my sister over everything; on the other hand, I also wanted to be a real support to my parents, because my siblings were bright, quite spirited, and kept us all on their toes. It was exciting to see how the character traits of the two manifested; how Philip developed his love of technology and Julia lived out her creativity in art and in making music. What my sister learned soon and above all, was how to assert herself against her big brother and against Philipp, and to enforce her will, if it was necessary by hiding his toys. My parents were sometimes at their wits end when Philip and Julia argued or provoked each other until one of them protested with loud screaming. All in all, it was a great time and I am glad that I was able to be a good brother to my siblings as I watched them grow up.

At home together with my three siblings and my parents

Michael "Kougi" Kogler, our grandmother and me

We all had to suffer a cruel stroke of fate; Oliver, my smallest brother, unfortunately lived only two and a half years. After a short but joyful and enriching life, he left this world. Oliver died in the summer of 2000 in a swimming accident, and left a big hole in our lives. The grief lasted extremely long. It was especially painful for my parents. Today, almost twenty years later, my entire family meets once a year and we walk together to his grave, so that we can all consciously remember him.

When my cousin Michi Kogler (at that time we did not call him "Kougi") went to elementary school, in the afternoons he was always with my grandmother Anni (on my father's side), and with us, so he was just another of us rascals. He and Philipp constantly drove grandma crazy with their mischief. Whether it was throwing the football into her carefully maintained garden, or destroying her pumpkin patch with hockey sticks (or some other type of sports equipment), these two young boys were always up to something rambunctious. It was during these years that the intense relationship that so closely links Kougi and me first developed.

In high school I developed my interest in mathematics, geometry, 3-D geometrical painting, and handicrafts, and scored the highest grades in all of them. But also, German and English were a lot of fun; I started to read a lot and was especially eager when we had to write long compositions in German. At home, I built model cars with Daddy and developed a love of detail. Even my Lego Technic toy cars weren't safe from me, as I used to dismantle them in order to reassemble them in new and improved ways.

I had subjects that interested me, and I also had some that I liked less. I think that each of us can tell of something similar from our school days. There was some discord between myself and my music education instructor. I did not know the scale, for instance, but in my youthful defiant stage of that time, I was actually proud of this. Decades later, I am back in contact with my former music teacher, and she is no longer angry with me. Pure learning subjects were not my strength either. In history, for example, I was interested in the time of the Greeks and Romans, but not particularly what followed.

The hardship of my high school years was Latin. Those students that have taken Latin are allowed to enter many university study programs, so I wanted to keep that option open. While I simply wanted to get a passing grade with as little effort as possible, the teacher was an obstacle to this strategy. She actually wanted us to learn something. I wasn't the only one trying to slide by—many of my classmates griped at her, and I joined them. To rebel against authorities comes easy in a pack, even if (as in this case) the teacher was neither unfair nor mean. The conflict between her and me rocked into an unequal power struggle: I refused homework; she threatened to fail me.

I am now grateful that she had been the more reasonable of us two. She had realized that I was swimming in the stream of class, funny and loud, but not vicious, just lazy. I still regret my behavior back then. Teachers do not have it easy. There are a few rebellious students like me who make stupid jokes, scoff at teachers, or blow up a toilet bowl with a Swiss firecracker (something like an American M–80) and see the school year as an excuse to wage guerrilla warfare. I sat in that all-boys class for two years and sometimes it seemed like we were chattering about how to get the worst grade in the class. Improvement in behavioral attitudes came in the upper grades when we were back with the girls in a mixed class. The onset of puberty and the presence of girls, who suddenly became more and more interesting, made us think differently and to forget the stupidities of the lower school years.

Emotional and melancholic lyrics were always my favorites; the REM song "Everybody Hurts" from their *Automatic For The People* album, for instance, or some songs from U2 or Oasis. I really don't have much of a singing voice, though I would sing these songs for myself sometimes, and actually, still do when the mood strikes. I listened

Free hour in the high school: playing foosball with two friends

to these songs whenever I could, mostly in the evening. I've always been a night person—getting up early has always been a real challenge for me. I bought CDs, dubbed them onto minidiscs, and then brought them back and exchanged them for others. Or, I "borrowed" CDs from music stores. Borrowing may be the wrong term—I did not bring them back. But honestly, it was no more than once or twice.

"Don't let yourself go
'Cause everybody cries
And everybody hurts sometimes ..."

I do not feel comfortable with unauthorized actions, so I try to avoid them as much as possible. Before non-stop races, I advise my crew to adhere strictly to all regulations and traffic signs so that we do not receive any penalties. Getting me an illicit advantage by illegal means doesn't even come to my mind in the least. That's why every time I left a music store with a "borrowed" record, I had a sinking feeling in my stomach. This happened at a time when my friends and I were skeptical and negative about the big multi-billion dollar retail chains and international companies, who we felt, with their focus on sales, profits and marketing slogans, had ruined the small record shops. Therefore, I accepted the guilty conscience because I really wanted to make a silent protest against the consumer society without harming a fellow human being.

At some point in life, however, everything comes back around. It happened that after one of my lectures a DVD we had for sale was missing. Someone who came for the lecture had probably taken it without paying, which annoyed me but only briefly. In memory of my youth, I took note of it with humor.

When I was 17 and 18 years old, I read a lot and came to my own worldview. I especially liked the novel *Ishmael* by Daniel Quinn. This is about a teacher-student relationship, where the teacher is a gorilla and the two characters communicate telepathically. This work, first published in 1991, is about the world and how it can be that man turns a paradise into a hell, pollutes the environment, exterminates living beings, and wants to convince other cultures to adopt his religion at the cost of their own. It is about the question of why "civilized" cultures follow a destructive drive to survive through infinite growth, and are subject to the unshakeable belief that only they know the right way of life. The people of the "takers" culture see themselves not as a part of the world, but as masters of it, which of course, they are not. At this stage of my life, I had rejected Bible tenets. I did not leave the church until later, at a time when my very religious grandmothers were no longer aware of it. But even then, I realized that on our planet, man, the so-called "crown of creation," is of no more worth than any other living thing. If there is an infinite number of Gods, I am sure, that they love every creature equally and do not prefer humans.

Ishmael has shaped me and asked me many questions: How should my life continue? Should I study or not? What can I personally contribute so that we do not destroy our world (even further)? The first answer was probably my decision to do my civil service at a non-profit organization abroad, instead of taking the more popular choice of military service.

Before that, however, there were still a few school years and the final exam before leaving high school. I struggled to get through drawing and music, history and Latin, and I think sometimes teachers did not give me a failing grade because they knew I wasn't slow, just lazy. I then managed to score well on the final exams.

As an athlete, I was popular and in demand during high school years. During gym class when it came to choosing teams for basketball, handball, or football games, I was always one of the first to be picked. At the TUS Kraubath, I started playing soccer in the U12 league (for kids under 12 years) and moved up with my friends through the age groups to the U16 team. As a defender, I had two role models. One was Trifon Ivanov, the "Bulgarian Wolf," who had reached the final of the European-wide international soccer cup with Rapid Wien

In the high school an assignment in painting education was to draw our favourite athlete. Even then I was a big fan of Wolfgang Fasching.

in 1996, but had been kicked off the team a year later because of some indiscipline. The other was Ronald Koeman, who helped FC Barcelona win their first ever Cup of Nations trophy in 1992 (the event equates to today's Champions League) with a free-kick in extra time. However, I didn't compare to my pro heroes—I did not have the robustness of Ivanov or the technique of Koeman. As a fullback I was persistent, but not fast—I lost most running duels. My shooting technique was in demand for free kicks and long shots, where I emulated my role models and also scored some goals. Instead of flanking dangerously toward the strikers into the top of the field, I often managed to clear the ball out of the danger zone. I put in additional training to improve myself at baseline, but the older I got, the more and more I often sat on the bench. I lived healthy, while others smoked. They were playing, not me. I was told that I had talent and that encouraged me to stay and not give up. But my interest decreased in proportion to the lack of fun. As much as I did not want to disappoint our trainer (we had a woman coaching us), I was also painfully aware that soccer was not my sport.

I would have been fit for the basic military service and it would not have occurred to me to try to sway my results on the acceptance test to try to get out of the one-year of compulsory service. I have nothing against the military; I just think it's superfluous. If it comes to military conflicts, then it is, with all due respect, certainly not the Austrian army which will make the difference. When I decided to use the gun or go to civilian service, it was clear that I wanted to do something more meaningful at this time than sitting around in some barracks, crawling through the bush in camouflage clothing, or risking heat stroke in hours-long marches. I wanted to change the world on a small scale, to be useful, to make a contribution. I wanted to go abroad, to Africa, to Asia, or some country in need, so I entered a preparatory seminar. The whole process is an exasperating bureaucratic nightmare. First, in your last year of school, you declare your desire for civil service instead of military service. Then, you have to wait to see if you must go into civil service immediately after school, or one, two, three, or four years later (depending if hospitals and nursing homes need staff at that time). While you wait, you can try to prepare yourself for the abroad civil service in these seminars. If you are lucky, that organization sends you abroad before the administration sends you to a place in Austria. If you are not lucky, the administration sends you somewhere in Austria before you may go abroad. So you do these preparation seminars at your own risk, no one can guarantee that you will really work abroad. Like I said, it's exasperating.

My wish of doing development or foreign aid abroad was not fulfilled. I ended up in the nursing home in Knittelfeld. And that was, hand on heart, not necessarily what I had imagined. True, I was helping some, but not as I hoped. I really wanted to make a contribution to the really poor of the big wide world, rather than having to work a few kilometers from my mother's kitchen in a home for retired people. And I saw this assignment as having missed another chance to leave my home country for a while. A year abroad at school, which I had sought, was also denied to me, because it would have been too expensive. As a substitute for the summer holidays, I attended a two-week language course in Malta, where I attended an English class in the morning, celebrated each night in the discos of the party mile, and fell drunk into bed after midnight. My parents let me do it. I was old enough, I paid for the language trip myself, and they knew that in the end, I would be responsible enough to take care of myself...mostly.

I could not come up with any stories about women and bed; neither in Malta nor before or after. I have never been a "player." The first time I fell in love was in elementary school, with a girl in my fourth grade class. I met my first big love as a high school senior. She was the ex-girlfriend of my best friend Peter. Even then, I thought it was not up to me to risk true, real friendships for a woman. But when you see the world through the rose-colored glasses of youth, you temporarily forget these good intentions, and so the friendship with Peter was subjected to a very tough test. In my love relationships, I have always sought relationships of trust, not one-night stands or sex adventures. I like being old-fashioned in interpersonal relationships, and that's what I stand for. I'm not impressed by those who boast about whom they have spent a night with. But to each his own.

In the end, I found my life partner. I'm happy with Sabine, and I feel secure, understood, and supported.

But back to the nursing home. It was, as I said, not my first choice, and yet my time there is one of the most important years in my life. While some of my former classmates and friends worked in the emergency room and had more stressful days, they also had more quiet, easy days; it all depended on the accident situation of the day. I was at work every day from 7:00 am to 3:00 pm. Often when I left the nursing home, I felt a light goose bumps on my back. "Although you have not provided for lasting peace in the world, nor worked toward relevant nature-preserving concerns," I thought to myself, "in your small way, you have done something useful with your life again today."

Working in a nursing home is no picnic. It ranges from walks with the residents, to helping with food intake, to making the beds, to physical hygiene and helping people dress themselves.

As the only male employee, I was the darling of the ward—with the patients and staff alike. I did what needed to be done and tried to do it as well as possible. Because I really liked the work, and had a bit of charm, the older people began to like me more and more...so much so, that one of the elderly women claimed to have fallen in love with me. She went so far as to make me a marriage proposal, and tried to kiss me on not once, but on many occasions. I had to master the practice of turning my head away at the last moment, so that her kiss landed on my cheek, instead of smack dab on my lips.

2002: Civil service in the nursing home in Knittelfeld

They tried to set me up me with their daughters. The daughters were then a fresh 70.

Minor incidents, which are rather funny when I look back, but embarrassing in the moment, also occurred. Each morning I had to bring two gentlemen their dentures, which are stored in water overnight for cleaning. My colleague on the night shift had swapped the containers, and the next morning the dentures of one man found themselves in the other man's mouth (and vice versa). The mistake was immediately noticed because of the different sizes of dentures. One of them had the dentures immediately fall out, the other one could not close his mouth and grinned unintentionally like something from an old TV comedy. My helplessness, and the excitement of the two gentlemen was short-lived, as I got the dentures out, again into the water and cleaned, and handed over to the rightful owners. Minutes later we all could laugh about it.

I learned how important it was to have a job and to be busy. The residents of the home were there for each other and enjoyed life. When these circumstances disappeared, and there was no longer any "sense of life," the patients quickly deteriorated

and died. What I also became aware of in that year, was the fact that pretending to be healthy and in good condition creates problems instead of solving them. It is no shame to admit weaknesses. Those who are too vain, only bring themselves and their environments into a dilemma.

> The year of civilian service was a learning year for future tasks. At the same time, friendships were created that continue today.

Reto Schoch and I exchange a few words just before the RAAM halfway point.

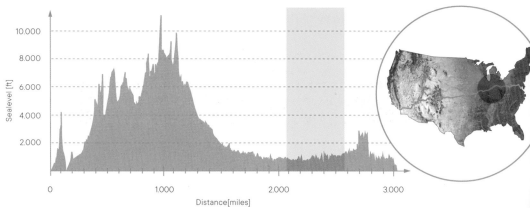

Sealevel [ft]

10.000

8.000

6.000

4.000

2.000

0   1.000   2.000   3.000

Distance[miles]

XIV
"FOR A FAIR RACE!"
RAAM, TIME STATIONS 35–44

Not all of my crew's attempts to motivate me are successful

I glared at the people around me and did not understand the world anymore. "Why? Why? Why the hell should I torment myself if RAAM was already decided?" Sure, I had to finish, but really, no one was near me and I had no competitors anymore. I was done, my body suffered from the rain, my soul suffered from the sleep deprivation. I had lost sight of my goal, and now these guys who called themselves my team tormented me, imploring me to continue full throttle. Why? Why the hell? I wanted to finish RAAM at my own pace.

A few hours earlier, my only remaining competitor at that time had held a piece of paper up to the camera congratulating me on my victory and my time of less than eight days: "Congrats to your sub–8–day ride. Epic performance."

At Time Station 40 in Greensburg, my lead over Schoch had been eight hours, one checkpoint farther, at Oxford, at 620 miles (1000 kilometers) from the finish, the Swiss rider gave up. When I received his message, I still had 497 miles (800 kilometers) to the finish, and my motivation was at zero. My big goal had been to beat Reto Schoch, and now he had beaten himself.

We celebrated and were euphoric knowing that the race was virtually won—we had a huge lead and no one else could grab the win anymore. All the other racers—Dani Wyss, Gerhard Gulewicz, Marko Baloh, and other riders—were already too far behind to be dangerous under normal circumstances.

Not dangerous, but just annoying, were my own people. How was this so?

My only competitor was Reto Schoch, and my relationship with him was anything but good. I would even go so far as to say that there were times when I deeply hated him. That's saying something, because it's not my trait to hate or devalue others. But with Reto Schoch, I made an exception. When I reflect on my behavior today, I feel some shame because I know in my heart how wrong it is to not show the respect to others that deserve it by their very existence.I am not overly concerned with moral or ethical values, but I do believe that every person deserves respect, regardless of what he or she does.

Yet, when I read what was on the website of Reto Schoch, to this day it still brings anger to my face. We are in RAAM 2012, at Time Station 39 in Bloomington, and Schoch describes the situation like this: "In Bloomington, the entire road network of the Time Station block was under construction. We drove therefore only one corner of the block and then continued to the east. That was the perfect time for the spies of the Strasser team who reported this behavior to RAAM Headquarters. After 6.8 miles, we were caught by marshals, had to pack Reto in the car and drive back to the block. This, as the president of RAAM, wanted to personally welcome Reto. But our joy was limited, we lost 45 precious minutes."

The Route Book and the rules of the Race Across America cover over two hundred pages. Each section of the route is meticulously documented—it could not be described in more detail what is allowed and what is not, and what penalties are imposed for what offense. Those who do not follow the route exactly will be disqualified and will be reported. Reto was less than "not exactly following the route"; he had cut the route, saving himself eight hundred meters. The route book said that the racers must circle around the block at the back of the time station. And then Schoch, or his internet person, is upset that we behaved unsportsmanlike? They had deliberately decided on a shortcut and even published this on their own website. His RAAM 2012 should have come to an end in the college town of Bloomington, Indiana, on a dusty, dirty construction site. Instead of being thrown out of the race, he lost only 45 minutes—and complained about it!

I do not like people who don't tell the truth. I do not want to be betrayed, but I could live with it if someone stands by what he has done. But, even that was not the case with Reto Schoch in 2012.

Sticking points of RAAM 2012: Heat and the duel with Schoch

I also have one important fact to record: The Swiss racer, who had participated as a rookie in this Race Across America, had been extremely strong from the start. I had won the RAAM in 2011, and knew that Schoch qualified for RAAM as the winner of the thousand-kilometer Tortour in his home country, but thought that I could be faster than him and control the greenhorn. I was in better shape than I was twelve months prior, and I was confident and dared to repeat the RAAM victory—especially since I was able to win the tough Race Around Slovenia a few weeks earlier. I am a grounded man and an athlete, but it is not easy to remain humbly on the ground of reality as praise pours in from all sides. Looking back, I confess that I may have been too confident. I think of the words of the Greek philosopher Socrates, "Anyone who thinks he is something, has stopped becoming something." I had believed in my subconscious to be a RAAM winner, and overlooked that I had to "become" again.

Schoch is just 5' 2" (1.60 meters) tall, and thus 9.8 inches (25 centimeters) smaller than me, and I doubt that he weighs more than 120 pounds (55 kilograms). He sped away from the first kilometer of the race. I let him go on in the lead. "I'll get him again," I thought, "At least on the long flats I'll be able to play my strengths over the mountain specialists." But then, I had quite different worries. After a hundred kilometers gastric and headache issues set in; I vomited my liquid food and on the second day, while waiting at a red light, and I collapsed due to the heat. Should I give up? After all, Reto Schoch had pulled away easily, and with every hour his lead grew larger. I did not want to surrender without a fight, and so I rode on and overcame this crisis with the help of my team.

In the mountains, the slender man from Eastern Switzerland had physical advantages, but in Kansas, I caught up to him and for fifteen minutes we even cycled side by side and exchanged a few words. He looked fit and fresh. "It's going to be a difficult race," I thought to myself. I pulled away, but then Schoch rode past against the headwind. He seemed to pedal effortlessly by, at a pace that was perhaps 6 miles (10 kilometers) per hour faster than mine.

We ran a neck-and-neck race for hundreds of miles. Whenever one took a power nap or a long sleep, the other took the lead.

The outcome of the race was fought out on the road. But the Swiss racer and his team still felt the need to post negative words about Team Strasser on the Internet. They were spreading what you would call "fake news" today: claiming something that is not true, or not reporting everything that happened. For example, the Schoch crew wrote that we were constantly shadowing Reto.

According to RAAM Rule 1470, regarding spying, a crew is allowed to overtake the competitor twice per hour with a support car that does not accompany the athlete to determine the time interval. We followed this rule to the letter. That we received a 75-minute time bonus, of course, also bothered Reto. We were in a heavy storm with a tornado warning and the police ordered us to stop. They had us follow them to a church in the next town—it was the only building made of bricks, and therefore the most stable. While I slept, my people became acquainted with the locals. Schoch also stopped about 19 miles (30 kilometers) from me, but not under the orders of the police, but on his own accord, so according to the rules, he received no time credit. Sorry, Reto.

There was another series of events that startled us. I was in front of him at a time station, yet he had passed by the next, though we had not seen him on the route. Later, conspiracy theories spread in our camp when my people saw that Schoch's bike had been loaded up and taken away for a short while during a sleep break. We developed a variety of theories, ranging from manipulated wheels to electronic drive assistance.

Another rule violation happened when Reto's cameraman was taken in a car, with no official race markings or racer number, to take pictures of me. While this does not affect the cyclist, it is still a clear breach of the rule as team members are only allowed to move forward in their own cars that are marked with the rider's race number.

What really bothered my crew so much was the appearance and the posture of Reto Schoch; always smiling, always relaxed, always casual. And later, when I saw the videos and photos after the race, it irked me too. Even under the most extreme physical effort, he showed no signs of fatigue. "I'm always laughing, that's my temperament," he once said in an interview. For me, it's different. If I give everything, I suffer and look like it. In a short film sequence, which was shown a few weeks after the race on Swiss television, Reto was seen during a break with a crew member discussing whether he should first take a shower and then eat, or rather the other way around. I never shower between Oceanside and Annapolis to avoid wasting time. And he wondered, which is the better sequence of activities? "Does he want to lure me?" I thought to myself. These scenes made me angry later.

I can only now describe how much we suffered from my competitor's psychological warfare. But I must say, that Reto's fans and my fans on the Internet guestbook pages did not mince their words and insulted each other. We knew that Reto Schoch was an intelligent man who had founded a microbiology start-up and was working with companies in Silicon Valley—and we obviously were pulled in by his tactics. The Swiss have laid the traps for us, instigated the provocations, and certainly had fun watching how we lost our cool and got worked up.

> In my subjective analysis, Schoch seemed to me to be more powerful and stronger than he really was.

While our media team did journalistic work and described things accurately (such as my problems during days one and two), Schoch's team ran proper PR. That was a lesson for all my subsequent competitions. Also in this aspect, the defeat in 2012 was the trailblazer for the victory in 2013.

But this was still very, very far away at this time.

When I appeared battered and disappointed at the banquet, we had seriously considered protesting the result. But too much did not seem conclusive, even though we had video footage that could support our theories. But there were questions that stopped us: Were the time changes always done when we changed time zones? Were we absolutely sure that Schoch had manipulated the competition in his favor? No, we were not. So, we did not file a protest. An hour and fifty minutes difference had decided a nonstop race of over eight days in Schoch's favor. I immediately focused on the following year, on my desire for revenge, and my need to take a clear and dominant win on the road.

I overcame myself, shook hands and congratulated him as Gerhard Gulewicz joined us.

A heated conversation between Schoch, Gulewicz and me

"Who are you anyway?" Gulewicz asked.

"Well, I'm the winner of the RAAM," Schoch replied.

"No, this cannot be."

"Yes, yes!"

"No RAAM winner looks like this. Turn around for me."

Schoch did as ordered.

When he looked Gulewicz in the eye again, Gerhard said; "No. That's not what a RAAM winner looks like."

Gerhard Gulewicz and I have a neutral relationship. He's never done anything to me. Though I was always surprised to hear what he told media outlets when he talked about his DNF's at the Race Across America, never blaming himself for his mistakes, but always his crew, but that was not my business.

That night in Annapolis in 2012, I could have hugged him in gratitude. In his own way, he had put my feelings and thoughts about Schoch in a nutshell.

"His cars and motorhomes are even bigger this year than last year," Gerald Bauer told me, who was staying in the same hotel as Reto Schoch before the start of RAAM 2013. Outwardly, I was struggling for composure, but inside, anger, contempt, and even panic rose. "What does he want to prove to himself and us?" I thought. "That he has more room to shower now?"

No question, my 2012 defeat hurt me for a long time after the race. My torment was not only mental, but physical as well. For one and a half months I could not hold any cutlery, four fingers of my right hand could not fully close, and I could not touch my thumb and little finger together. In physiotherapy, I received electromagnetic treatments, and for the first time in my career, I realized that sport can cause lasting damage.

> **Close defeats are among the most motivating in sports.**

In the meantime, Reto Schoch had won Tortour again and set a new course record, and in doing so, dethroned my idol Jure Robic, the previous record-holder. But it got even worse; he announced that he wanted to finish RAAM 2013 in less than eight days. Right before the start in Oceanside, he reiterated this goal. He said in an interview that he had won the race before, and only the goal of setting a new record could be motivation to do RAAM again.

"To dishonor Jure is one thing, but this goes too far," were my first thoughts when I heard of his goals. These were feelings of a 31-year-old romantic, whose role model had died just two years earlier. Records are there to be broken; even my best marks are not etched in stone for all eternity.

Schoch's announcement made me train like a fiend. If he had the goal of staying under eight days, then it was mine to beat him. And if that meant that I had to do a "sub-8" RAAM myself, then so be it. My bike sponsor, Specialized, persuaded me to deal with the possibility of riding suitable sections on a time-trial bike. I did not share a word about that, nor many of the other things that were going on in my preparation. In 2012, Team Strasser had been authentic, open, and honest in its outward appearance—but in the end, that naivety, self-assurance, and arrogance were to our detriment. We would take a different path in 2013.

We could also play psych games, as Schoch experienced the evening before the start at the racer's meeting. There, the organizers go over the rules, explain race time, provide any late updates, and here, the riders get to meet each other and wish each other well. But no one talked to Reto Schoch—the defending champion was treated like an insignificant fellow traveler. When I chatted with Marko Baloh and Schoch joined us, I ignored him at first. Then I shook hands with him, grabbed his right forearm and squeezed. "This time I have you," I thought. "To a fair race!" I said, then released him and turned around to talk with Baloh. I had not even given Schoch the time to open his mouth for a reply.

Seven Austrians at RAAM 2013: Eduard Fuchs, Gerhard Gulewicz, Franz Preihs, Christoph Strasser, David Misch, Gerald Bauer and Franz Wintersberger

In 2013, many Austrians were on the starting line. Alongside me was the already mentioned Geri Bauer, also David Misch, who became Rookie of the Year, Franz Wintersberger, who could win the age 50–59 category, and also Eduard Fuchs, Franz Preihs, and Gerhard Gulewicz. I tried to repress this self-constructed duel against Reto Schoch, remembering the words of Gerhard Gulewicz ("I'm going for victory in 2013"), and yet, I did not manage to free myself from my thought prison. Before our collaboration ended, mental trainer Thomas Jaklitsch helped me in this phase to calm myself, and to mentally push Schoch away.

When the race started and we reached the end of the eight-mile parade zone, Reto Schoch shot past me like an arrow. I was impressed. Was he so strong, or was I so weak? I had to use all my mental strength to stay calm and not panic when he rode away.

One hundred and eighty kilometers later, he stood with his team on the side of the road, overcome with cramps. He had been shot down at the beginning of a race that was nearly 3,000 miles long. After I had heard this positive news (for us) from Rainer, I turned up my effort thanks to this "mental tailwind."

In order to give no impression of weakness, we showed only moments of strength and determination in the pictures and in videos that we posted. We even staged a pre-planned power nap to look like a sudden crisis, when in fact, everything was perfect. It was all a show to make Reto perceive an apparent weakness and give him hope, only to then leave at full speed. In fact, I never saw Reto Schoch or any other rider ever again that year. That's why, tired and hallucinating in the Appalachians, I could not understand it when my team explained that we were in a cycling race.

We had arrived at Time Station 44, when we heard that Reto Schoch had given up three checkpoints behind us (at least for the time being). The official RAAM Media team had posted the headline: "Reto Schoch Has Lost His Laugh!" Among us, we had interpreted the matter a bit more directly; we had driven out his laughter. The beaming man no longer beamed. The man who had won all his races confidently, and always looked unnaturally fresh and happy, was now grumpy and tired.

Two Austrians were responsible for Schoch resuming his RAAM, and to eventually finishing third behind compatriot Dani Wyss. For years, Karl and Hansjörg Schlederer have accompanied RAAM as officials, and they talked to Reto when he had stopped at Time Station 41. After the finish, the two officials shared what they had told him: He, as defending champion, had the duty to honorably finish the race. It could not be that he threw away everything in the face of defeat, because he had a responsibility to himself, the competitors, the organizers, and the history of the race. We jokingly came up with a fantasy word that, thanks to the persuasion of the Schlederer brothers, Schoch had been "Schlederized." Definition: /Schled-der·ized, verb, past tense: Schlederized; past participle: Schlederized; to convince a RAAM racer to continue on to the finish. Used in a sentence: If an ultra-cyclist, who wants to give up the Race Across America, is persuaded at length until he finally continues on, then he is "Schlederized." ;)

The pressure of competing against Reto Schoch and my own will to win was so great that I decided to fly with Kougi in March, to train in the US and devote myself to riding the particularly challenging sections from the Mississippi River, over the Appalachians, and on to Annapolis. Much of the course there is an ugly area, the humidity provides ideal conditions for insects of all kinds, and as if that wasn't enough of a challenge, it is also hard for a cyclist to be on the road. The motorists—truckers

An enthusiastic fan in Kansas

especially—do not exactly love cyclists, and show little regard for us, for decency, or for the passing-distance rules. Crashes and accidents can happen at any time.

Still, my crew is happy every time we reach Lebanon, Ohio where Cathy, a good friend of Team Strasser, lives. We had met her during my 2013 training camp. Actually, we had wanted to stay with another friend, but his house was being renovated. He arranged a replacement for us, and so our friendship with Cathy began. She is a caring person, a really good cook, and extremely friendly when hosting my people. "How are you doing?" She calls out every time Kougi and the others knock on her door. As I continue, my people have time for a quick shower, or even a dip in the pool to cool off. Whenever we come to see her, some bike shop and crew shirts change owners. That makes her proud. RAAM may not be a national event in the US, but in Ohio, there are many who are interested and stand on the road cheering for the riders. Cathy is one of those people, and she cheers for all of the RAAM riders, but she cheers especially loud for us—at least I think so anyway.

My vengeance against Reto Schoch was satisfied. I would win the race, I would experience karma first-hand that "what goes around, comes around." Everything was good. Almost everything.

"Vogs" with the right words at the right time

On the ascent to Grafton, a small town in the Appalachians, where Time Station 46 was located, I slowly tormented myself. I could no longer recognize the meaning of my actions. Why did my people want to push me? I was so far in the lead that I could just roll easily at my own pace to the finish, and still win. Reto Schoch was out of the race, after a long and hard fight I had prevailed. He had failed in himself and in his goal. So why on earth did my crew really want me to ride so fast? What was that about? Who cares if I finish in seven, eight, or nine days? The main thing is first place; the main thing is being faster than the others. The rest did not matter.

My team stopped me unplanned. The camper was parked diagonally in a bus stop, and my people stood by the side of the road. "What's the problem now?" I thought to myself. "Are we getting a penalty? Is there a problem with the police?" Markus "Vogs" Vogl approached me. He is one of the most endearing and loyal souls on my team, he was part of my first, and all my following RAAM participations, he is a big supporter, and a fixture in my crew. Working in the background he ensures a good mood and good food, keeps the RV in good condition, and does all this out of friendship. As a chef, he does not profit professionally from the fact that he can write on his business card to have been on a winning RAAM team. This man, who creates great things in the background, came into the foreground at that moment—apparently, he had important things to say to me. He smelled of cigarettes, his hands were shaking, he was visibly nervous: "Please, you have to do this for us now. We all want to create this record together with you. We all want you to do your best for us one last time. We know how tired you are, but we are all here just for you to help you realize your dream. Feel the moment that you will make it less than eight days!"

He handed me a note with the signatures of all my crew, who also shared this message. From then on, the note was stuck on my bike.

Vogs and the team pulled a switch in me. I knew again why I was here. I was able to accelerate again. In the end, my winning time was seven days, twenty-two hours, eleven minutes. Not only did I beat Schoch, I also took what he wanted so much for himself.

> As great as the disappointment and frustration in the previous year was, I still have to thank Reto Schoch, because if he had not snatched the victory from me in 2012, I would certainly not have been so driven and motivated in 2013. This defeat was the breeding ground for my breaking of the eight-day sound barrier.

Without my people, I would not have been able to achieve this seemingly impossible time.

XV

"... BUT IT'S MORE IMPORTANT TO BE NICE!"

SOCIAL CRITIC, SPORTS FAN, VELOBLITZ BIKE MESSENGER

After the bell in my high school in Knittelfeld had heralded the end of the school day, on sunny days I'd sometimes hang out with my friends in the meadow near the public pool. Between the beach volleyball games, we philosophized about life, made plans, and finally moved our discussions into the adjoining park. We exchanged popsicles for more substantial refreshments, and sipped our cans until our six-pack of beer was gone.

It would be wrong to say that we were revolutionaries. We just wanted to be different and smarter than those who created the prevailing system in which my friends and I felt trapped. We did not want to accept the hardships and grind of everyday life and looked for ways out—mainly on a theoretical level. We wondered if it really was the purpose of life to work until retirement, strive for material wealth, but never really be happy. "Why," we mused, "are those people from poorer countries, who are less fortunate than we are in Europe, happier than we are? Why are so many people depressed and dissatisfied despite all of our prosperity here?" With all our talk, I already realized that I could not say goodbye to existing social orders so easily, and that existential questions can never be answered absolutely right for everyone.

What remained was a desire to spend time with friends and not with one's own career. I was drawn to the approach of living in a community made up of a small, fine team, in which everyone would be essential and not interchangeable, and of living in a camper bus and not in an expensive, chic house. We did not want to start a political party or movement, but simply to improve the world (on a small scale). But making the "system obsolete" and claiming to save the world from ruin is hopeless, and a waste of energy. The knowledge grew to choose the lesser evil, and to lead a reasonably self-determined existence in everyday life. I wanted to adopt an alternative lifestyle and not be part of the system that forces us to destroy Earth to survive.

> **I became aware of how responsible I was for my own actions, and how, through my thoughts, words, and deeds, I could inspire others to think and perhaps imitate.**

Daniel Quinn's *Ishmael,* states that there is not one single right way for people to live because there are different cultures, tribes, and circumstances. That's why I was not, and am not, someone who tells others how to live. It is important to me that I live sustainably in my influenceable environment, and I wonder why others want to impose their political, religious, or nutritional attitudes on their fellow human beings. Let everyone live the way he or she wants! It remains important to be able to stand behind one's own actions, and to answer for them morally and ethically, and to not rob anyone of his or her freedom.

One question that I regularly ask concerns my attitude to global challenges. Overpopulation has become an unsolvable problem: Eight billion people overwhelm the earth's ecosystem and resources. The most beautiful times of our planet are already behind us, many processes are irreversible. Rainforests have been cleared, animal species die out, nature reserves are dissolved for economic use, and the oceans are polluted with plastic. What is happening is sheer madness, and it does not fuel my desire to bring children into the world.

It could be even worse. If the civilized people have the opportunity to emigrate to other life-sustaining planets, then there would be similar issues to what we currently see on Earth. Doing the same thing over and over and expecting different results is a sign of insanity, Albert Einstein once said. However, so is believing we know how to live, and forcing this lifestyle on others, even if the global outcomes are fatal.

I find it fascinating that on the one hand, we humans are becoming so much greater in number, but on the other hand, we're growing together more culturally. Modern means of communication have made it possible for the world to become a village. As a further consequence, all people should not necessarily follow the same rules of the game—rules dictated by the society of the First World. There are many controversial issues and occurrences around the world, for which I have opinions on what should be done. But do I have the right to impose my opinions and values on the people that are directly affected? I am against any form of corruption, but doesn't this word and the associated actions have a different appeal in every culture?

Back then, I supported Greenpeace and still do so today. Starting in 2002, I started to study environmental protection during my university days at Montanuniversität Leoben, but I quickly realized that I had been mistaken in my appro-

First longer bike ride on the Grossglockner

ach to this study. I listened attentively to the lectures, thought along, but did not learn the books at home. In the first semester, I took all the examinations, but I was not up to the task of memorizing chemistry. In compulsory and grammar schools, one can make it through with logical thinking and cooperation during class, but at the university, one has to learn. The study was technical, numerical, and fact-based, and provided few concrete approaches to making our planet a better world.

In Leoben, I had shared a two-person flat with my university colleague "Bertl," lived a modest student life, and found more and more joy in my bike training. I was able to train ten hours a day, but was unable to learn ten pages of a textbook. As a marginal employee, I worked for a refurbishment company for 350 euros a month. I scaled down rock samples, sifted sand into grain sizes, and made pellet balls from dust. I was enrolled for twelve semesters, and when I celebrated my first success as an extreme athlete in 2007, going to university was merely my plan B, which I could follow up on, should my cycling ambitions not pan out. My studies had triggered internal blockages; it was not what I wanted to do. The training on the bike, however, fascinated me. Forty hours of training a week made me tired and exhausted, but the whole package called "life" was fun.

Is it a pattern, or simply the naivety of the age that many young people doubt the prevailing system, have core values, and want to bring about change, but are later disillusioned and so only look at their own needs? I read numerous books on the topic and shared my favorite work *Ishmael* again and again; I studied magazines like GEO and continued to educate myself off the curriculum.

My pride and joy: Mercedes 207D camper-van, built in 1978

With long hair, a beard, and backpack, I saw myself as a pilgrim on Spain's famous Camino de Santiago, discussing with others what is going wrong in life, that the construct of our civilization is like a flying object that does not conform to the laws of aerodynamics: we flutter like the former aviation pioneers, although faster, but also continue to fall. Although I did not make my way to Santiago de Compostela, I bought a camper bus. That was in 2003. I was 21 years old; the bus was 25. From then on, I spent many years traveling with friends and our bicycles in Spain, Portugal or France. In 2004, we drove together to the Olympic Games in Athens. We did not see a single competition because we could not, or did not want to, spend our meager money on tickets, but we had made a sport out of tricking the system. What would have been unimaginable today was possible "at the safest games in history." At night, we sat at the ledge of the Olympic pool where the world's best swimmers fought for medals during the day. Peacefully and quietly we enjoyed our "triumph"—a fabric banner, which we "liberated" as a souvenir, and which then adorned my room for several years.

That I did not see a single competition, I felt then, as today, was not a big drawback. Many sports are rather boring from the audience. Rather, I'm a fan of the protagonists of a discipline or a beautiful game—or of the huge atmosphere in stadiums.

Already at school in woodshop, I had built a football arena out of balsa wood and worked on this at home. The result was a small model with continuous grandstands, a second level, an LED floodlight system, and a removable dome roof. It was the impressive stadium of FC Barcelona that I liked at first sight on TV. In the meantime, I've visited Camp Nou twice in Barcelona: on one of my bus trips in 2004, and eight years later, on my 30th birthday, when I got tickets for Barcelona against Real Madrid. The game was outstanding, the mood in the stands, a disappointment. The spectators behaved as if they were in an opera performance. "There are more emotions in the Austrian football league," I thought to myself.

I would rather watch international football matches than a cycling race—they are more engaging. My attitude to the protagonists has changed over the years. When I started cycling, I thought how unfair it was that these guys had to train so much and yet remain unnoted and underpaid, while the football (AKA soccer) stars trained much less, yet were adored by tens of thousands of people and were royally rewarded. But to be a footballer has a higher price, which I need not pay as an ultra-cyclist. If you are a star, then everyone knows you, and I do not envy anyone who cannot go anywhere without having to engage with fans. For me personally, sometimes it is too much when I am sitting in a restaurant with a pizza and autograph or photo requests are brought to me. I'm sorry, but sometimes I get rude, even though I'm actually an accessible type, but when I dine with friends, I'd like to enjoy our meal in peace. But the thing is, I'm a nobody compared to superstars like Messi, Ronaldo, Lewandowski or even pop stars and Hollywood actors. How must it be for these people, how can one psychologically endure such circumstances? Why would anyone wish to be famous, and yet be unable to go places in the world without being recognized?

In cycling, I'm a fan of Fabian Cancellara. His style is powerful, his bike control impressive, and his way of riding is especially beautiful in the classics and in time-trials. I'd like to see him at the Race Across America, but that will probably never happen. It is often said that professional cyclists are inferior in the ultra-distances, but I see it differently. I would say that he has the ability and a chance to win, if his motivation was strong enough. The physical fitness would definitely exist. Apart from that, in my favorite sport, I am interested in the many years of personal duels of the great characters: Armstrong against Ullrich, for example, or Boonen against Cancellara. Personalities captivate me more than race patterns, but I realize that these two aspects must be considered coherently. But as I said, I do not watch cycling on TV for its own sake, and I do not know how other, more prominent athletes are with their TV habits. Did Lindsey Vonn like to watch a skiing event when she was not competing herself? Does Formula 1 ex-world champion Niko Rosberg watch motorsport races?

In the world of sport, my greatest veneration is the greats of tennis, especially Roger Federer. For me, he is the best tennis player of all time. He has accomplished so much more than anyone else, yet despite all these successes, he does not tire of continuing to compete at the highest level and to win. He still loves his sport—you can see and feel that. He does not have to prove anything to anyone but himself. His intrinsic motivation is probably compounded by the current situation in world tennis, where Rafael Nadal is a permanent rival, and Novak Djokovic is once again an opponent at eye level. This spur from the outside is lacking in my current situation. Severin Zotter and Reto Schoch challenged and beat me years ago, but both are not racing anymore, and there are no aspiring riders with great potential for a sub–8–day finish in sight at RAAM right now.

Federer excites me with his passion for sports and his mental strength to be able to give his best in decisive moments. He fascinates me because he has developed new techniques, even in the late years of his career, and knew how to surprise his opponents with different strategies. He never tires of working on his game, and does not shy away from changes. Conversely, this means that Roger Federer must be extremely disciplined in training, but also takes breaks in his tournament schedule at the right time.

> Self-motivation, as seen in Roger Federer, is the hardest form of motivation. Federer's love of the sport is most likely the reason he still carries on. And that's exactly how I see it with me. If that enthusiasm fades one day, then it's time to devote myself to other activities.

The Swiss is much more than an outstanding tennis player. He is correct, good-natured, and noble. His role model effect does not stop when the match is over. In his biography, I found the following sentence: "It's nice to be important, but it's more important to be nice." This quote is not from him, but an adage first attributed to US journalist Walter Winchell in 1937. But no matter whom the author is, this statement unites all that Federer is for me: greatness and importance, decency and virtue, and humility. That's why I try to pattern myself after his positive qualities, to bring love for my sport, to achieve goals, and to remain humble.

But you can learn a lot more from Federer: In his late career, he cleverly splits his powers, changes his tournament calendar, plays fewer tournaments than before, but with full focus and at the highest level. He estimates his resources correctly, and knows that he cannot (anymore) dance at all weddings. The fact that he renounced the clay court season in 2017 and 2018 may make other people angry—but I admire him for that. Since taking a break because of an injury in 2016, in his comeback, he was able to win three more Grand Slam titles with this strategy.

Anyone who has earned more than a hundred million euros purely in prize money and was World Sportsman of the Year does not still play for financial reasons, or for his ego. Someone like "FedEx" plays out of sheer love for the sport.

Cycling was ever present, even on my holiday adventure trips in my camper bus, I did long rides in beautiful places—for the fun, the experiences, and to keep my training edge. After all, bicycles have played a role in my life since I was five years old. I like to think back to some of these key moments and relive being the child that I was then. The whole thing went like this:

"Now open the surprise egg!" My father encouragingly said to me at an Easter party. My joy was limited. I wanted to get a real present and not chocolate and some little toy. "Don't you want to open it?" My father had obviously done a lot; he had carefully divided the chocolate in halves, put a key inside, and reassembled the surprise.

When I saw what was locked by the key, my joy was unending: The Easter Bunny had brought me a brand new bike! I immediately made a lap around our home to try out the sparkling neon-colored vehicle. However, this first ride did not go without incident. The usually closed garden gate was open, and the neighbor's dog, a shepherd, barked at me and bit me on the knee. Tears shot into my eyes, but I did not fall, and rode the few yards home. After all, it was not a big drama—I came away with a pair of torn pants and a few scratches, and the neighbor apologized. But I still have the respect for dogs when they cross my bike's path. Again and again, I see some of them on RAAM, because the area between Monument Valley and the Rocky Mountains, which is passed through on the third day, is full of strays.

On my confirmation, my grandfather gave me my first mountain bike. It was without suspension forks and had 21 gears. Twice I raced on it at the 24-Hours of Fohnsdorf. And when our local football teams were merged, and I had to go eight kilometers away to St. Lorenzen for practice, I often cycled there. "Cycling makes you slow," my soccer coach admonished. But these words of reprimand had no meaning later, when I left the team. I also cycled to my grandmother's house, who lived on her farm up a mountain. Again and again, I set new goals for that ride. "I will only get off twice," was my goal, and when that was done, I wanted to do the 4-kilometers-long climb with only one dismount, and then with none.

Cycling grew to become an alternative way of life for me, which is why I did not find it to be a problem to leave the 2-person flat I shared in Leoben, and as a 26-year-old, move back in with my parents after having been standing on my own two legs for seven years. In a phase of my life in which I wanted to position myself as a cyclist, and earn my livelihood with smaller jobs such as a summer job at VOEST (a steel company in Linz, Austria), this step seemed a sensible compromise because it allowed me to spend my money on cycling events and training camps. I always had the support of my parents and so they were not against me coming back home. "You do not have to be involved in the household budget," my dad said, "but you're old enough that you've got to earn the money for your sport yourself." I could live well with that. Money has a higher value if you work for it than if you get it for free. I never borrowed money, never went into debt. Either I could afford something or I had to save for it. That's one of my basic tenets. Money is not a factor in my life that interests me, and if I were to win the lottery (which would be difficult since I don't play), I would not know where the money would go. A new city bike? A new winter jacket? But, these are things that I do not have to win the lottery for anyway.

As good as my relationship with my parents was, on some days it was difficult to live with them. I've always been able to leave a chaotic mess. I'd borrow my dad's tools and then lose them, or the garage and basement were often full of my bike gear, which occasionally led to "discussions." Before the good climate between us began to suffer from these trivialities, and thus lead to quarrels, I felt it best to become independent again and no longer a burden on my parents.

At the end of 2008, I decided to follow my girlfriend Sabine to Graz. One year later, we fulfilled the dream of a shared apartment.

I have known Sabine since my school days. She is the younger sister of a schoolmate, and we have known each other for many years. Just before Christmas 2006, we became a couple.

In the first years of our relationship, my career had been uphill. Then, I won the world championship title at Glocknerman and qualified for RAAM in Slovenia. We worked together to forge my sport into a profession and started my online shop, which Sabine helped me with, while completing her studies and also working a part-time job.

I am always asked why my life partner is not present at my races. There are a few different reasons. In any case, in the early years, it was not always easy for us to bridge this separation. That was a learning experience for both of us. We realized that it was better not to experience this intensely challenging and painful part of life together on the ground. Nevertheless, Sabine is a tremendously important support for me during a race. If my support crew is not able to lift me up, they pick up the phone and call her. She manages to motivate me to give everything in the hardest stages at the

Sabine and I on our way in Southern Europe

end. But if she were there at the race, it could be a burdensome situation for both of us. I don't really know how my girlfriend would react if she saw how bad I really am sometimes, then I'd be too preoccupied on the bike with how the whole thing would be for her. That's why we both decided that she stays at home during the races.

In addition, there is another very simple reason: We now run a two-person company, and in the time before and during the RAAM, we are working in the online shop, doing customer service, updating the website, and managing editorial activity for my social media. We are so busy that it would not work if she didn't remain at home to run the office.

Sabine also has her qualities as a crew member, as was evident in the 24–hour race at Le Mans 2009. She was the only caregiver and was completely on her own. The lack of hospitality and helpfulness in this race wasn't what we're used to, which presented us with a real challenge. I almost received a penalty when I rode too fast through the pit lane; nobody had thought to inform us of that. The neighboring teams in the pit lane avoided us Austrians—even though Sabine spoke fluent French and could therefore communicate. In the prevailing August heat, I suffered in the last hours of the race and did not really put pressure on the pedals. But instead of pitying me or taking a break, she did something completely different: she asked me what position I wanted to finish in, and at the same time told a white lie about the lap times, claiming that my pursuer was on pace to catch me and I'd still lose second place if I kept rolling like that. What can I say? She knows me too well and her tactics worked. I mobilized my last strength and took second place with some advantage over my pursuers, who

were actually much farther behind me than Sabine had led me to believe. The next day, we started a spectacular trip home for Sabine—she drove for 18 hours in one go, with the exception of two restroom breaks. And I was a fairly useless passenger. If I had not just fallen into a comatose deep sleep, I ate through our supplies, and out of cravings for something acidic, I even drank the juice from our jar of pickles.

I was also fortunate to have Sabine on my team of supervisors in Grenchen, where she had the race-saving idea to ease the nausea I'd been fighting with homeopathic stomach drops and peppermint oil, which improved my condition.

One of her greatest strengths is in letting go, taking a step back, and letting me and my team go, but still seeing herself as an essential part of our business. She is the part of the team that has the most difficult job: She has to motivate me 365 days a year, discuss with me, and sometimes kick my ass. She comforts me after failures, slows me down when my mood perhaps soars too high, and gives me grounding and stability. I am grateful for this support and the great freedom that I have. Many of my cycling friends have problems in their relationships for exactly this reason. This is not an issue for us, because Sabine, like me, is a freedom-loving person.

We both like to travel and have a great love for our neighbor, Italy. Once a year,

whether in training camp or on vacation, we are somewhere in Tuscany. Here, we are happily unbound, and have spent many of our vacations on campsites or, as in our Corsica Trip 2007, with my old Mercedes bus. It is always a bit of an adventure; a luxury hotel is not in our vacation planning.

We value not only our love of freedom and our desire to travel, but above all, our sense of humor. Sometimes we can laugh for hours, sharing our sarcastic humor with each other and imitating Austrian comedians.

Fifty meters to the ice cream parlor, a hundred meters to the bookstore, two hundred meters to the cinema, restaurants in every direction—in Graz we lived at a crossroads to the old town center, thus right in the center of the second largest city in Austria. We enjoyed the convenience and the flair of the city center, which, however, also

235

had its drawbacks. Once as I returned from a training trip, I found the traditional Austrian pre-Christmas Perchten festival was in progress, something I'd forgotten about. I stood in the midst of the crowd with my helmet and bike. And as I watched the traditional evil-looking Perchten creatures with their wooden carved masks, their long tails and fangs, and their carriages burning with metal bins and fireworks, I understood how these ancient mythical beings are so effective at frightening children into behaving better. Yes, the Perchten demons are very much like the better-known Krampus, but I think of Perchtens as the more high-end pro versions of Krampus! I like Austrian customs, but this evening, this celebration barred me from accessing my apartment, and to the shower and my much-needed dinner.

After three years, we moved from the city center to the university district to be closer to Sabine's lectures. Later we moved to the city's outskirts, where we have our own apartment with a garden shed.

I had known of the Veloblitz bike messenger company scene before. At 24-hour races, some of these bike couriers had successfully competed in the relay competitions, where they stood out with their long hair and cool demeanor. "I would like to be one of those guys," I mused. Years later, the time had come. After my DNF at Race Across America 2009, I was hired at Veloblitz. I realized that these were not just cool guys, but absolutely cool guys, who had parties in the head office after their shift, drinking beer, smoking cigarettes, and enjoying life. They did their jobs during the day, as I did, but after that, they had their fun. Meanwhile, I pedaled the ergometer for at least an hour.

> With the move to Graz, I found an activity where I could combine work and training: I became a bike messenger.

I used to work as a courier twice a week, so that my job would be on the bike and my training on the bike. Depending on how fast and smart I rode, and depending on how many orders could be combined, I received between 5 and 15 euros per hour. I enjoyed the feeling of having to get up and ride to honestly earn 80 euros for a day's work. During those days, there were no thoughts of any university exams, or e-mails I had to write to sponsors or the media. I was one with myself and my job.

As a messenger, you're always in a hurry, but I think I only disregarded road signs or traffic lights when I was absolutely sure nothing would happen. Like the other couriers, I rode wild, but with complete self-responsibility. I knew that I was always weaker compared to cars. Once, I carried a two-meter-long roll of paper, tied to my backpack it almost dragged on the chain and protruded a meter above my head. Express orders paid 3 euros more if they were completed within a certain period of time, for example, if tissue samples from a hospital had to be analyzed in a nearby laboratory during an operation. Although the distance between the hospital and the laboratory was only one kilometer, I still gave it full throttle. The dispatcher was glad to have a messenger who was an ultra-cyclist with much endurance—I was assigned many of the special orders to cities farther away. A cell phone needed to be brought from the shop to an advertising agency, and I built the relevant 35 kilometers into my intended training session. The experience as a messenger also influenced me. Although I never did the "Alley Cats" events held at night—a kind of scavenger hunt on wheels—because they were too dangerous for me, during the day I learned enough for future tasks, namely, how to behave in the busy traffic between cars and trucks, so you do not need to be nervous when the streets are busy. Others may gasp when passed by more than one car an hour, but being among many cars became routine for me.

There have always been discussions with the police, even before my time in Graz. Once, I was training on a country road between Leoben and Kraubath, when a car came up close behind me. The driver honked aggressively for no reason. I did not respond. A little later, the scene repeated itself with another car, whose driver got extremely, and dangerously, close to me. Slowly I became agitated. Immediately he honked again. Without turning around, I raised my hand angrily and held up my middle finger. The car drove by and slowed down in front of me. It was the police. I apologized, told the officials that I had some issues with bad drivers that day, and the matter was settled.

Several other times I was ordered to pay fines. Once during winter training near Leoben, I put on my gloves at three degrees Celsius and rode without my hands on the bars for a few meters. The police saw this and stopped me: 35 euros.

"But I have no money with me and I just put on the gloves, so my fingers do not freeze. Can't you just give me a warning?" I asked.
"Where do you live? We'll come with you to collect the fine."

My apartment was two kilometers away, but the policeman could not change a 100-euro bill. So they had to follow me, again, to the next grocery store. With the money changed and the fine paid, the policeman was happy. By law, you're not allowed to ride with your hands off the handlebars, that's right. But on a completely empty street, is this really a crime that requires a fine? I think a policeman should be a friend and a helper, not a debt collector.

Paragraph 68 of the Austrian road traffic regulations allows cyclists to ride side by side when on racing bikes and in training. Although, I assume that all police officers know this statute, I also have the experience that there are those who may not have read the text thoroughly enough. During a workout, a friend and I were stopped. As

2009 to 2012: On the job as a bike messenger for Veloblitz in Graz

the angry officer got out of the car, we noticed his unhealthy complexion.

"What you're doing is forbidden!" He barked, exuding a not-too-subtle scent of alcohol. I briefly tried to enlighten him, which was unsuccessful.

"Do we want to be right or do we want to continue in peace?" I thought, and calmed down. "You are right, Inspector, our mistake. We won't do it again." The official stuttered a few reprimands and then disappeared back into his car.

There are pain thresholds, red lines that I do not cross. But I do not have to engage in a discussion with a cop, just to get it right. Strengthening my ego is irrelevant. I prefer to avoid stressful situations.

At Veloblitz, where I also met Severin Zotter, the confrontation with the city police was limited. We respected each other and our work, and so I did not ignore red lights very often.

All in all, I was on the road for three and a half years as a courier and still rode as

Some photos shot for Veloblitz during route reconnaissance before RAAM 2011

RAAM winner for the Graz messenger company. In the years 2011 and 2012, Veloblitz was represented on my jersey. We took pictures in the desert of California, and we launched a small advertising campaign with the slogan "We do not have an order too far." At the end of 2012, I finished working with this company; we are still in contact. You do not forget the nice times easily.

High humidity and high heat in the Appalachian Mountains

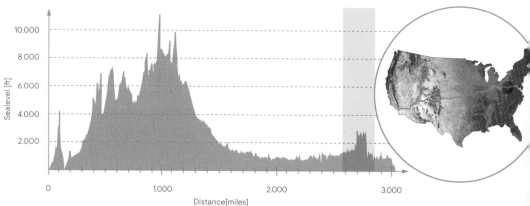

XVI

"I WON'T PAY FOR ANY OF HIS BEER!"

RAAM, TIME STATIONS 44–49

"Take Me Home, Country Roads." the famous John Denver song, had been planting itself in my head while I was fighting my way through West Virginia. Sometimes having a song stuck in my head is torture, but this one I don't mind at all. Its lyrics about mountains and rivers call to me, and make me think of my farm-life boyhood in Austria, which somehow makes all that I'm enduring a little bit easier, and the song puts me in a good mood. I've recently learned that my John Denver earwig about going home was also a favorite of Jure Robic's, and that he had a Slovenian version that his crew would play for him over their loudspeakers during RAAM. I suppose it reminded him of his own country upbringing in Slovenia, which probably put him in a good mood as well.

To get me in a good mood, there are few combinations better in RAAM than waking from a power nap and then having a cup of espresso freshly brewed on the RV's gas stove, followed by some good music. Simple pleasures, you know?

> "Good mood" is a relative term in The Appalachians. By this time, I'd been continuously in the saddle for six or seven days and sleep deprivation had taken its toll.

You cannot train to stay awake; at least, I don't. In my everyday life, I tend to go to bed late, rarely before midnight. Staying up is a nice thing, I've always wanted that as a child—perhaps out of concern of missing something important. Fatigue and sleep deprivation and the associated challenges in RAAM follow the body's natural rhythm. The first night, the eyes want to close and the stressed organism realizes that it will not get eight hours of sleep. Since the physical performance is highest on day one, and the biorhythm is still intact, the brain defends itself against insomnia by all means. The second night can be the hardest if you overdo the fight against fatigue and have not taken a short power nap. The third night actually gets better, as the body adjusts to the new situation: continuous load, on the one hand, little to no sleep, on the other. The danger of falling asleep on the bike decreases insignificantly, but I am also becoming thin-skinned, more peculiar and also forgetful. After five or six nights, chaos reigns in the head, especially when the route book turns to the Appalachians.

In my first RAAM, I was told that the event really starts in the Appalachian Mountains. Nonsense! In order to survive this non-stop journey, it takes a top performance right from the start. But it is true that the route has more climbing per mile in the Appalachians than in the Rocky Mountains, and the climbs are more difficult and steeper than those in the west. Flat sections are rare, and the route goes almost continuously up and down. And because it is already spinning from sleep deprivation, the brain creates its own reality.

"Who are you?" I asked a man who ran beside me in an uphill passage and cheered me on. "Somehow your voice sounds familiar to me ..."

Sleep deprivation leads to more and more psychological lows

"It's me, George. I'm part of your team," he answered.

"Aha, good to know," I mumbled. As he slowed down, I also slowed down my pedaling.

"Keep riding, keep going!"

"I can't leave you here alone."

"Keep riding! I'll get in the car, I'll manage."

"What car?!"

A moment later, I realized that I did not remember how to steer my bike. With my elbows outstretched and my back arched, I rolled toward the curve that opened in front of me. Fearful and confused, I talked into the headset of my radio and begged for help: "Please, how do I steer? I have to go to the left, how do I do that?"

Somehow, I intuitively made it around that turn, going so slowly it's a wonder I stayed upright—I could have easily walked faster. I realized that something was wrong with me, but I could not untie the knot in my head. I heard my mind say good-bye and then it was if I was just a passenger in my body, pushing the pedals down with sheer muscle memory. But it was impossible for me to consciously intervene in the process. Ten minutes later, I realized what was happening around me, and then I was again, the master of my situation. From then on, I was only sick and cold, I was trembling all over because my circulation was not up to scratch. After another ten minutes, all my systems began to work again, my metabolism kicked in, and I felt myself warm up. I asked questions and demanded answers; soon the first jokes came back. By the time we started making fun of each other, everyone knew that I was back with them and survived the "waking up and clearing up,"—arguably the toughest phase in RAAM.

Confusion and disorientation often occur after sleep breaks

The Appalachians are where I so often perceive the support vehicle as a menacing pursuer, and my crew as unknown spies. It was there that I crashed after a power nap and luckily was not injured. It was there that I heard an announcement from my crew that I had to turn right at the next intersection, misunderstood, and immediately steered right—directly into the curb. It was there that I was convinced that my crew had put me on the wrong bike. And it was also there that I tried to get onto my bike backwards! Did you know that a right cleat will not click backward into a left pedal? But at least that time, I knew it was for sure my bike.

Yes, once I did not even recognize my own bike. During a sleep break, my companions thought they were doing me a favor by replacing the old, dirty, sticky handlebar tape with fresh tape. As I was riding on, not feeling the dirty, sticky material on my palms, I protested, saying that this was not my racing machine. I had to be appeased and once again persuaded to continue. It made me grumpy that now I was sitting on a strange bike. At the next break, the crew members fetched the old tape out of the garbage bag, wrapped it around the handlebar, and I was able to continue happily.

All ultra-cyclists struggle with hallucinations, some more than others. Wolfgang Fasching did not perceive the cinema playing in his head during RAAM as a delusion, he once said. Jure Robic, on the other hand, was plagued by self-made realities.

According to the replies he gave in an interview with The New York Times, he thought there were armed enemies who wanted to obliterate him and his family. Instead of reassuring him, his crew had encouraged him in this assumption: "Ride faster, you must flee!" The ethical aspect of this behavior may be questionable, but his people's request served one single purpose: victory. It worked; Robic had gone faster and won—once again.

If RAAM is a close race, then the decision is made in The Appalachians. In 2011, Gerhard Gulewicz gave up 180 miles (290 kilometers) from the finish after falling back from second to fourth. In 2012, Reto Schoch decisively pulled away from me in this phase of the competition. In 2013, I was plagued by the most severe hallucinations. In 2014 and 2017, I was confronted with a new route, which led to even more confusion than usual.

Between Time Station #46 in Grafton and #48 in Cumberland, the classic route was via Time Station #47 in Keyser, but the new route was a bit more northerly via McHenry, which included more altitude on a similarly long distance. But also in 2013, when I should have known the route, I asked, "Why do I have to go back up there? Do you think I do not notice that you have sent me the same ascent four times? And why is the whole nursing home over there cheering for me?"

I was just on the section of the Appalachians on which the RAAM organization determines the winner of the Jure Robic Award. It was named after the legendary Slovenian because this section of extreme climbing had been his favorite part of RAAM. In the spring of 2013, I came to the US with Kougi and had a training week riding from Ohio to Annapolis. I wanted to see this part of the route with a clear head and get a sharp picture of it without being sleep deprived. I knew that this stage is actually special. Shortly before that, it goes from West Virginia to Maryland, and that changes a lot. The streets are turned from potholed to carpet-like and smooth, dilapidated wooden houses into well-kept properties. West Virginia is one of the poorest states in the US, Maryland one of the richest. The obvious differences always cause confusion in my mind, and then suddenly, I feel out of place.

On the "Robic stage" there are four climbs, each containing 300 meters difference in altitude, which closely resemble each other, and on the third mountain is a large house on the left side of the road. In front of this house were the members of a cycling club

From West Virginia to Maryland

with some senior citizens who cheered me on. I thought back to my time as a civil servant in the nursing home...

"We are on RAAM and you're already on the last day. Now we just need to get to Annapolis—you already have all the mountains behind you. Tomorrow we will be there!"
"What? What are you talking about? I do not understand a word! And the retirement home?"
"These are fans, cyclists, who we saw here last year. They just come here to cheer for you because you're going to win RAAM. You are in the lead, clearly!"

Christian "Scheb" Schebath did his best: He talked to me in a calm voice, trying to get me out of this hole of disorientation. But his help was in vain. For me, at that moment, he was like a stranger telling me untruths, telling me something to get him out of this alleged race faster. "He's tired of this crazy carousel and wants to get off," I thought to myself. Actually, Scheb is one of my most loyal companions, and has been on my crew for five RAAM's, RAA, Ireland, and Glocknerman. We have a close friendship, but in those moments, I suspected him of wanting to do me evil.

Hours later, after the crew shift had changed, Kougi asked me, "I heard from Scheb that you did not feel well on the Robic stage, and that you did not know your way around. How are you now? Is everything okay again?"
"No," I answer, "Christian told me some nonsense. I will not pay for any of his beer at the finish!"

"Come on, let it go, you're arguing with a madman up front," I heard from the back of the car. How true. While at this point I wasn't strong or fast, but at least was on the bike again and pedaling forward. When we finished in 2013, the first thing I did was apologize to Christian and promise him two beers.

Hallucinations can be bad, but over the years I've learned to deal with them. I keep going, concentrating on the road and not looking left or right, paying no attention to the delusions in my brain. I know that I see strange things next to me and ignore them. Disorientation, however, is another phenomenon that I do not know any cure for.

If RAAM is already decided, then the question of the meaningfulness of pushing my pace is great, especially in the Appalachians. "Why do I still have to work so hard, even if it would be enough to go on comfortably?" "Why am I doing this?" These are the questions that come to my mind in the quieter moments of RAAM when I'm alone in my head. I have realized that Race Across America would be a part of my future and my life plan. To keep the privilege of making a living from racing my bike, I must give it my very best and endure such tough moments.

For many extreme athletes, it seems they are torn apart in life as if they are escaping from something, or breaking out of something, as if they were replacing one addiction with another, and do not know exactly where they actually want to go in life. That wasn't, and is not, the case with me. I did not run away from anything else, because I always knew where I wanted to go. I wanted to make cycling my profession (and as Plan B, I had an unfinished degree of study that I could still turn to).

Unfortunately, many, too many, appear only temporarily on the ultra-cycling scene. The German, Pierre Bischoff, was 31 years old when he won RAAM in 2016 and said to RAAM Media, "After this, it is time to become an adult."

Is it time to grow up after RAAM? Or does RAAM help one to mature as a person and athlete?

Pierre Bischoff and I are good friends. I, as well as Severin Zotter and others, conveyed motivational messages to him when he was on his way to success, and in other years, I received uplifting words from Pierre. This mutual appreciation is really remarkable.

RAAM 2017: Using the last of my strength on the steep climbs of the Appalachians

I followed RAAM 2016 at home in front of my laptop and updated the live tracker almost every hour. Watching that race from home, took more out of me emotionally than others that I suffered through on the course.

Pierre arrived in Annapolis after 9 days and 16 hours as the first German winner in the history of RAAM. I was very happy for him, yet I was still torn by his performance. My personal attitude is to give the best, under whatever circumstances. I did not always see this devotion with my German colleague in 2016. Pierre has a different charac-ter than me: he takes things more relaxed, he sometimes chooses friendliness over the competition, and at many time stations he stopped, took pictures with fans, and signed autographs. In between, videos were released that showed him joking and fooling around with his team—he was cycling with his beard glued on or telling jokes. I find this behavior disrespectful to the slower riders. At the back end of the field, older athletes and hobby riders struggle against the cut-off, and getting through, for them, is a serious matter, and their chances of earning an official finish often slip away. If the leader presents himself as a joker on the way to victory, that does not throw a good light on the others. On the other hand, I have to admit that Pierre never spoke of a RAAM victory before the race; that was not his declared aim. He always wanted to ride a good race, to experience an adventure, and to have fun with his team—that was, of course, what makes him likable. He maintained this approach, even when he took the lead.

My favorite book, *Ishmael*, states that there is not one single right way to live for all people. Similarly, it must be true that there is not one right attitude for all athletes, and that's a good thing.

Just as it was with Pierre's casual goal, which had burned into his subconscious mind be-fore the race and could not be changed during the competition, so was it with me in 2011. My goal at that time, was to arrive healthy and ideally to land on the podium, possibly first. As I climbed into the lead through the Appalachians, a remark came from Rainer Hoch-gatterer. His colleague Dr. Helmut Ocenasek—a RAAM expert and supporter of Fasching, who crewed for Wolfgang for many of his podium finishes and victories—had just written to Rainer that a finish time of fewer than eight days would still be possible.

I was horrified and protested, "What do you want from me? I am in position to make it to the finish, win the race, and instead of praise you want more?! Are you satisfied with nothing? I'm I not going to stress myself. I will ride on as well as I can, and I'll be the luckiest person in the world if I win!"

RAAM 2014: My crew shows humor while I crank

Even if I refused to think about the breaking of the "sound barrier" at that moment, this was a topic for me to contemplate in the months that followed. I started to seriously think about this goal. The seed was scattered and soon began to germinate.

It is interesting that the participants of the RAAM start the race with varying expectations. Many are driven by the thirst for adventure, and the question of whether they would be able to accomplish this challenge within the maximum allowed time of twelve days. Others want to explore their own limits and get the most out of themselves, while others make their personal success dependent on placing well in their category. What

The later it is in the race, the more difficult it becomes for my crew to get through to me

is common to all, however, is the fact that you can no longer move from one approach to another during the race—the goal formulation develops over months and is firmly anchored in the subconscious.

At any rate, my mother was happy when I could not compete in 2016. "Great, boy," she told me in all seriousness, "then someone else can finally win." I was perplexed. "You know," she added, "I'm so sorry for the others."

I said, "With all due respect, Mama, but the others have to make an effort if they want to beat me. I will not let anyone win so easily." I thought back to when I was a small boy playing the fox-and-hen board game with my dad and he sometimes let me win. I had not been pleased, but was instead sad and a little annoyed.

Bischoff's 2016 RAAM win was a joy not only to his followers, his fans, and my mother but also to RAAM Media, led by Vic Armijo. This small group, which reports annually from the RAAM, does not have it easy. Even though the crew is in constant contact with the race director, and therefore knows what's going on, ideally they stay where the race is most interesting.

> **Just as in my childhood, it still applies to me today: If I want to be successful, then I have to deliver a real performance as well.**

When I won in 2013 and 2014, Armijo and his people interviewed the racers behind me, then raced through the US with little time for eating or sleeping, to catch up with me so that they could cover the last part of my race. With a grin, Vic told me in 2017 that the media team had thoroughly enjoyed the competition the year before. "Having Pierre in the lead, and not as fast as you were on the road, was a pleasant change for us. For once we had time to get a good night's sleep and to actually have sit-down meals. We definitely were less stressed."

However, for me to take my time to facilitate the work of others would not come to my mind. In the Appalachian Mountains, for example, I would go mad if I was told to slow down. In 2017, our doctor, Florian Wimmer, recommended the team boss grant me a longer break. For him, it was terrible to witness my sleep deprivation and its consequences. Florian did a great job with me and with the entire team, and he played a big part in my success that year, but at times he almost became too coddling, which was absolutely understandable in his role as the doctor responsible for my health. Crew leader Kougi knew me better, and the team stayed with the agreed plan. It was clear how I would have reacted. "You ruined my race! Why do I do push so hard for days if you're just going to let me sleep too long?" I would have yelled at them all. I could not have held my tongue if they had let me sleep too long.

The last sleep break before the finish line

In 2011, I sat on the bike thinking, "Where's my bike? Didn't I just have a sleep break? And now I'm here, but where is my bike?" I grumbled at my crew, "Can you tell me where my bike is?" Thankfully, I had experienced people around me. Others would have laughed and said that I was sitting on top of it, and an endless discussion would have probably unfolded.

But Thomas Jaklitsch answered, "We'll call the people in the mobile home—they'll take it. You just keep on riding."
I was reassured, "Yeah, okay, it's okay."

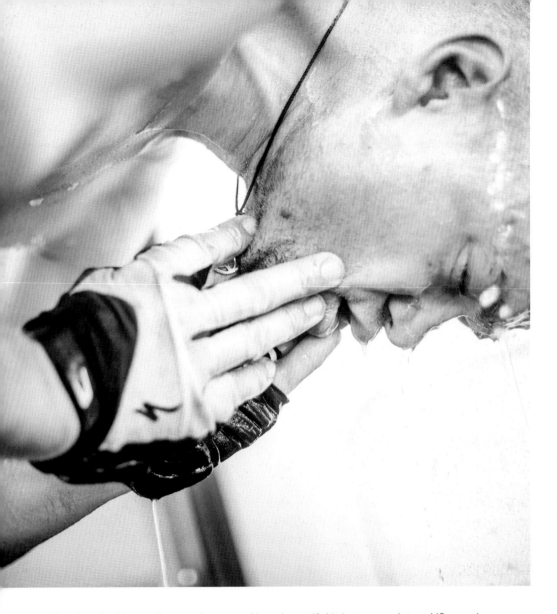

The Appalachians offer no glimpses of how beautiful it is to complete a US crossing, nothing of the joy of a possible forthcoming victory. These climbs, they are tough, brutal, and cruel. Every single time, I was glad to be able to leave a climb behind and get strength for the remaining 137 miles (220 kilometers), before I'd take my final sleep break of the race.

XVII
"DOWN UNDER SEVEN"
ACROSS AUSTRALIA

"Where did he get this emu from? And how did he actually catch one?!" I thought to myself as I saw Jürgen from my film crew, groox, holding a wriggling animal in a headlock.

My brain wanted to ask further—I could not imagine how he had managed to capture the second largest ratite in the world, which had been running alongside me a few minutes ago in the steppe.

But as I approached, I realized that it was not a bird he was holding under his arm, but the three-legged tripod of his camera. My mind was already so confused by this time.

It was my fifth day of long-distance cycling, and as it happens, when sleep deprivation meets physical exertion, hallucinations come around to play their little games. Again and again, I shied away from the continuous white painted road stripes, because I thought they were dangerously high sidewalk edges, and again and again I felt sorry for the Italian beach vendors on the left side of the road. They'd traveled thousands of miles to get here and spread their carpets with fake clocks and cheap jewelry, and I was not even allowed to stop for a moment to chat and haggle with them. Although I did not want to buy anything, but at least politely pretend that I was interested in their goods.

"Come on, keep going, do not stop pedaling!" I was told. I rode on, and in the next moment had another odd sight. The koalas on the hoods of the trucks waving to me amused me; all of the cute bears were looking at me and signaled to me that they would like to be petted. The reality was different. We'd been on a highway for the previous 124 miles (200 kilometers), but with the increased number of trucks, the left-hand traffic, and with the sudden change from federal roads to large federal highways, an enormous amount of stress was put on my fatigued psyche and my confusion continued to grow.

> **Why should it be different in Australia than in the Race Across America? And why the hell did I want to have this adventure?**

Once, when mountain climber George Mallory was asked why he wanted to climb Mount Everest, he replied, "Because it's there." Why did I want to cycle through Australia? Because it was possible, as Wolfgang Fasching and Gerhard Gulewicz had already proved before me, and because, after my severe training accident in autumn 2015, I was working on a meaningful 2016 annual plan. In the hospital, I had already come to terms with the reality of having to forego RAAM, which took place about eight months later, for the sake of my health. This would be a good opportunity to face an Australia crossing, I mused. Australia was not just an issue since my accident; the down under cycling challenge had been on my wishlist for years. However, other competitions and their preparations prevented it, and now I was able to move this project up on my list of priorities.

Sometimes things just have to play out, and even if I could never have imagined it, the serious accident and the long rehab break really did bring something positive. The old wisdom, that from a setback comes new possibilities, that when one door closes another opens, is really true. Taking RAAM off my schedule brought the opportunity to cycle across Australia.

Australia would not only become just another long bike ride, but in many ways be a highlight for me. "It would be a great workout for the RAAM," I told myself, "as a team, we could grow together, be more practiced and prepared, and work on solutions to the extreme heat issues that plagued me physically during RAAM 2015." Our goal would be to better stabilize the fluid balance in my body, and to further optimize the concept of external cooling.

At the same time, a world record (certified by the UMCA) was at stake. In 2007, Gerhard Gulewicz had completed the 2,448 miles (3,940 kilometers) from Cottesloe Beach near Perth in the west, to the Sydney Opera House in the east, in seven days, eight hours and 49 minutes to break the earlier record. He did an incredibly good job, considering he set this time despite suffering a bad crash due to a front wheel failure. He completed the last 320 kilometers after a short stay in hospital, being treated for serious wounds on his face, and then, with an unwavering determination, he completed the tour—an impressive display of toughness and determination.

Last but not least, Australia would also become a journey into the unknown and therefore, a true adventure. I was interested in the history and culture, fauna and flora of the country, and I read some reports and books about the distant continent in my run-up to the venture. As much as I was looking forward to meeting koalas, I developed a great respect for the venomous scorpions and other animals that I knew I would rather not meet.

The preparation was on schedule—similar to that for a RAAM, and yet, different. We decided not to use a third vehicle, which we used in America as a media car, navigation aid, and to watch competitors. The eight-man team drove in a car and an RV. The route had to be planned and supply options had to be researched. Gerhard Gulewicz supported us with valuable tips on route planning. We were also looking for, and found, an Australian PR agency, with which we shared content and provided media attention about our Australian challenge.

On New Year's Eve, Team Strasser sat on the plane. It was not only a long trip, but also a nervous trip. Over and over, I wondered if we had packed everything we needed, and if all our equipment—661 pounds (300 kilograms) in total—would arrive safely at the other side of the world. The hygiene regulations for luggage are particularly strict in Australia, where a dirty bike tire can be a problem. I was relieved when we saw our boxes on the oversized baggage rack. Ten days of acclimatization and preparation time were planned to switch from European winter to the Australian summer. On the first ride I took with mechanic Gerd Skant, we looked at each other and let some curses fly, "It's so damn hot here, what was I thinking? Why did I choose January, the hottest month in Australia?" The answer to this question was objectively clear, because the necessary vacation days my crew members had to take from their jobs were only possible at that time, and it was also the only time possible during my season considering my other sporting goals. When I saw the thermometer, however, I temporarily questioned this decision.

The landscape was beautiful and unique, the sea inviting, the towns and centers around Perth maintained and lovely, the people open, nice, and friendly. These first impressions I got from Australia were just a dream. Winds came from the south, from the west, sometimes not at all. And the heat rose with every kilometer that we traveled from the coast towards the interior of the country.

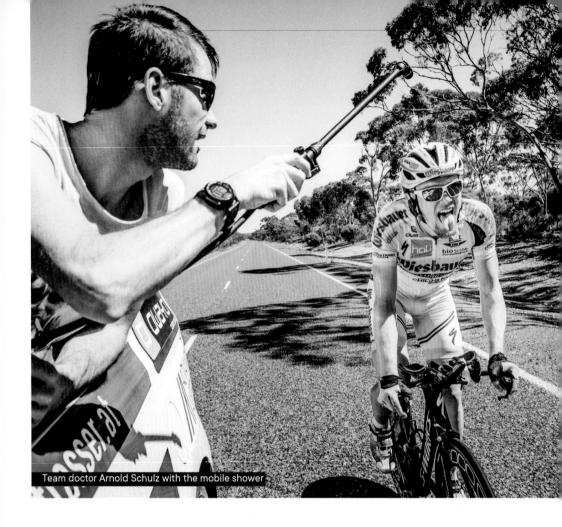

Team doctor Arnold Schulz with the mobile shower

Before large ventures begin, there are usually equally large speeches full of motivational slogans like the ones found in books and Hollywood scripts. Also, I always try, together with my team, on which I am dependent, to set a special mood and to make everyone clearly understand our goal. We then talk about role distribution and team tactics. In Australia, we did this at a picnic on the shores of South Perth. The team spirit was good, we were all bursting with energy, and at the same time, it was a relaxed and quiet atmosphere.

"The whole thing will be difficult, friends—for me, as well as for you. There will be pain, fatigue, monotony, loneliness. It will be hot and windy. The roads will be bad, my diet

Fans and friends from Austria played traditional Austrian music on their accordions at the start in Perth

monotonous and your meals will be dependent on the scarce supply in the Australian roadhouses (gas stations). Nevertheless, it is a mission that we are happy to face. Let's leave out of this dramatic undertone and put it this way: We are on our way, from Perth to Sydney. And there, we'll go for a cold beer!"

My crew—team boss and team doctor Arnold Schulz, Christian Loitzl, Markus Kinzlbauer, Gerd Skant, Jürgen Gruber, Manuel Hausdorfer, Michi Pletz and Markus Vogl—had to laugh at these words. That was a different approach: cycling through Australia for a week, chasing after a cold beer. Our good mood was further enhanced by these relaxed, positive moments.

I was not so arrogant as to announce my goal of finishing in less than seven days. Due to the lack of experience with the route, the weather and the strong winds, it was difficult to formulate a goal. Above all, I could not really judge how much the loneliness and the lack of competitors would affect my psyche. First of all, cycling, doing my best, and looking at what will be, made my attitude a lot better. It was clear,

Everyday life in Australia: long straights, dead kangaroos

that even if the crossing of this continent served a higher purpose—namely, crossing another continent—I was not allowed to take the world record attempt lightly. I knew that I would have to ride consistently to attack the Gulewicz's record. Still, secretly, I hoped to finish in under a week.

The world record attempt started with a few, but interested people, and some media representatives at 2:00 pm. I was sent off to accordion and violin music, and by my compatriots waving Austrian flags.

I also received great attention and affection from the Austrian community that exists on the fifth continent. There was a contact to the international department of the Austrian Federal Economic Chamber, the Außenwirtschaft Austria, and a department of the Austrian Embassy, which not only invited us to a finish party in Sydney, but also organized a small event at the start, where around two dozen "expats" arrived on January 10. They were proud that the RAAM winner had come to Australia, and that we had attended one of their round tables the day before.

The shift change strategy of the crew and my sleep strategy were the same as in a Race Across America. The climatic conditions were, at least initially, the same. On the first two days, the sun burned at 104 to 113 degrees Fahrenheit (40 to 45 degrees Celsius), which made cooling methods and hydration, not just relevant, but essential to my survival. Australia turned out to be the wild adventure I expected from the first kilometers.

"Just stay on this road, we'll drive to the gas station quickly and refuel the car—we do not know when the next station will come!" I heard over the loudspeakers before my crew left me alone for a few minutes. We had about 373 miles (600 kilometers) behind us, the first night was over, and I was in a good rhythm. So far, there had not been a single turn from Perth—no intersection, no change of direction, the route on the navigation device was drawn like a ruler. I vaguely remembered the route planning, and knew that after about this distance the first turn would come. I saw a sign with "Norseman" written on it. This place was familiar to me. So I turned off knowing I was in serious danger in case of error. If my team did not find me afterward because I rode down the wrong road, it would not take long before my fluid reserves would be used up. Shortly, I was afraid and anxious. Should I turn around? Should I wait?

Not too long after, I heard Arnold's voice, "Your pedaling looks very good," So I was on the right road. The car was obviously fueled and everything was good. We had plenty of time to conscientiously prepare ourselves before reaching the next turn, 124 miles (200 kilometers) ahead.

Who needs swimming pools in the Australian Outback?

The wildlife in Australia is unbelievable. We saw flocks of birds, emus, and kangaroos, as I rode through bushes 6, 12 or 30 feet high. Since the route was initially wavy and hilly, I could not keep a really high average speed. After a day I had covered 466 miles (750 kilometers), and we passed the largest gold mine in the country at Coolgardie. What struck me was the consideration of the truck drivers, who passed me at a reasonable distance. And that was reassuring for me and my crew, because in Australia it is mostly road trains with a length of 100 to 230 feet (30 to 70 meters) that drive through the sheer vastness of the country. The cargo was sometimes interesting; who knows why and where large-swimming pools are transported, when hardly any people live in the interior, and almost no water is available?

The differences between my Australian adventure and RAAM began to manifest. In the US, I often had the impression that truck drivers were almost trying to push a cyclist off the road. In Down Under, they announced themselves at an early stage and overtook in a large arc, waved, and honked to express their enthusiasm for my project, which they knew by the stickers on the accompanying car and from the radio announcements.

The hot east wind from the front and from the side, and temperatures beyond 104 degrees Fahrenheit (40 degrees Celsius) are features of the Nullarbor Plain, in which there is not much except for small hamlets along the railway line. At 91 miles (146.6 kilometers), this part of the Eyre Highway is the longest straight in Australia. The group AC/DC, on tour at the time, wrote the song *Highway to Hell* here, and I can understand the sentiment.

I had been looking forward to this section, as I like long and flat straights especially, though I know that this is hardly comprehensible for anyone else. Due to my stature, my strength lies on the flats. I love to put out a constant effort for hours without having my rhythm broken by ascents. The reality was not very exciting.

The only highlight in almost 150 kilometers was a kangaroo that crossed the road. Since it was dark, nothing else was visible. And because the road before, and after, was equally monotonous and free of turns, Australia's longest straight did not really stand out for me.

"That's unexpected," was the dry comment from the gas station attendant in Madura to a downpour, which in the truest sense of the word, was unexpected. In this town, the time zone changed, my crew adjusted the clock by 45 minutes (Yes, this time zone really is 45 minutes different than the previous one!). As I left the Madura Pass with its "mighty" 130 meters above sea level, more and more marsupials crossed our path, and vultures waited to be able to feast on the animals killed by cars or trucks. The refreshing rain shower turned into a steady rain, which did not stop me, and somehow reminded me of past RAA adventures. After 48 hours on the road, I'd ridden 839 miles (1,350 kilometers).

The precipitation continued, and my crew had trouble drying my wet clothes in the follow cars due to the high humidity. I have never had such joy when riding for hours in a downpour. Fortunately, the dreaded heat was over, and the weather turned to wet, but pleasant. When fatigue set in, my companions kept me awake with puzzles and questions from the Who Wants to be a Millionaire? show. "Now I'll need to use my LifeLine. I have a friend who will know that," I joked and added, "Without phone reception, this is rather difficult." But despite my mental state and the continuous physical exertion, I knew the answers to many of the questions—sometimes better than the crew.

While we joked about phone reception, the lack of existing mobile network coverage became a problem for us. Thus, the communication between the two team cars was repeatedly put to the test—for example, when it came to planning breaks. My crew could not use Wi-Fi connections at gas stations because the service station staffers were rude, denied our requests, and said that they needed it themselves. So my peo-

Heavy rain and powerful trucks in Central Australia

ple stayed in contact via satellite phone and updates on the website, or in the social media done by Sabine in Austria, which was kept up-to-date via text messages. The phone bill at the end of the adventure was amazing!

It was a new feeling for us to not be able to use modern means of communication as usual, and to be cut off from the rest of the world. In the Australian outback, you are actually completely alone—on the other hand, the deserts in America are data highways.

After four days, 1,606 miles (2,585 kilometers) had been covered, leaving about 870 miles (1,400 kilometers) to Sydney. But it was still too early for arithmetic.

Strong headwind taunted me. It was the kind of wind that makes you battle as if you had to climb a 20% gradient; the type of wind that prevents a fast ride, even in the evening with pleasant temperatures; the kind of wind that brings a constant, penetra-

There were some strange, still unidentified animals at the roadside in Australia

ting noise in the ears. It was in those moments when I wondered what I was doing there, and where we were actually going. Hallucinations set in. "I cannot get the earbud out of my ear," I barked at my people, though I actually wasn't using any. The sleep deprivation and the constant wind had driven me half mad.

"Left, right, left, right— that's all there is," a friend had written via WhatsApp. How right he was, and yet this "left-right" is so much easier when there is variety.

The mountains of the Southern Tablelands represent the last range before the east coast of Australia; they are almost like the Appalachians of RAAM. Only in Wagga Wagga, 248.5 miles (400 kilometers) from the finish, we began to make calculations in earnest. Because I—with cold beer in mind—apparently, had effortlessly climbed the 2300 feet (700 meter) high mountain range, we could expect a finish time of well under seven days. After exactly six days, only 177 miles (285 kilometers) separated us from the Sydney Opera House.

Drawn by fatigue and physical hardships

When I reached the metropolis, I rode through Chinatown around midnight and asked my crew, "Are we in the right place? Looks more like Beijing than Sydney."
They laughed and reassured me once again, "All is well, just make sure you keep pedaling."

My quest for a world record ended in the darkness of a parking lot at the Opera House, with no glamor, no finish-line band, and no fans waiting to cheer me on. I've always had the image of the brightly lit, world-famous building in mind, but that night the lights were obviously off, we were at the back door, and not in front of the pompous facade. The journey ended after six days, ten hours, fifty-eight minutes to an audience of security personnel who did not allow us to celebrate. The security sent us politely, but determinedly, away from the site—they said we would disturb the residents with the popping of our champagne bottle. They also kept us from shooting photos with the opera house in the background, due to our "World Record Down Under," saying that such images would be commercial use. We tried to celebrate in a parking lot but were also driven out by locals there. In the house we'd rented in a Bondi Beach neighborhood, we finally got our cold beer, and realized what beautiful and emotional moments of joy we had experienced during the tour. Reaching the finish was once again less exciting than the journey itself.

"Victory Photo" in front of the world-famous opera the day after the arrival in Sydney

The next day, we ate a leisurely breakfast, then strolled through Sydney and shot the obligatory photos in front of the opera, outsmarting the security people by quickly rolling out our banner, and then just as quickly disappearing. During the walk on the beach, Arnold told me that he wanted to set other priorities in his life and was no longer available for my crew. Difficult vacation planning with his employer, and a desire to spend more time with the family, demanded his presence at home. These were moments that made me sad and thankful. As my team doctor, Arnold had contributed many ideas, insights, and dedication to my activities. His support for me was important and valuable. Knowing that he would be absent from RAAM, just five months away, I asked myself, "Who would, who could, replace him? Who would have the knowledge and the character to tackle RAAM with us?"

So I flew back to Austria with mixed feelings of great joy and a big question mark.

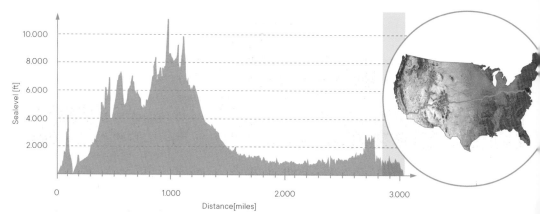

LIVE COVERAG
Race Across Americ
Race Across the W
@RAAMrac
Ride
CHARITY
Team
Strasser

XVIII
"IT'S NOT MUCH FARTHER NOW!"

RAAM, TIME STATIONS 49–55

Confusing house facades

The Mojave Desert, the Rocky Mountains, the Great Plains, the Appalachians are all behind me—it's about 124 miles (200 kilometers) to the finish line. However, there is no joy, quite the contrary. I'm just sitting on my bike, pedaling and frustrated. "Everyone is against me," I tell myself, "they're leaving me here. I'm sure we have passed this red house with the white fence before. Where are we anyway? In Norway? In Iceland? The road surface is different than before, no longer gray but brownish red, the landscape is hilly, winding and idyllic, the overall picture looks clean and tidy to me and not shabby and dirty as on the days before. There! There is that house again! We've certainly passed it before! They've sent me up this mountain for the fourth time now. For sure, these mountains! They are more poisonous than those in the Appalachians, only a hundred meters long, but with a slope of up to twelve percent. And as soon as one of them has been climbed, they send me in circles, and probably laugh, too."

These illusions were especially hard in 2011. I got off the bike, got into the car, and burst into tears. Rainer and Max meant well and wanted to motivate me with a game. I had to score points; there were ten for each climb, one more bonus point for getting out of the saddle, and an extra point for every short sprint. Unfortunately, this game caused me resistance and confusion, I felt a bit scared. After a clarifying conversation, we agreed that I would go on as normal, without stress—and I'd asked for the hundredth time, may I please listen to my favorite music, and not this strange and fast drum & bass techno that my crew had been playing, hoping that the beat would increase my speed.

One year, in the final miles, I'd fixated on RAAM Media's Vic Armijo as he stood in a left turn. Instead of following the road, I steered right at him, went up onto the grass, and at the last moment, swerved back onto the roadway in front of him as if nothing had happened. I just barely avoided falling. "This is a stupid situation," my confused

I almost fell and I almost hit a RAAM Media member. Almost.

and tired brain thought, "When the people in the car notice that I'm no longer strong at cycling, they're sure to get upset and scold me. Or worse, they'll condemn me to a break and delay the end of the ride even more." So I hid it from them and pretended that nothing had happened. I hoped that nobody had noticed my little detour, failing to remember that my follow car drove mere meters behind me, and all the crew members in it had experienced my faux pas live with horror.

For a cyclist crossing the US, Maryland does not fit the expected image of this country, especially when that cyclist is struggling with sleep deprivation and hallucinations. Maryland has a strong European influence, and my head could not handle all these seemingly contradictory impressions.

The Gettysburg National Military Park commemorates one of the bloodiest battles ever to take place on the American continent, which occurred in 1863 during the Civil War. The RAAM route passes through the memorial, its roadside lined with cannons and sawbuck fences. This historic place is special, and the race directors instruct the teams to be quiet and respectful. Instead of commemorating the many victims, I was only annoyed.

The route does not take the shortest route to Annapolis at this point, but leads north in a loop. This is unnecessary, and I wonder every time why we can't go directly to the finish? In general, I feel the route as a burden, because the traffic increases, and to be on busy roads, especially at the end of the race, is dangerous. I also think about the slower riders who get through here, after eleven to twelve days and are even more tired than me. I do not know if there are alternative routes, but in my imagination, I see myself cycling on side roads directly to Annapolis. The reality is unfortunately different. In the Race Across America, the goal is only reached when it is reached. This also applies to the record runs in 2013 and 2014. I knew that a finish time of under eight days

Gettysburg National Monument, site of the famous US Civil War battle

was possible, and felt it was almost an insult that my people pushed me on so. They meant well, but in this phase of RAAM, I did not realize this anymore and emotionally withdrew from them.

And then, someone said to me while I pedaled wearily, "It's not much farther now!" At that moment I cursed everyone and everything. "You have no idea what it is to be on the bike all the time, and we're still not there. And as long as we are not there, it is far. Every kilometer, every meter hurts!"

> **"Please be quiet and let me do my work!"**

However, in 2017 my crew chief managed to really cheer me up. The colorful fireworks that my people placed at the road's edges were a highlight and, if you like, the only one. I could hardly believe my luck, and rode through their trellis of sparks, cheered and had tears of joy in my eyes. I tried to hold on to these euphoric emotions and carry them and myself to Annapolis. Again and again, at even smaller intervals, the RV and the media crew were at the edge of the road, and crew members ran up the climbs next to me—we celebrated the approaching success. These moments of joy were overwhelming, but they did not last long.

The closer the finish line comes, the more instructions and rules there are in the Route Book. At Time Station #52, Mt. Airy, any time penalties that have accumulated

Celebratory fireworks just before the finish

since passing through Durango, Colorado must be served. Each team is required to contact the race management and clarify whether penalties have been incurred. Punishment is fast and hard. Patric Grüner was sentenced to two hours in the "Penalty Box" in 2017 for public urination. This was spared on me one occasion, when I had to take an unscheduled pee stop in some bushes. This went unnoticed. As I swung myself onto the bike, the support vehicle turned and the beam of light fell onto a big building, and it was then that we suddenly saw the name of a bank. I had relieved myself in the flowered landscape of the Bank of America. "Thank you Bank of America – it was a pleasure to do my business with you."

As I approached my first RAAM finish in 2011, I believed that the race was over in Mt. Airy, and that I just had to roll down to the finish line. Not even close. From there it's another 55 miles (89 kilometers) to the finish, which is not a big distance in itself, about the same distance as the Oceanside Pier to Time Station #1 at Lake Henshaw. But this comparison is weak, because how could a cyclist in this condition, with aching knees, numb fingers, and sore buttocks, be able to cover this incomprehensibly long distance? With my first RAAM victory in mind, in 2011, I almost broke down upon learning of this distance.

Time penalties can be crucial, as tight racing finishes have proven in the past. Two hours may not sound like a lot, with a total time of seven, eight, nine days, but to ride hard enough to make up two hours is tedious, cumbersome, and likely impossible in RAAM.

"But it is not much farther away, now." I was silent, too tired to complain, but I would have preferred to put the crew member who told me this into a stranglehold. RAAM finishes about 30 miles (50 kilometers) east of Washington, D.C in Annapolis, the capital of the U.S. state of Maryland. The finish arch and the stage where finish interviews are held are on City Dock, which overlooks Chesapeake Bay, right next to the US Naval Academy. The overall setting is very nice, with many historic buildings (some dating back to the city's founding in 1649), and there are many restaurants and taverns nearby where finishing racers and teams can celebrate. It's a cool atmosphere, and I'm told it is much nicer than where RAAM used to finish in Atlantic City.

However, what is not so nice, are the last few miles of the route leading to the sea on the main streets of Annapolis, which are peppered with traffic lights, and depending on the time of day, can be full of heavy traffic. With the varying traffic, to keep things fair for all of the solo racers and teams, the RAAM organizers have chosen to basically have two finish lines—one on the outskirts of town where they record the actual finish time, and the other being the sort of ceremonial finish on City Dock. By doing this, the racer who finishes in the middle of the night when there's virtually no traffic, won't gain an advantage over the racer who finishes during rush hour.

The initial finish is on a wide road with a very wide shoulder, and the last few miles leading into it usually have light traffic. The location was chosen so that if there are solos or teams close together, there can be a safe sprint such as the one that came in 2013 between Edi Fuchs, 8th place, and Gerald Bauer, 9th place. After nine days and twenty-one hours, there was a minute between the two. This "timing line" of the world's most important ultra-cycling race is in front of a tavern, the Rams Head Roadhouse, where the RAAM organizers put a finish stripe on the road and place a pop-up tent with a few lights. An official is assigned to staff the finish, and depending on when a racer finishes, there may be a few fans and spectators there to cheer—or not. This has been a cause of confusion for some of my fans who watch our Live Feed, see me rolling across the line to be greeted only by my crew, an official (usually RAAM owner, Fred Boethling), and a handful of fans. "That's it?" some have commented, "Strasser rides 3,000 miles to a tent and 12 people?"

But the RAAM race is really only neutralized there. RAAM officials record the racers' arrival times and then adds another 26 minutes to each solo rider's time to allow for the actual time needed to reach the ceremonial finish, 6 miles (10 kilometers) away. What sounds totally unbelievable is that for me, those last ten kilometers are the hardest. The race is over, the finish time is set, but you still have to continue. What a pain! Therefore, racers are instructed to not stop at the Rams Head Roadhouse, but only about 1.8 miles (3 kilometers) later, at a gas station. There, depending on the circumstances, I can freshen up, put on a clean jersey and wait for an official car to escort us to the finish. While I wait, my crew always buys the most important items: drinks and food in the gas station shop. In 2011, Rainer wanted to pay with my credit card.

The preliminary RAAM finish line: The finish time is recorded here and the remaining miles to the ceremonial finish are neutralized

"I need the signature of the cardholder," explained the operator.

"He's on the bike. He's just won Race Across America."

"Whatever. I still need his signature!"

The dispute almost ended in a brawl between the two, and it made clear that after RAAM, I'm not the only one with frayed nerves—the crew is ready to be done too. My people forgot about their purchases because I was sullen and in a bad mood. No one dared get me off the bike even though they needed my signature for their snacks and drinks.

Every third traffic light is red, and I have to dismount and wait and start again, again, and again. "Is this really necessary?" I begin a meaningless discussion with the official. "Do you really want to scare me in the last kilometers? What are you actually thinking?"

His answer? "It's not far now!" Jim, the head official, had accompanied us for days and had done a good job. He not only monitored our compliance with the rules, but was also responsible for our safety. He was dedicated to us and we really liked him, too. But in this now-it-is-not-so-far-moment, he brought me to despair.

RAAM 2018: A dream comes true - with the fifth win I'm tied with Jure Robic

> If a tennis player plays much better than his opponent, he only needs three instead of five sets to win. RAAM is not a tennis match. RAAM always takes five sets.

That's easy for him to say! I know that the race is virtually over. Nevertheless, I have to reach City Dock, although my head and body are beyond finished," I thought to myself. The fact is, not even the last kilometers of the Race Across America are a pleasure. At that time, I knew that I had won, so I could have reflected on the past few days, recalled all the beautiful pictures, and patted my team and myself on the back, and maybe get a champagne shower from my people while riding. But, no! RAAM is a torment from beginning to end, it frustrates me even when I've done well and should be proud of my performance.

"Done, finally done!" The port of Annapolis was reached. The finish line arch on City Dock is in sight. We stopped and hugged each other. The entire team gathered and I was immensely proud of each and every one of us for having survived this tour together. Internally, I was just relieved that it was over, but I really had to make an effort not to be in a bad mood and be nasty. I felt the need to tell the organizers that I find the last few kilometers very complicated. But then, I forgot that anger and realized how happy my companions were for me, how they had sacrificed, fought for me, and put their own needs aside for days. I owed it to them to show irrepressible joy—yet the fatigue was too great to let my emotions run wild. Sleep would have to wait until a few hours later—that was clear to me. We held Austrian flags and together we covered the last ten meters through the finish arch. The clenched fist, the tortured smile, I had to force myself to do this for the organizer's media team, for the race director, who hung the finisher medal around my neck, for my team that had given its all for the past ten days, and for me.

As I said earlier, the atmosphere of Annapolis and City Dock is nice. But having experienced the finish of some of the larger European events, such as the Race Around Austria, with its large crowds, music, exhibitors, and its huge concert stage, the RAAM finish seems a bit lacking. But I also understand, that in America, cycling is a fringe sport, with ultra-cycling being even more so, which explains why there are usually so few spectators on City Dock. And with the huge distances between the finishers, who has the time to wait for hours or days to watch one ultra-cyclist after another?

Overwhelmed with fatigue during the finish-line interview

If I was not a racer, but a fan, would I wait out on City Dock to see a racer's finish? Probably not.

I sat for my finish interview with RAAM emcee, George Thomas (a past RAAM solo finisher). I told the few reporters and media representatives how happy and satisfied I was, and of the honor of winning RAAM. It is all very pleasant, but again, it was missing something compared to the races back home. What there is are other "Rules and Regulations"; where to park which car for how long, where to pick up the material that was packed away in Oceanside and transported to the destination by the organizers, and where to pick up the tickets for the banquet that takes place a few days later. The doping control, which the winner has to undergo, has also become routine. The final conclusion of this nerve-wracking finish, was a shaky walk to the RAAM Media RV for doping control. After that, I was finally allowed to go to sleep.

You might think that I sleep like a log the night after RAAM. I only wish this was so! Much of that first night in a real bed, I toss and turn and sweat and roll from side to side— that's when I'm not getting up and tottering like an old man to the bathroom, again and again.

After five or six hours of fitful sleep, I realized that despite my exhausted state, getting regular sleep was out of the question. So, I sat down with my laptop to read e-mails and surf the social networks. I caught up with what I had missed during the previous days. As I sat on the bike, I was dependent on what my crew wanted to tell me, and their communication was selective. Finally, I had the opportunity to read everything (or almost everything). At that time, I was slowly realizing what had happened in the past few days, realizing what we had achieved and how many people were happy with me. Hundreds of messages, emails, SMS and guestbook entries, thousands of comments on Facebook, and many more likes and reactions were piled upon me. Tears of joy came to me, for a few hours I was the happiest person in the world, and could hardly believe it. Many people were deeply touched by my actions and expressed their feelings with thanks, even the Austrian Federal President congratulated me in a personal e-mail. Hours later I saw TV reports on ORF (Austrian Broadcasting Network), front pages on daily newspapers, many reports in print and online media. I slowly understood how different my own perception was from that of the public. Sometimes, I found it unpleasant to think back to the negative situations of the previous days. No one on my team deserved for me to snarl at them, and it was absolutely unnecessary that some of my bad mood was seen in live stream videos. But now, there was enough time to savor the success and to spend two or three beautiful evenings with my crew in Annapolis.

Anyway, after the Race Across America, the body feels as if it is in full jet lag. Therefore, several times a day, I have to allow myself an hour of sleep—until the biorhythm has changed again, and my cognitive center has realized that normality has returned so that enough rest will be granted during the night. I do not even notice the jet lag from North America to Europe anymore—that's just a bonus. It is also strange that two days after the finish, I still have problems with my balance, the sensitivity, and coordination in the soles of my feet and toes comes back slowly, but the recovery of the knee joints and the seat meat within that same period is surprisingly fast.

About two weeks after the end of the Race Across America, I do not need an afternoon nap, but the competition is still present in my thoughts—also because of the physical injuries, such as my bruised and battered palms and some numb fingers. In terms of performance, after about six weeks at the most, I am back where I was before RAAM, and the nerve pathways on my hands have fully regenerated.

Before normality re-enters my body and mind, the RAAM banquet is on the agenda. In a hotel room in Annapolis, the first place finishers are honored in the various categories and for the fastest. There is a wooden board cut in the shape of the USA, on which the route of the Race Across America is traced. For me, participation in the banquet from 2013 on was no longer possible, since we started the journey home in a timely manner because my people had to return to their work routine as soon as possible. Therefore, I got the trophy on City Dock the day after the finish. Every time I pick them up, I grin inwardly, thinking, "In the old days, everything was better,"—that's what my grandparents used to say. Wolfgang Fasching has also received a board for his successes in the 1990s and 2000s—but I've seen his, and they were three times as big! The first time I received one I joked to myself, "Nowadays, you save money wherever you can." The wooden board works well on the wall in my training cellar, but I jokingly refer to it regularly as a snack board, on which you can slice my sponsor's Wiesbauer sausages.

Each category winner receives a glass trophy and each finisher gets a finisher's jersey. The latter, however, will be produced after the race and subsequently sent. Anyone who reaches the destination is asked for their jersey size, which is recorded on a list. "Why don't they order their jerseys before, so we can have them immediately, as is the case in other competitions?" I thought once. But now, I'm sure that the organizers actually only want to have only as many finisher jerseys in circulation as is called for—no more, no less. Nobody should ever be able to get such a jersey without finishing the race, and since about 50% of the participants do not make it to the finish line, only the correct number of finisher-jerseys is produced.

This garment is something very special, and I hold those jerseys that I have fought so hard for in honor. Though it's always a bit anticlimactic when the jersey comes in the mail, with but a few words: "Congrats and best regards." I always wish it could be more celebrated. But what could they do? Sprinkle glitter into the box, or maybe enclose a device like those in musical greeting cards, only this one would play "Land der Berge, Land am Strome," the Austrian national anthem?

"Land der Berge, Land am Strome,
Land der Äcker, Land der Dome,
Land der Hämmer, zukunftsreich:
Heimat großer Töchter und Söhne,
Volk, begnadet für das Schöne,
vielgerühmtes Österreich."

"Land of mountains, land by the river,
Land of fields, land of cathedrals,
Land of hammers, with a promising future!
Home to great daughters and sons,
A nation highly blessed with beauty,
Much-praised Austria!"

XIX
"TELL ME, HOW ARE YOU DOING THIS?"

ULTRA-CYCLING AS A PROFESSION

"Uh. Hmm. I'm sorry to say, I forgot …"

"How did you forget?" My German teacher, who taught me my first year of high school, stared at me in astonishment. "Forgot?!" he asked again.

Yes, forgot it. In a poetry contest at our school, I landed among the best in my class and went on to the next round. I simply forgot this later round, which is why I stammered in front of the professor and said that I would rather not compete. Two weeks after the pre-selection, I should have recited the same poem, but I only partially remembered the words. My half-hearted reading of the text just minutes before it was my turn did not really help. In competition, there are no excuses! The jury or timing determines winners and losers. Leaning unsteadily against the wall, I stood on the stage, stammering to myself. My performance was lacking—to say the least—and I was immediately out of the competition. I survived it. While it may sound strange, this experience was the beginning of my lecturing.

Having to talk to other people—this has been scientifically researched and proven—triggers one of the biggest fears a human being can have: the fear of failing, and consequently publicly disgracing oneself, by being seen stuttering and stumbling when what they planned was to deliver an astonishing (or at least competent) performance.

However, there is nothing better for me now than sharing my adventures and experiences with others and telling them about my ultra-competitions.

When I was a member of the small cycling club, RSC Klausen Leopoldsdorf, at the beginning of my career, I held my first lecture at the end of the season. More precisely: I spontaneously showed some photos and talked about them—it wasn't much better than something an elementary school kid would share during "show and tell," and my simple report lasted only five minutes. The following year it was fifteen minutes, and again twelve months later, not only racers but also their spouses or partners were there. In the fourth year, I spoke to sixty or seventy people and showed the film of my Glockerman participation. At one of those lecture evenings, I realized that this could be another mainstay in my ultra-cycling career.

I am fascinated by learning new things. I read books about interesting and inspiring personalities, and educate myself by visiting seminars and watching presentations by other sportsmen and adventurers. I especially liked the seminars and lectures of Wolfgang Fasching, whose influence inspired me to enter ultra-cycling, and years later to emulate him as an in-demand lecturer. What I learned from Fasching, is to preserve authenticity and the sense of reality. Of course, his events carry titles that can be well marketed: *You Can Achieve What You Want!* for example, but Fasching himself has an addition to these words: ... *But It Will Be Tough*.

> A 200-pound man will never be a champion gymnast, and a 100-pound man will never become a Sumo wrestling champion.

In principle, I do not believe in motivational memes that read, "When you achieve this or that, you can do everything in your life." That's nonsense. Just because I can ride a bike for days across the US does not mean that I am capable of excellence in other areas. Wolfgang Fasching sees it similarly. You can achieve what you want if it is within the range of your own possibilities.

But my intention is not to hold motivational speeches and to coach my listeners to peak performance in whatever field they happen to be in. In my lectures, I simply portray my life and my experiences in front of the audience. I talk about the Race Across America, about all the difficulties that my team and I encounter, and how

Autumn 2013: A speaking engagement together with "Kougi" in Graz

we overcome them successfully. These multi-media evenings have something of a sports-themed travelogue, and those who go learn more about the vastness of the US, and, at best, how to face and manage challenges. If everyone that attends one of my lectures would say that it was a pleasure to listen to me, this would already be enough praise and recognition for me.

At corporate events or in-house workshops with companies, I also discuss the parallels between sports and work, and talk about mental training, the importance of visualizing, mental goal achievement, my methods for increasing motivation, and how these techniques can be applied in one's working life. Equally important to me, is to learn to respond to setbacks as they are unavoidable but extremely important for long term success. Personally, my "getting back up" after failures has allowed me the greatest learning experiences on my way to my successes.

I especially like it when I give lectures together with others—with my team leader Michael Kogler, for example, or with my nutritionist Dr. Markus Stark from the Evosan Center. He represents the approach of Paleo nutrition, which is why we are on the same wavelength. Creating an evening together with others undoubtedly has more advantages than disadvantages. When two people talk in turn, the audience stays more attentive, and you can present a story from two different perspectives.

I have to admit that I'm always a bit late in preparing for my lectures. Although I demand the highest level of professionalism from myself in this area, and am also very precise in the selection of video clips and photos that are shown, I find the words for the pictures only at the last moment—sometimes on the stage itself. Much of what is in

Enjoying the overwhelming atmosphere on the stage

my lectures comes spontaneously at the time, the evening's presentation depends on the audience's mood and whether they are quietly listening to my statements or are lively. Thus, I would not like to prepare a well-formed lecture before, but adjust myself to the energy of my listeners, so each lecture is unique. I continue to work to develop my structure further. When lecturers always tell the same thing, day in and day out, it is not only boring for the speaker, but also for those guests who, out of enthusiasm, visit such events more often.

When I think back, there was a single performance where I had really bad stage fright and which I would have liked to cancel: in 2014, I was supposed to give a lecture in front of twenty bankers from different European countries—in English. So I refreshed my foreign language skills, practiced my presentation, and set off. On the drive there my courage left me and feelings of being ill prepared suddenly rose in me, I could not remember my words or English vocabulary, and was thinking of my embarrassing experience at the poem competition in school. I got very nervous and wanted to call and cancel, say I had a car breakdown and had to turn back, or I was terribly ill and would have to go to the hospital. A death in the family would make my appearance even more impossible, and so on. A lifetime's worth of excuses came to my mind.

> No excuse was strong enough to keep me from my first speech in English, so I gave it—and received the highest praise for it.

However, one of the principles in my life is: I cannot be ashamed of any embarrassment. That's not to say that I'm trying to fail, it's meant to express that every action has the potential to become a success or a disaster. A possible failure must not be the reason not to do something from the outset.

Over the years, I've held hundreds of lectures and seminars, some for my sponsors such as Wiesbauer or Specialized, or for big international insurance agencies and banking institutes like Raiffeisen, Magna or Wiener Städtische, and also to students and schools. I still feel it is a pleasure and an honor to be invited, and it's rewarding for me to share what I like the best. I like to look into the interested faces, but sometimes the feeling comes over me that I am given more importance than I am worth. It seems that fewer and fewer people are religious, but more and more people are adored, like substitute gods. Some worship basketball stars, like LeBron James and Kobe Bryant, or tennis legends like Roger Federer and Rafael Nadal, and in my scene, some choose me as their idol. I find this circumstance questionable. I do not want to be lifted onto a pedestal and act unreachable for others. What I want is to inspire others.

The business executives who task me with giving a keynote presentation to their companies never specify what I am to say. I am only told which clientele my listeners will be, and what they might expect from me. I do not represent myself as anything that I am not or do not have, and I put myself out simply as a role-model.

It's not about motivating people to do the same as me. My lectures are not just aimed at athletes but are meant to give everyone the opportunity to immerse themselves in another world and to learn what achievements are possible in a well-functioning team, and that man can achieve anything if the passion for his "thing" is burning, be it professionally or privately. My motto is that every ordinary person can do something extraordinary if he is willing to work hard, is passionate about the goal, and is not afraid of setbacks. The path to dream fulfillment or goal achievement is seldom easy, but the challenge enriches the experience along the way, and is retained for the rest of one's life.

My lectures consist of the stories and insights of my life. In fact, it's always interesting to see how others behaved in certain situations or how they coped in extreme moments. Life means learning from oneself, also from others, maybe from me, too. And if my lectures perhaps do not help, then they certainly do not hurt, but at least provide entertainment and let the audience members escape into my cycling world for a moment, which for many, is something less comprehensible and tangible than, for example, the even more well-known Tour de France.

"Tell me, what things do you take with you on your rides?" I was asked years ago, again and again by training companions. My conversations with sports colleagues focu-

sed on sports science planning, equipment, nutrition, and much more. I talked about products that I trusted, and more often the conversation ended with, "Next time you order, can you order for me too?" I integrated a contact form on my homepage where supplements, sports drinks, T-shirts, cycling jerseys, and DVDs could be ordered. In the beginning we were so excited when orders came in; we'd pack up the purchases and send them off with the invoice inside. Of course some people took advantage of my inexperience and never paid. We've learned from those mistakes and now have a well-run and successful online store.

The requests became more frequent, and the effort larger. After my training, I often stood at the post office with two suitcases full of packages, annoyed that the queue extended out to the entry area. Together with Sabine, I thought about creating a webshop that could cover the needs of cycling and ultra-cyclists. In 2015, the sales portal www.ultracyclingshop.com was created with the competent input of Günter Weixlbaumer and his agency ChiliSCHARF.

> "I bought that at the Strasser Store, but it's actually crap." Such a sentence should not, and will not exist.

We now have a professional payment system, a parcel service picking up the items in our warehouse, and offering products in the categories "Books and Movies," "Clothing," "Sports Nutrition," "(Bike) Accessories," and "Lecture Tickets." The assortment has been personally selected by me, all products that can be found in this shop have

been tested, worn, designed, written, read, and approved by me. I offer nothing that I have not tried and approved myself. After all, this is also about my good name.

Sabine and I manage all aspects related to the webshop. We buy, store, receive and ship the various products. There are no intermediaries or distributors. For this reason, we can also serve customers very quickly—usually within a day or two. Especially in summer, and even more so at RAAM time, the email inbox overflows with orders. We are pleased, because it proves that we are recognized for our reputation and our prices are competitive.

A long-desired dream came true for me with *www.ultracyclingshop.com*. Not only is it possible for me to live from cycling because I have turned my hobby into my profession, but this has also created a job for Sabine, who is responsible for our company with great commitment, and a burning passion to build on what we have already created.

At the finish of RAAM 2018

XX
"SUCCESS IS A LOUSY TEACHER!"
HUMILITY AND RESPECT

There are names that have shaped a sport or the epoch of a sport. So, I think that there is no "greatest of all times," because times—and with them, the equipment, the training science, the sports medicine knowledge, and so on—are changing. There will always be the unanswerable debates about today's stars versus yesterday's stars. Who would win if we took tennis great, Björn Borg from his 1970's prime, put him in a time machine, gave him today's training and sports knowledge, and put him up against Roger Federer? Or, if we did the same to the great Babe Ruth, would he hit more home runs than Barry Bonds? But these comparisons make little sense, really. Other times, other requirements.

At RAAM, there was Rob Kish, who started the race twenty times(!), finished the race nineteen times, and won it three times. There was Wolfgang Fasching, with eight starts, eight finishes, always on the podium, and three times first. There was five-time winner Jure Robic. And then there's me, who in 2018, was able to catch up with the Slovenian's five victories. Robic is dead, and the very interesting question that will re-main unanswered is: Would I have been able to beat him? As I said, this is a question that cannot be answered—and in the end, it does not matter. I've set new standards in ultra-cycling in the past few years, and I'm hard to beat right now, but there's also going to be a competitor someday who'll beat me.

Just because you have played the role of favorite for years, is no guarantee that it will remain so in the long run. That's just fine in my opinion, because it encourages an athlete to continue to work hard, and to be able to delay the moment when a better one comes along.

To be the best in my discipline for the years that I have, however, does not fill me with pride as much as with happiness and humility. I feel lucky that I can do what I love professionally. When one's dreams become reality, it is a feeling that is difficult to put into words. To do so is humbling because it is neither easy nor natural to be able to achieve and experience this. It demands hard work, hardships, understanding and support from family and friends, and a team that stands behind you and guides you without hesitation. I do not take my achievements for granted, because they did not come easy. They are a combination of physical fitness, attitude, passion, teamwork, and the irrepressible will to fulfill these dreams and to set goals again and again.

Physically, I bring the conditions that are essential to ultra-cycling; I have robust health and a strong immune system. My skeletal apparatus is intact, knee pain has become increasingly rare over the years, as the tendons and ligaments get used to the long-term strains. These basics cannot be trained for, but of course, can be ruined. However, I am too heavy to be a cyclist specializing in one-day races or classic tours. For an excellent, fast endurance athlete, I fall short of another requirement: my lung volume is absolutely average.

What I can influence, however, is my focus and attitude towards what I do. At the moment, I like to be a hard-to-beat competitor in the Race Across America, but that's relative. I was at Oceanside eight times, yet I did not win every time or even finish every time. In 2012 and 2015, I was put through a tough schooling and learned all too clearly that pride comes before the fall. I also had to learn to accept physical ailments that prematurely ended my dream of RAAM, or did not even allow me to compete because of injury.

Thus, I find it always incomprehensible when people tell me that I am unrivaled. You can never be sure of that, even though there may not be any known names on a start list. Reto Schoch was not known in ultra-cycling, yet he dealt me a sound butt-kicking.

If I'm the measure of things right now, it's because I've worked hard for this status, learned from mistakes and experiences, and evolved, perhaps a little further ahead of others. I was a stranger to the scene many years ago and worked my way up. Undoubtedly, there will be an ambitious rider in the future who will achieve that.

"You have it easy, you have good sponsors and you are a pro!"

The duel with Reto Schoch shaped and motivated me for many years

I don't understand why I hear this statement from competitors. You are not given sponsors, you develop your own sponsors by working on yourself and achieving success—only then do you have the opportunity to gain financial support. For my first RAAM, which cost me about 40,000 euros in entry fees, flights for the team, rental cars, accommodations and equipment, I used half of my savings and my bank account was nearly overdrawn—and then, I did not finish. My journey began rocky, and even now, I earn very little from my sponsors and make my living through lectures.

I am a professional because I can live on many activities that all revolve around cycling, but not because I have nothing to do except train and race.

I am proud of what I have achieved with my team so far. I am not in favor of discounting my own achievements, but I am not a friend of false pride and arrogance, or of bragging rights. I'm not one who likes to shine in the limelight. I never wanted to be known or cheered. I just wanted to be able to do what gives me the most pleasure in my life.

After successes like RAAM, I always need a short break from my sport, where I become a gourmet chef. That's when I come back from the United States with a body weight of 167 pounds (76 kilograms), and three weeks later I weigh 180 pounds (83 kilograms). And yet, I try to get back into my training routine as soon as possible. In recent years, for example, I enjoyed attending a bicycle-training-camp in the Austrian Alps in Tyrol as a

Even after successes, periods of weakness are inevitable and breaks are necessary

guide. Together with a group of amateur-racers and century-riders, we climbed famous passes like the Stelvio, and prepared for one of Europe's biggest bike-marathons, the Ötztal Marathon, a 148-mile (238-kilometer) event in the Austrian Alps.

Routines are nice, but they also lead to a deceptive self-image, to the subconscious assumption that as a defending champion you are holding the best cards for the next RAAM. That may not seem so wrong at first glance, but it is dangerous. In 2012, we underestimated Schoch; in 2015, we underestimated the race. Once a rookie kicked our ass. Another time we beat ourselves. Both defeats hurt. "Success is a lousy teacher. It seduces smart people into thinking they can't lose," Bill Gates wrote in his 1995 book, *The Road Ahead.*

Looking back on my career in ultra-cycling, I am pleased to have proved that even a young athlete can race to success. I have broken the myth that in ultra-cycling only older racers with decades of training behind them are capable of celebrating big victories. If I regret things, then it is those times that I was a victim of my own arrogance—in my eyes, a cardinal sin. Not only did my arrogance depreciate others, first and foremost it also weakened me. Any defeat resulting from arrogance was therefore highly deserved.

My successes have enabled me to create a profession that is unfortunately only for a few, since sponsors for this sport are not easy to find, and a career exclusively on the bike is hardly possible. Jure Robic was a member of the army all his life. Wolfgang Fasching used his RAAM victories to position himself in a sustainable manner as a speaker, alpinist, and extreme athlete.

And, I too, am in the fortunate position of now being a popular speaker, and have been able to build up an additional mainstay with my online shop. The fact that I can afford to be an ultra-cycling professional is the result of hard work that I could not handle on my own.

To be successful, daily training is a must. The race may bring action, excitement, and adventure, but the up to thirty-five hours a week I spend on the ergometer are at times grueling. It's getting harder and harder every year to not get lazy. In the winter, I crawl into my training cellar when it's still dark, and when I come out, it's already dark again. "Why am I doing this?" I ask myself repeatedly. Then I answer, "Because every missed training session makes the race more difficult. Because bad preparation takes the fun out of the Race Across America. The longer it takes me to ride through the USA, the more I will suffer." As I suffer and train, one hour after another, I think of marathon runners; those who finish in three hours are less tormented and have more fun than those who need five.

Nevertheless, I remain fair and reserved for the benefit of the entire sport. I see myself as an ambassador of my discipline, but that does not mean that success isn't valuable to me, or that I want to simply hand success to others. I know that I can count on the many people who accompany me on my support crew, and I count on my faithful sponsors, and so I strive to do my best not only for me, but out of debt and gratitude to them. That's why my job is year-round; I do not punch a timeclock and do not count weekly hours, but keep working on my skills and my fitness, and make myself a better ultra-cyclist.

> Some say that I'm supposed to mock my competitors by putting hours and days between myself and them. The opposite is the case! For me, it is a sign of respect to everyone else, to be optimally prepared and to waste no time during the race.

"Success is a lousy teacher," said Bill Gates. The cousin of success—complacency—is a much worse instructor, I say.

RAAM 2018: On the way to the first major sleep break, after crossing The Rocky Mountains

Sealevel [ft]

10.000

8.000

6.000

4.000

2.000

0   1.000   2.000   3.000

Distance [miles]

XXI
WHY NOT FIVE?
RAAM 2018

Now I am a five-time winner of the Race Across America, and those who confidently predicted that I would win again will feel validated. Looking at the results reveals that it was a clear success. Numbers do not lie. However, it is wrong to believe that I only have to fly to the USA and cycle a few days to pick up the next title. It is always difficult to win a RAAM—however great the gap between the runner-up and me may be.

One of my biggest achievements in the first half of 2018, was to withstand the pressure that came from outside of me. Everyone expected the win or a record—the only question seemed to be the margin by which I would win. Some organizers of my lecture series in the fall, already wanted to announce me as the five-time winner on their posters, even before I even went to the start. The work on this book also created a certain amount of stress, because winners can certainly be better marketed than losers. Had I not won, this chapter would be called "Still Four" or something less enticing like that.

But I set the bar high for myself. Despite my respect of the other racers, the start list was sobering—no past winners or contenders, though I did expect Luxembourg's Ralph "Dizzy" Diseviscourt to be the fastest of my competitors. In order to stay motivated until the end, I wanted to complete the non-stop journey in less than eight days. I knew I needed my best possible performance for that, and yet I did not have a guarantee of reaching my goal. Looking back over the previous weeks and months, I realized I had done all my homework, but unlike the 2015 race, I was not confident of victory. "First, arrive healthy," I told myself. And maybe, one of the other participants would actually challenge me, so I would have to stand my ground and fight. Dizzy, for instance, knew RAAM (he'd finished once before), and had won both Tortour and the Race Across Italy. Only after a hopefully ideal start, and a smooth crossing of the Rocky Mountains, would I want to look at the clock.

I love you and think of you. The nervousness is good, but now you must push everything away that is not relevant before the race. Together, we will manage all of that, but now you have to focus on RAAM! This eighth participation gives you the chance to catch up with Jure Robic's victories. You can do it. You've invested so much, I've invested so much, and the team is investing so much in reaching Annapolis. And in the end, that will happen—you will reach Annapolis, which you have worked so hard for. Now that's the focus—only that.

The waiter on Lanzarote said it best, "Why not 5?" Why not! Because you can do it, deserve it and above all else, want it!"

My partner Sabine, wrote this to me a few days before the start of Race Across America 2018, and when I read it, I had to think back to those days that seemed so near and yet so far away. In February 2014, I was in Lanzarote for my annual training camp, and Sabine had accompanied me on this occasion. While I was there cycling between five and eight hours a day, Sabi studied or took walks. On the rest days, we visited the island and had some really good times.

In the evening, we usually stayed at the hotel for dinner—after all, there was a buffet that included fresh fish and grilled meat, and because of my demanding training, I felt a constant hunger. But I had a problem with the wait staff, which changed daily. There was an elderly, grim-looking lady some days, and when she was there, I had never dared to order more than two pieces of fish or meat. When I asked her for a larger portion, she glared at me as if I had criticized her cooking or kidnapped her daughter. The fact that she had held a large, sharp knife in her hand further discouraged me from asking for more.

On the other hand, I did not shy away from her nice, polite colleague but ordered three pieces each time. Finally, at the next dinner, I went a step further, declaring that because I cycled around the island I was very hungry, and since everything tasted so good, I asked if I could possibly have four. The waiter laughed heartily, smiled at me and answered: "Yes, of course! Why not five?" From that moment on, I always got five slices of meat or five pieces of fish from him.

In February 2014, some months after having won my second Race Across America, I had moved on from my trauma with Reto Schoch, and—honestly—did not even think about becoming a record holder. But the, "Why not five?" evolved over the years into a running gag between Sabine and me, and when this year's fifth RAAM success was actually possible, she chose "Why not five?" as our motto.

RAAM 2018 was first in my thoughts in December 2017, when I began following Markus "Max" Kinzlbauer's sports science advice and training plans. It was not easy, the training changes pushed me physically and mentally. I had to go to my performance limit much more often than before, due to his prescribed high-intensity intervals, and I had no rest days for weeks. Previous plans had one or two rest days a week, but now instead of just relaxing, I had three to five hours of easy pedaling. So in the longest phase, I rode 35 days in a row before I had my first rest day, which really did earn its name.

After the training camp in Cyprus in February 2018, my crew chief Michael "Kougi" Kogler wrote to me:

I have to get something off my mind. I'm not a sports scientist, not a watt-per-kilogram cyclist, not even a cyclist. But I am me, and I've seen you pedal for 13 years—and the last time you were so motivated and so greedy on training sessions was when Rainer Hochgatterer dictated your training. The effect of having to work as directed, and not just by the way you're feeling, is definitely obvious. Your torturous work during your training camp is incredible, because there is so much motivation behind it! And that's why it's not like a recent RAAM, that's why it's not a daily routine. You take joy in doing, riding, and fighting. This distinguishes you: you do not stop, and do not rest on your laurels, but give it the gas, the fight, and the bite. And when I read through your postings, then I am again as focused and motivated as I was in last year's Race Across America. I want to bite, fight, kick, and scratch with the whole team, and direct the whole operation so that we dominate the course—not the opponents—so much that everyone, whether athletes, competitors, or spectators, is left wondering, when we're on the road, is the asphalt supposed to burn from all of your speed.

It's not a whole new team this year. A few are experienced, a few are rookies, but we all only want one thing: 5!!!!! 5 victories. In a few weeks, your name should be Christoph "5-time RAAM Winner" Strasser. The Strasser, this little boy from Kraubath, who nobody knew, has conquered a scene and as an individual has more fans than all other sports together! The Strasser, this little boy who loved to ride his bike, has grown up, yet still has fun, and he inspires us all! No matter who, no matter where—everyone from your team of supervisors is with you, and it's all about one thing: to you, to us, to passion, to fun, to pressure on the pedals, and above all to a number. To the #5 !!!!!

Talking to crew chief Kougi

Here too, I have to get something off my chest: I confess that in recent years, there have been moments when I have not given Kougi the respect he deserves. There are many reasons for this. We've known each other from an early age (we're cousins), he was present at my first races, we know everything about each other (you can compare us to an old couple), where the tone becomes more casual. One understands the other in amazing ways and we trust one another, but the word of the other sometimes has less weight than a statement that comes from an outsider. That should not be so. Michael Kogler has matured in the past few years from the joker, and youngest crew member, to a leader who is respected by the team, who ensures good team spirit with his charming, enthusiastic, and dedicated nature. Depending on the situation, he makes tactical decisions such as sleep breaks, and crew shift changes with a combination of planning and of gut feeling.

> I promised to respect my younger cousin, as well as I would a doctor who is many years older than me—and I think I've succeeded.

If I focused even more on the training this year, it is because my partner Sabine supports me with all her time and energy. She coordinates appointments and lectures, answers emails, and manages the online shop, so that I can have my head free for my many tasks that revolve around RAAM.

At the beginning of April, after another training camp in Mallorca, I could look back on another impressive number. Never in my life had I put out a one-hour threshold power (FTP) of 395 watts. In my 4×16 minute all-out intervals, I held 410 watts all the way to the end. And in an overlong seven-hour unit, I recorded over 300 watts.

How much this would affect a puzzle like RAAM was unclear, but the homework was done; physical fitness—33% of the potential success—was in place. The mental fitness—another 33%—had been honed through the training, and grown in me over the years. And the team—which makes up the final 34% was also well prepared. The important position of the doctor was especially well-filled by Dr. Robert Url, MD; I had met him in the spring and saw him to be a prudent, cheerful, and calm man. He'd been a cyclist in his youth, and had been recommended to me by my physiotherapist Christian Loitzl, who knew him from their days at the UKH Graz, the local emergency hospital in my hometown. After meeting with my former medical advisors, Florian Wimmer and Rainer Hochgatterer, I was convinced that Robert was well prepared for RAAM.

The week before the start

Coach Kinzlbauer's new concept did not include any classic "tapering" that is, greatly reduced pre-competition training. This year his idea was for me to train more in Borrego Springs than in the years before, and thus staying in the rhythm, so that certain difficulties I'd had in the first days of RAAM in previous years could be avoided. Of course, due to the heat of the desert, the amount of exercise was decreased, and the inten-

sity was lower compared to my spring-training back in Austria. On the one hand, I wanted to acclimate to the heat, and on the other hand, I wanted to prevent overloading. Nevertheless, in the week before the start, I still sat in the saddle for 25 hours, and the day before the start, I completed a three-hour ride. Apart from the training, I took care of sponsorship and media contacts, and even continued to work on this book—at least until Sabine messaged me and encouraged me to push everything aside.

MONDAY, JUNE 11
FOCUSING

"Lie down and relax, we'll take care of all this," my people told me. They were all busy putting the logos and stickers on the cars, and installing the necessary electronics, making purchases, and putting them in their designated places in the vehicles. And me? I sat in the room mentally playing through the upcoming race. But there were so many more thoughts going through my mind: I missed 2016 due to an accident, in 2015

I returned home with a "did not finish." I remembered that I had been extremely cautious in 2017. There had been a lot going on, and I had definitely wanted to finish the race, and that implied that I had to minimize every possible risk. So now, in 2018: My self-confidence and that of my team was great, we knew that I had no weakness in my lungs, and we could counteract any lung problems by paying special attention to my fluid balance. I wanted to stay healthy, keep my foot on the gas, ride properly, and even push my own limits. For me it was a question of honor—if I am at RAAM, I must do my best.

TUESDAY, JUNE 12
A PUNCTURE AND A SPECIAL PICTURE

The start in Oceanside went very well. Going to the first Time Station to Lake Henshaw and down to Borrego Springs, I was able to keep my pace up and set the second fastest time behind Ralph Diseviscourt. When I switched to my beloved time trial bike, my team had prepared everything necessary. In less than a minute, I was back on the road and wanted to push my pace to take full advantage of my aerodynamic equipment. "Now the race really starts for me!" I told myself.

But after three minutes my effort was temporarily over; I had a rear puncture and had to call my crew, who had already driven ahead due to the leapfrog control, and they had to come back to change the rear wheel. I was a bit annoyed, because I just wanted to get out on this fast section. But my frustration did not last long—in such situations, it's best to forget what has happened and look ahead. The race lasts long enough to regain any lost time.

A few kilometers farther, the route led through a depression. It went two hundred yards down a ten percent grade, and one kilometer later there was a two hundred yard, ten percent grade uphill—nothing out of the ordinary, except that at this point my photographer, "Lex" Karelly, was waiting to take a special shot: the cover art for this book. Before RAAM started, we had spent two days trying to get the perfect picture at this point. I had ridden up and down eighty times, and Lex had taken hundreds of pictures. All the photos were good, but they did not look authentic.

In the race, he snapped the perfect picture with a single attempt! "Two days of work for nothing," Lex told me with a laugh while I pedaled on. He had flown into the US a few days before the rest of the team so we could get this photo.

"The time could have been better spent," I joked back, contemplating all the time devoted to getting photos we wouldn't use. At any rate, it made me proud and happy to know that we'd gotten a real racing photo for my autobiography, and not some staged image. Although it may be immaterial to others, this circumstance makes a big difference to me personally.

TUESDAY, JUNE 12
THE FIRST NIGHT

As feared, the first night was one of the toughest times of the whole race. Between Time Station #2 and #3, I was not able to put much pressure on the pedals. I kept thinking about, and was even about to ask for, a sleep break. I wondered how in heaven's name I was to finish this race, when on the first night I fell into microsleep and had such a loss of concentration.

There is no option but to continue, I told myself. If I take a break now, I'll be mad at myself later—wasting time is an unforgivable sin in this race. And the first night is always tough; you just forget how hard it really is. You always remember the beautiful moments; the worst ones are quickly suppressed by the subconscious.

I cursed how my brain works, but it was my decision and my will to do RAAM again. I had worked extremely hard and consistent for eight months—now I had to go through it all again for eight days. "Play some music!" I asked my crew, and the German rapper Kontra K. resonated from the speaker. One of his songs was to be my hit of RAAM 2018: "Erfolg ist kein Glück", which basically translates to, "Luck Doesn't Bring Success." The lyrics tell of how success comes through sacrifice, and how in life one receives what one gives. These words mean so much to me. I strive to live them, and to show others how real they are.

> I get annoyed when I feel that I'm not doing my job perfectly. That's what I'm working on, because a RAAM without lows has never happened before.

After the first night, everything went better, and just before Time Station #8 in Camp Verde, we used an official instruction from the Route Book to our advantage: "Due to a construction site and heavy traffic on a narrow lane between mile 42.5 and 54.5 (which is 19 kilometers), all racers are to be transferred by their team in the car before they resume the race at the Walmart parking lot." We studied this passage before the start and had planned for me to take my first power nap there. I dozed in the car while being cooled down with ice cubes and coolpads. Falling asleep, I was happy about the race and the fact that the first crises could be mastered so well. It was nice to feel that our good preparation paid off, and our plan of taking my short sleep break along the construction site worked well.

WEDNESDAY, JUNE 13
FULL THROTTLE TO FLAGSTAFF

Our strategy was to reach Flagstaff, Arizona as quickly as possible, so as not to be subjected to the full heat of the third day. My aggressive riding position on the bike was—as my crew wrote on the live ticker—a real eye-catcher for the crew, the media, and every cycling fan." With an overall average of 19.41 miles (31.25 kilometers) per hour, I was not only three kilometers per hour above the average of 2017, but at this point in the race, I had ridden the second fastest RAAM ever! I liked it. "So foaht ma Radl!" ("This is how you ride a bike!") I said, and continued to crank with all my strength, as the sun went down behind Lake Mary, creating a beautiful panorama. It was pleasantly mild when we reached Flagstaff at nightfall, and I benefited from the tailwind on the downhill to Tuba City. With a smile, I thought back to the previous year, when we arrived here at midnight, having suffered a drop in temperature from 104 degrees Fahrenheit (40 Celsius) to 32 degrees Fahrenheit (0 Celsius), and that night, I did not get that helpful wind.

THURSDAY, JUNE 14
A WIND VEST IN THE WRONG PLACE

It was still dark when we entered Monument Valley, and Flo allowed himself to joke that our photographers had missed the moment when I rode past the "Forrest Gump spot". In the film starring Tom Hanks in the title role, Forrest had finished his run at this very spot in the Valley, and had turned around to go home. Of course, we did not stop or go home—but only continued east. Anyway, we were traveling so fast that we were through  Utah before it got really hot. At sunset, we reached Wolf Creek Pass, and at the end of the night, the third of the Rocky Mountain passes, Cuchara Pass.

A moment of panic occurred in Durango: On the descent from the 7,382 feet (2,550 meter) high Hesperus Hill Summit, I had put on my wind vest, which I later took off and stuffed in my jersey pocket during my short time riding through that very nice little town. My crew stopped at the time station to make a crew change, so I was alone for about twenty minutes. Suddenly, on a straight, level section, I started skidding. My rear wheel was locked up. I was afraid that a car had touched me from behind and I panicked. In desperate need, I compensated for the skidding, and somehow came to a stop without falling. When I saw what had happened, I felt relieved: The vest had slipped out of my jersey pocket and had been sucked into the rear wheel. Immediately I thought of Gerhard Gulewicz, who crashed heavily in a similar mishap and that ended his 2008 RAAM. In his incident, his jacket had wrapped in the front wheel—resulting in a front somersault, and severe head injuries. I cursed my carelessness, which had almost caused a similar drama, and continued the ride with shaky hands. "Stop in the future and lose ten seconds, instead of haphazardly stuffing your things into your jersey!" I scolded myself.

RAAM 2018: Impressive rocks in Utah between Time Station Mexican Hat and Time Station Montezuma Creek.

FRIDAY, JUNE 15
FANS OR NO FANS?

Halfway through the race, we were four hours below our 2017 time. A wasp sting could not stop me, especially not when an annoying crosswind quickly turned into a helpful tailwind. Between the time stations in Trinidad and Kim, Colorado, I rode at 24.8 miles (40 kilometers) per hour through the Great Plains. In Kansas, however, as it is every year, there was little to see. The small towns were relatively full of fans. At the Maize Time Station, at a crossroads, I saw a family with two children waving Austrian flags and holding up a sign saying, "Go, Christoph!" Another person cheered for me from their car. Then I saw a whole fan club— five people stood in front of a gas station, all of them held big signs and hopped, screamed, and wildly waved at the roadside. I was honored, even though I did not exactly hear their message.

When my team caught up with me after filling up at this gas station, I was happy to talk about the many fans and the big group.
"They were not fans. These people were having a car wash, and were trying to lure customers from the passing motorists. They were not there for you. They wanted to make a few bucks."
I grinned, "Well, it was funny anyway!"

SATURDAY, JUNE 16
THIRST!

On the dry and parched Kansas plain, where there is nothing but cattle herds, cornfields, and dust-raising combine harvesters, I hoarsely said to Kougi, "You know, sometimes during RAAM, I used to fantasize about having a huge steak with salad from my own garden, then there were years when I was so tired, that I wanted nothing more than a bed that I would not leave for weeks, and in which I would sleep for days. But this time, I just want to guzzle gallons of sparkling water. I have had a dry mouth for days, my throat is rough, my tongue sticks to my palate, and my lips are almost impossible to open because they stick to each other. I feel as dry as the bushes in Borrego Springs. I would like to have three liters of mineral water with some deliciously juicy lemon, freshly picked in California. I just want to drink everything you have in the cooler. But do you want to know something else? I know it's better this way, I know that you take care of me and have a grip on my fluid balance. I trust you. But I just wanted to tell you how I feel right now. Now I have to stop talking, otherwise, my voice will fail completely. But may I have at least a chewing gum or a cough drop?"

A few times—I openly admit that—I acted independently. I had two bottles in the bottle cages. One was full of ice cubes and water, and it was just for pouring over my head to cool me, and keep me awake. There was usually nothing in the other bottle, as I always drained the small amount of carbonated electrolyte drink in one gulp. I only ever got a quarter liter. According to the nutritional protocol, I received one liter of fluid per hour. Sometimes, it was more than intended, for I opened the bottle of "cooling water," took out a handful of ice cubes, added it to the electrolyte drink, and let it melt. Suddenly, I had gained two small sips more than I was actually allowed, and I celebrated this little sin like a teenager secretly smoking his first cigarette. It was wonderful!

SATURDAY, JUNE 16
A COKE AS A REWARD

It was also one of my personal successes when I negotiated for a whole can of Coke with Robert after five days. This drink has absolutely nothing positive in everyday life—I avoid it, and really don't like the taste anyway. But in the race, this mixture of sugar, chemicals, carbon dioxide, and caffeine, has a refreshing effect not to be underestimated. On those rare occasions, it came freezing cold from the ice-chest, usually as a small reward for bravely ridden miles. But Robert was strict. Whenever I asked him, there was either none or only half a can. That was a good thing, even if I would have liked more. But when we crossed the Mississippi River, the deal between Robert and me was already made: I had already asked him at the beginning of his shift, whether it would be possible that I could

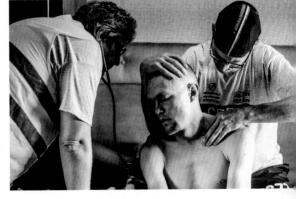

get a whole can of Coke after the Clark Bridge. Robert smiled and agreed. He was thoughtful and responsible, but also extremely empathic and knew what joy it would bring me. I cranked and cranked, and was finally as happy as a little boy on Christmas morning, when the carbon dioxide in the can hissed loudly, and I was allowed to drink it. My luck was so great that I even proudly told the night shift about it. There was a lot of laughter, because no one could really understand how I could be so happy about a can of sugar water.

In a movie about another Austrian RAAM rider, there is a scene on the same topic. The rider goes to the lowered window of the follow car and orders a coke, and a chocolate bar. The crew denies the request and reminds the rider of the liquid food, which is much better for his performance, and the rider responds with, "If I do not get a Coke from you now, I'll get off the bike right here and stop riding!" The team members give in, the cyclist forced his will, only to give up the race a few days later, his body bloated with water retention after giving in to his cravings too many times. The best coach cannot help you when you do not let yourself be coached!

SUNDAY, JUNE 17
UNEXPECTED LUXURY

Missouri is a US state that I do not like at RAAM, and then I like it again. Nowhere else are the car and truck drivers more aggressive and unfriendly than here, and sometimes I really have the impression that they purposely want to run me off the road. This was no different in 2018. But also in Missouri, are many RAAM fans, more than practically any other section of the route. They come to the route every day and night to cheer for me, they gather at the time stations, and at the one in Washington, there was even a pool! My crew jumped, more or less, fully clothed into the

cool water, and I could at least cool my head. That's why I was not tired and withdrawn at the beginning of the next night, but instead, was in a good mood and joking. My team jumped into a pool the next day again, when we saw our good friend Cathy in Lebanon, Ohio.

TUESDAY, JUNE 19
GHOST RIDE

The Athens Ohio Time Station has a special meaning for me; It is the starting point for the journey over the Appalachians. In Athens, so to speak, the finish of the RAAM is heralded—and that has it all. The Appalachian Highway is a busy highway. The cyclists have to ride to the far right or, where possible, be on the shoulder of the road. But the shoulder is often strewn with broken glass, stones, shreds of burst tires, and other debris that I have to dodge again and again. Many times, to miss whatever wreckage was on the road edge, I had to ride over the rumble strip, andcross grooves cut into the pavement to shake up tired drivers who drift onto the shoulder. It was also hell this year: the cars were loud, the trucks in the majority, and the fear that another road user would rear-end us was constant. And as if that was not enough, every time I crossed the white line it rattled my ears, my buttocks, and my whole body. The shock went through my skin and my legs, and my palms were already sore from the consistently rough asphalt, and here they got their final overload. On the next break, my handlebar tape had to be given another layer of padding to keep the numbness in my fingers from getting worse.

But riding slowly is not an option there. For the top riders in the Race Across America, the time from Athens to Annapolis is less than thirty-six hours. Jure Robic and Dani Wyss even mastered these mountainous sections in their mad race of 2009, in a time of thirty hours! This strong finish is absolutely fascinating for me, and I always thought of approaching this record myself, even if it will probably never be achievable for me due to my strong stature, and the slightly different route used now.

Last night, there was a tough situation: Tom was getting annoyed in the passenger seat over the live stream, which was supposed to broadcast my ride on Facebook.

Our Wi-Fi hot spots in the car worked well, but there were always holes in the network coverage. Also, Kougi was working on the nutrition protocol in the back seat when he suddenly shouted loudly, "Left!"

Tom, who is a perfectly safe and flawless navigator, could not argue, as he was not fully focused on the route at that moment. Navigating was not necessary in the current situation—it was all straight ahead. The right-hand lane looked like an exit, Kougi explained later, and he had wanted us to stay to the left of the green strip and stay on the right lane. This turned out to be the opposite lane—and so we had been traveling for a hundred meters as a ghost driver. Fortunately, no one else had been on the road beside us, and we had noticed the mistake immediately and corrected it.

> "Guys, watch out!" I shouted to my crew. End of story.

This matter is not really worth mentioning, I only bring it up to address an important point: those interested in me and the race love the live streams. There are thousands of likes and comments, and the attention given to the entire coverage is enormous. That's good for me and my sponsors, and that's why we attach great importance to this feature, and have sometimes even commented on it. The audience could ask questions that my people or I answered by radio. It was a mix of entertainment, distraction, and pastime for me, but it also took a great effort from the crew—a real concentration eater. The fact is, we would not have lost our way without having been distracted by online messaging, and that made us realize just how fast performance can suffer in secondary locations. Only if the route is easy, and everything is running smoothly, can we afford the luxury to press the "live" button on the phone (even if many viewers and fans would like to have more of it). Even then, there is still a residual risk.

WEDNESDAY, JUNE 20
NEARLY A SUDDEN ACCIDENT ON THE LAST DAY

The lead over the previous year's victory time in West Virginia was seven and a half hours, and it actually seemed as if we could stay under eight days. The 2018 route was 93 miles (150 kilometers) longer than my record runs in 2013 and 2014—making it nearly impossible that a new best performance could be expected.

But around Time Station #46 in Grafton, it seemed to me that our calculations for another possible finish under 8 days would become obsolete. I was on a nine percent climb, riding out on the white line. A truck approached me from behind with great noise, and I saw another truck approaching from the opposite direction. The road was not very wide. The thought, "This is damn tight!" shot through my head. But, what to do? To my right, there was no room, no room at all—just a small ditch, then a sheer wall. "One shake to the left and the truck gets me," I thought to myself. Should I throw myself in the ditch? It seemed to me that I had to choose between the plague and cholera. The roar grew louder, despite the lack of sleep, I concentrated more and held my line. The truck pulled by, and touched neither the on-coming vehicle nor—much more importantly to me—me.

On the front wheel, pointed metal sleeves pro-truded from the lug nuts—it reminded me of the ancient chariots. The load consisted of poorly se-cured wrecked car parts. As the truck rattled past, the hoods, side doors, and bumpers shook in the back, and their pointed ends threatened to tip off the edge.

I was sick, I had to stop and sit at the roadside. "You could have be run over so fast," I thought.

Incidentally, my team was not with me for this incident, because my crew had stop-ped to do a shift change. At this point, I did not know that Thomas Mauerhofer had left the race after a car accident. Mauerhofer is a rider from the Austrian state of Sty-ria, whom I had thought could be a close competitor, and a very likely candidate for the Rookie of the Year award. During the race, I had repeatedly inquired about him, was happy to know that he was in third place for a long time, and already saw the two of us together on the podium. But since crossing the Mississippi, he was listed as a "DNF" on the results. My team told me that the reasons were unknown. In fact, it soon became apparent that he had been hit by a car, and had been taken to the hospital with broken cervical vertebrae. The people on my staff withheld this information from me because they did not want to further strain my nerves. That was a good thing, because after the close pass by the truck in Grafton, I would probably have had to deal with even more fear.

Even as I rode my own lonely race, I regularly asked how the others were doing. On the one hand, it was important to find out, to have a look at the classification; on the other hand, it interested me personally. RAAM 2018 was a challenge for all of us! To say that I was pleased when I heard that Mauerhofer would fully recover from his injuries is an understatement. I was thrilled not only by his performance up to his DNF, but also by that of Nicole Reist, who finished the race in nine days and twenty-three hours, which put her in third place among all the solos—beaten only by me and by the Luxembourger, Ralph Diseviscourt (nine days, twelve hours, thirty-three minutes).

WEDNESDAY, JUNE 20
A WORK OF MASTERPIECE FROM MY TEAM

It was not quite enough. It took me eight days, one hour, twenty-three minutes to complete RAAM 2018. I could curse, and angrily proclaim that I was too slow by eighty-four minutes. But it is not so. I can live very well with my time, and with my performance, and for several reasons. On the last day it had rained in buckets, and that had slowed down my journey. But even more important to me, is the fact that though I had endeavored for a time of under eight days, I gave the best performance that I was able to bring, and had wasted no time unnecessarily. Even though I had signed a few autographs at two time stations, these stops had been identified in advance, and were limited in time. "I'll wait for a maximum of fifteen seconds," I had let the fans know, and on the sixteenth second, I was back on the road again.

Our race plan called for a maximum of eight hours total spent on breaks. After 24, 36, and 48 hours, there would be a twenty-minute power nap to help complete the three passes of the Rockies. Then, there could be the first one-hour break. For team boss Kogler, who at that time was analyzing and planning from the RV, the main question was how long I should sleep before the Rockies—whether it should just be a power nap or a longer sleep break. He was afraid that I would not get over the mountains as planned, and so got in touch with the follow car to ask about my strength and condition. He was encouraged by Robert and Florian and the others. We all wanted to get over the mountains as quickly as possible, and Kougi's strategy of calculated risk worked. It gave me a little more time than an ordinary power nap, but less than a regular sleep break. Bingo!

After that, we planned for twenty minutes in the afternoon, and one hour during the night. But my sleep breaks were not identical to the entire length of the stop. I had to get off the bike and get some food before the actual rest period started. Part of our strategy was to make the entire break as short as possible. If one hour of sleep was planned, we did not want to spend more than eighty minutes stopped.

A RAAM is decided on the road and in the breaks. Ralph "Dizzy" Diseviscourt came up with a similarly fast net riding time as me. According to our own records, I was in motion for seven days, nine hours; we were able to limit the idle time to around 16.5 hours. According to RAAM's GPS tracking, Dizzy was in motion for seven days and fourteen hours, but was not moving for a total of two days. So my team was, roughly calculated, almost three times faster at break management. It is undisputed that with his additional frequent breaks, Diseviscourt probably slept more, and regenerated better than I did. In a non-stop race, however, it is not enough to be fast only when sitting on the bike.

The last sleep break can theoretically end in disaster. What if I wake up in confusion, and slip into a crisis after a couple of hours after getting back on the bike as was the case in 2017? What if I do not get it clear in my mind for hours? What if I fall then? Before the last sleep break, Kougi tormented himself with as many negative thoughts as I did. At midnight, I found myself in the motor home again and within a few seconds, I fell into a deep sleep. Not wanting to disturb my sleep for any reason, Robert skipped the usual medical check. Our physiotherapist, Tom Marschall, gently treated my knees and back during the break and then slowly tried to wake me up by intensifying his grip. I was not so easily awakened, but as Tom massaged my muscles tighter, I slowly came to. I still looked dead tired, but my head was clear. Getting dressed, taking Ensure, drinking coffee, peeing, and getting on the bike took fifteen minutes. By then I was fully in race mode again and everything was fine.

The people I had around me in 2018 were always in the mood for jokes: they built an artistic six-man pyramid on the side of the road, launched the "High 5 Handshake" with a Hulk Fist, and threw themselves into the koala costume and dangled at the Cuchara Pass sign.

> **My team was one of the most important factors for my—for our—fifth RAAM victory.**

The fact is, things can get badly out of hand as was painfully experienced by Franz Preihs in RAAM 2018. I appreciate him as a competitor and friend, and his "DNF" hurts me too. His downfall was not due to a lack of cycling skills or a whim of nature. But as he wrote on Facebook, on tactical, and subject-specific wrong decisions within a crumbling crew structure from the beginning, which ultimately led to the formation of two separate groups. It must be a bad feeling when a cyclist notices that the mood in his team tilts, and this leads to an exit from the competition. In my RAAM appearances, there have been a few much smaller issues that I learned of only after the race. In 2018, however, everything went smoothly in our team. The supplying of the crew from the mobile home was excellent. Thomas "Kahli" Kahlbacher and Philipp Bergmann had always packed our "Mothership" with food. There was a warm meal for the exhausted crew members at each shift change, while the three persons who changed into the follow car also received food. The motorhome was always clean, tidy, and was controlled in a reasonable driving and listening mode, so it was always in the place that Kougi had arranged, in front of me and ready for my sleep break. During the day it also stopped for a few hours to give the crew an opportunity to get some sleep. The RV management was incredibly important to keeping a good mood within the team.

Three people formed a day shift, and three formed a night shift. The distribution of tasks was well regulated. In the day shift, Thomas "Bob" Hämmerle was the driver, and our expert in engineering and electronics. Florian Kraschitzer was the deputy team leader for tactics, navigation, the live ticker, and live streaming. Dr. Robert Url was the supervising physician, responsible for my food, keeping the nutritional record, and monitoring my breathing and blood levels at every break. On the night shift, team boss Michael "Kougi" Kogler was responsible for the overall strategy, and thus also for the feeding and the break planning, and of keeping a record of these. My coach, Markus "Max" Kinzlbauer was driver, motivator, and coach—but in principle, was the "do whatever is needed" guy. Thomas "Tom" Marschall was our physiotherapist while we were stopped, and while we were driving, the navigator, who also took care of the live ticker and the live streaming on the Internet.

On both shifts, which always alternated at twelve-hour intervals, the communication microphone was passed along. Everybody tried to get involved again and again in

Celebrating good times: Using Hulk's fist instead of a high five

The crew of the night shift: Thomas Marschall, Michael Kogler, Markus Kinzlbauer

talking to me (if I needed it), to tell me about the race, to entertain me with funny news, or to read my Facebook messages and guest book entries to motivate me.

The media team consisted of Alexander "Lex" Karelly, who acted as a responsible media officer and photographer. Stefan Schmid shot video; Manuel "Hausi" Hausdorfer was the driver, and the second photographer. So we were also well positioned with media technology. The media car was always close by at key moments to document the journey, and were flexible enough to respond in emergencies—such as when the support vehicle punctured its tires. Photos were shot, edited and uploaded, video footage was edited, set to music, and the finished video was put online on YouTube, and TV material was sent to ORF and other media outlets. All this happened while driving in the car, and not in a production studio. The photos and the webisodes were very well received and garnered a lot of praise. We had other important support at home from my partner Sabine, and from Martin Rosenender, who distributed RAAM broadcasts to the media.

RAAM 2018 was a great success for us all. My physical condition was always ideal, allowing me to reach my limits. The fatigue had been great, but never precarious or even dangerous, and due to optimally chosen breaks by Kougi, I had not become disoriented in this race, and the question of meaning had hardly surfaced. I also managed to refrain from becoming really grumpy and obnoxious.

The crew of the day shift: Florian Kraschitzer, Dr. Robert Url, Thomas Hämmerle

My mental state was also very good: I had not questioned my entry into the race, had not begged for sleep breaks, and did not try to play off my crew, just to make my ride easier.

I had known what I wanted to accomplish: to be able to say to myself that it could not have gone any better—no matter if in the end, it all took a little longer than eight days.

What now?

Relax, enjoy, celebrate, and let body and soul hang loose! The next goals will come soon enough...

But just as an idea, I say: "Why not six?"

**5-Time RAAM Winner
Christoph Strasser**

The bike and me—that's a long-term thing.
At first, we were looking through rose-colored glasses.
In time, it became real love.
As in every relationship, there is a lot of work behind it,
toward pleasing the other.
Sometimes I have to force myself to train
and there are also moments when I say to my bike:
"Today I want to be alone for the day!"
Then there are those moments when we are together
flying over the road and I can't imagine
living without my bike.
But maybe I should not take myself
and my love for this beautiful sport too seriously.
"There are only two tragedies in life," Oscar Wilde said.
"One is not getting what one wants,
and the other is getting it." I add:
"But who cares, if the journey fills us with happiness?"
Life consists of many more things than cycling alone,
even if this can be one of the best hobbies in life.
And for me, it's not just a hobby,
but passion, life content, and love.

APPENDIX
NUMBERS, DATA, FACTS

...

YEAR	EVENT	DISTANCE	TIME	mph
1962	birth Herbert Strasser (father)			
1964	birth Helga Strasser (mother)			
1982	birth Christoph Strasser in Leoben			
1982–87	childhood years on my grandparents' farm (from mother's side)			
1987	Moved to Kraubath to my grandparents' house (from father's side)			
1989–1993	Elementary school in Kraubath			
1993–2001	High school in Knittelfeld with Matura (final degree)			
1993	Birth Philipp Strasser (brother)			
1994	Birth Julia Strasser (sister)			
1997	Birth Oliver Strasser (brother, *1997 +2000)			
2001	First semester Montan University Leoben, moved to Leoben			
2002	Civil service in the nursing home in Knittelfeld			
2002	24-hr race Fohnsdorf, 9th place	260,98 mi	24h	draft
2003–08	Further studying at Montan University Leoben, no final degree			
2003	24-hr race Fohnsdorf, 7th place	323,11 mi	24h	draft
2004	12-hr Kraftwerktrophy, 9th place	259,73 mi	12h	draft
	24-hr race Fohnsdorf, 3rd place	372,82 mi	24h	draft
2005	24-hr Kraftwerktrophy, 7th place	478,46 mi	24h	draft
	RATA Race Across The Alps, 14th place	326,22 mi	1d:3h:32m	11,85
	24-hr race Fohnsdorf, 2nd place	394,57 mi	24h	draft
since 2006	Relationship with life partner Sabine			
2006	24-hr Kraftwerktrophy, 3rd place	543,70 mi	24h	draft
	RATA Race Across The Alps, 6th place	326,22 mi	1d:1h:56m	12,58
	24-hr race Kelheim (GER), 1st place	472,24 mi	24h	draft
	24-hr race Fohnsdorf, 1st place	416,32 mi	24h	draft
2007	Race Around Slovenia, 3rd place	714,58 mi	1d:21h:50m	15,60
	Glocknerman Ultra-Marathon-WC, 1st place #1, track record	627,58 mi	1d:10h:19m	draft
	RATA Race Across The Alps, 2nd place	326,22 mi	22h:59m	14,20
	24-hr race Kelheim (GER), 2nd place	450,49 mi	24h	draft
	24-hr World Cycle Race Schötz (SUI), 2nd place	590,30 mi	24h	draft
	24-hr Kainachtaltrophy (AUT), 2nd place	553,64 mi	24h	draft
since 2008	Moved to Graz together with Sabine			
2008	Race Around Slovenia, 2nd place	736,32 mi	1d:18h:50m	17,19

YEAR	EVENT	DISTANCE	TIME	mph
2008	12–hr Kraftwerktrophy, 1st place	257,87 mi	12h	draft
	Training ride around Austria, nonstop	1553,43 mi	4d:4h:30m	
2009	Race Around Slovenia, 5th place	736,32 mi	1d:20h:43m	16,47
	RAAM, DNF #1			
	24–hr race Le Mans (FRA), 2nd place	530,65 mi	24h	draft
2010	Race Around Slovenia, 2nd place	764,29 mi	1d:23h:00m	16,32
	Glocknerman Ultra-Marathon-WC, 1st place #2	627,58 mi	1d:13h:46m	draft
	Transaustria, UMCA Record	475,97 mi	1d:0h:42m	19,27
2011	Race Around Slovenia, 3rd place	707,74 mi	1d:17h:36m	17,01
	RAAM, 1st place #1	2989,42 mi	8d:8h:6m	14,94
	Tortour Suisse, 6–person-relay-team, 1st place	621,37 mi	1d:7h:4m	
	24–hr Radtrophy Kirschenhalle (AUT), 3rd place	451,74 mi	24h	draft
2012	Race Around Slovenia, 1st place	738,19 mi	1d:16h:08m	18,39
	RAAM, 2nd place	2993,14 mi	8d:8h:19m	14,94
2013	Race Across Italy, 1st place	391,46 mi	17h44m	22,02
	RAAM, 1st place #2, first man under 8 days	2962,08 mi	7d:22h:11m	15,54
	Race Around Austria, 4–person-relay-team, 1st place	1351,48 mi	2d:18h:47m	20,23
	Race Around Ireland, 1st place	1340,92 mi	3d:21h:16m	14,38
2014	RAAM, 1st place #3, track record	3019,86 mi	7d:15h:56m	16,42
	Race Around Austria, 1st place #1	1349,62 mi	3d:15h:56m	15,33
2015	24–hr UMCA road record, Berlin Tempelhof (GER)	556,75 mi	24h	23,20
	RAAM, DNF #2			
	Race Around Austria, 1st place #2	1351,48 mi	3d:14h:44m	15,34
	Training crash, broken patella, shoulder surgery			
2016	Race Around Austria, 1st place #3	1326,63 mi	3d:12h:41m	15,66
	Cancellation 24–hr indoor-track World Record attempt			
	24–hr WC Timetrial, Borrego Springs (USA), 1st place #1	550,53 mi	23h:57m	22,98
2017	Across Australia Perth - Sydney, UMCA record	2454,42 mi	6d:10h:58m	15,84
	RAAM, 1st place #4	3082,00 mi	8d:9h:34m	15,23
	24–hr indoor-track UMCA WR Grenchen (SUI)	584,71 mi	24h	24,36
2018	RAAM, 1st place #5	3069,57 mi	8d:1h:23m	15,94
	RAA Challenge, 1st place (Austrian Champion Ultra)	347,97 mi	15h:54m	21,88
	24–hr WC Timetrial, Borrego Springs (USA), 1st place #2	567,31 mi	23h:40m	23,97

RAAM 2009: Alexander Karelly, Christian Schebath, Daniel Guarise, Jürgen Gruber, Ulrich Schönfelder, Thomas Jaklitsch, Albert Schober, Dr. Viktor Weinrauch, Markus Vogl, Zita Bereuter, Markus Kinzlbauer

RAAM 2011: Markus Kinzlbauer, Christian Schebath, Dr. Rainer Hochgatterer, Markus Vogl, Michael Pletz, Thomas Jaklitsch, Clemens Haid, Christoph Kohlbauer, Ulrich Schönfelder, Harald Tauderer, Alexander Karelly

RAAM 2012: Harald Tauderer, Jürgen Gruber, Roman Rubinigg, Alexander Karelly, Dr. Rainer Hochgatterer, Michael Pletz, Christian Loitzl, Ulrich Schönfelder, Markus Vogl, Thomas Jaklitsch, Michael Kogler

RAAM 2013: Christian Loitzl, Jürgen Gruber, Christian Schebath, Dr. Rainer Hochgatterer, Harald Tauderer (standing); Michael Kogler, Michael Pletz, Alexander Karelly, Markus Vogl, Johannes Reiser, Roman Rubinigg (sitting)

RAAM 2014: Florian Kreis, Dr. Rainer Hochgatterer, Christian Schebath, Michael Kogler, Dr. Bernhard Schauer, Alexander Karelly (standing); Christian Loitzl, Johannes Reiser, Jürgen Gruber, Harald Tauderer, Markus Vogl (squatting)

RAAM 2015: Michael Pletz, Alexander Strasser, Jürgen Gruber, Christian Loitzl, Florian Kraschitzer, Philipp Strasser, Michael Kogler, Christian Schebath, Dr. Arnold Schulz, Johannes Reiser, Florian Kreis, Alexander Karelly

RAAM 2017: Georg Michl, Manuel Hausdorfer, Michael Kogler, Stefan Schmid, Thomas Kahlbacher, Florian Kraschitzer, Thomas Marschall, Thomas Hämmerle, Jürgen Bruckbacher, Marc Komrij, Dr. Florian Wimmer

RAAM 2018: Stefan Schmid, Michael Kogler, Markus Kinzlbauer, Florian Kraschitzer, Thomas Marschall, Thomas Kahlbacher, Philipp Bergmann, Thomas Hämmerle, Dr. Robert Url, Manuel Hausdorfer, Alexander Karelly

ANALYSIS RAAM 2014

POWER DATA AND FACTS

Recorded riding time [h]	168,9
Recorded distance [mi]	3014.27
Average speed netto without breaks [mph/kph]	17.83/28.7
Calories burned	108.971
Calories burned per day	14.291
Power, average [W]	162.9
Time without pedalling (rolling) [%]	9.1 %
Highest climb Wolf Creek Pass 10,857 ft [h]	1 h 5'
Power output while climbing [W]	229
Recorded total climbing [ft]	118.110
Right-left-pedalling-balance minimum	49%
Right-left-pedalling-balance maximum	54 %
Cadence average [bpm]	70
Heartrate average [bpm]	116
Temperature maximum [°C/F]	44/111
Temperature average [°C/F]	21/69
Off-bike-time total [h]	15.0
Off-bike-time per day [h]	2.0

The RAAM 2014 data recording was done with "power2max" power meters and Garmin Edge 520 bike computers. This track record is still valid in 2018 and above all shows one thing: Keeping the off-bike-time as little as possible is essential for a fast finishing time. The power output is reduced in the Rocky Mountain and kept fairly constant in the second part of the RAAM.

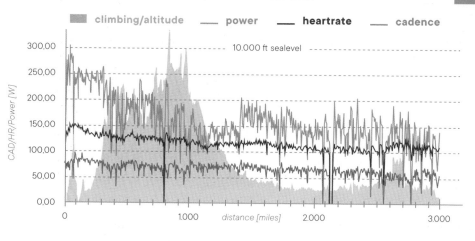

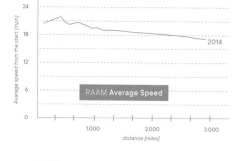

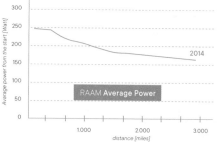

TS #	TS NAME	miles raced	miles left	Arrival time	Riding time	mph Ø total	mph Ø this TS
55	Finish,	3020,00	0,00	06/18/2014 8:23	07:15:56	16,42	13,15
54	Annapolis, MD	3014,30	5,70	06/18/2014 7:57	07:15:30	16,43	15,00
53	Odenton, MD	3004,80	15,20	06/18/2014 7:19	07:14:52	16,43	14,02
52	Mt Airy, MD	2965,30	54,70	06/18/2014 4:30	07:12:03	16,47	14,64
51	Hanover, PA	2928,70	91,30	06/18/2014 2:00	07:09:33	16,50	12,09
50	Rouzerville, PA	2888,40	131,60	06/17/2014 22:40	07:06:13	16,58	11,64
49	Hancock, MD	2839,90	180,10	06/17/2014 18:30	07:02:03	16,70	12,58
48	Cumberland, MD	2802,80	217,20	06/17/2014 15:33	06:23:06	16,77	13,64
47	McHenry, MD	2757,10	262,90	06/17/2014 12:12	06:19:45	16,84	13,66
46	Grafton, WV	2697,90	322,10	06/17/2014 7:52	06:15:25	16,92	10,47
45	West Union, WV	2651,50	368,50	06/17/2014 3:26	06:10:59	17,11	14,47
44	Athens, OH	2565,90	454,10	06/16/2014 21:31	06:05:04	17,21	15,72
43	Chillicothe, OH	2506,70	513,30	06/16/2014 17:45	06:01:18	17,25	17,00
42	Blanchester, OH	2448,60	571,40	06/16/2014 14:20	05:21:53	17,26	16,28
41	Oxford, OH	2398,40	621,60	06/16/2014 11:15	05:18:48	17,28	17,20
40	Greensburg, IN	2348,80	671,20	06/16/2014 8:22	05:15:55	17,28	11,76
39	Bloomington, IN	2285,70	734,30	06/16/2014 3:00	05:10:33	17,51	14,71
38	Sullivan, IN	2218,30	801,70	06/15/2014 22:25	05:05:58	17,61	17,68
37	Effingham, IL	2145,50	874,50	06/15/2014 18:18	05:01:51	17,61	18,72
36	Greenville, IL	2096,20	923,80	06/15/2014 15:40	04:23:13	17,58	16,76
35	Mississippi River,	2050,20	969,90	06/15/2014 12:55	04:20:28	17,60	17,90
34	Washington, MO	1977,70	1042,40	06/15/2014 8:52	04:16:25	17,59	11,61
33	Jefferson City, MO	1900,50	1119,60	06/15/2014 2:13	04:09:46	17,97	17,21
32	Camdenton, MO	1843,70	1176,40	06/14/2014 22:55	04:06:28	17,99	16,37
31	Weaubleau, MO	1794,60	1225,50	06/14/2014 19:55	04:03:28	18,04	16,56
30	Ft Scott, KS	1729,20	1290,90	06/14/2014 15:58	03:23:31	18,10	17,73
29	Yates Center, KS	1669,20	1350,90	06/14/2014 12:35	03:20:08	18,12	18,72
28	El Dorado, KS	1604,60	1415,50	06/14/2014 9:08	03:16:41	18,09	10,57
27	Maize, KS	1570,60	1449,50	06/14/2014 5:55	03:13:28	18,38	15,30
26	Pratt, KS	1493,60	1526,50	06/14/2014 0:53	03:08:26	18,57	16,60
25	Greensburg, KS	1461,40	1558,60	06/13/2014 22:57	03:06:30	18,62	15,55
24	Montezuma, KS	1395,30	1624,70	06/13/2014 18:42	03:02:15	18,79	17,31
23	Ulysses, KS	1345,20	1674,90	06/13/2014 15:48	02:23:21	18,85	20,33
22	Walsh, CO	1291,00	1729,10	06/13/2014 13:08	02:20:41	18,80	20,22
21	Kim, CO	1222,60	1797,50	06/13/2014 9:45	02:17:18	18,72	14,50
20	Trinidad, CO	1151,30	1868,80	06/13/2014 4:50	02:12:23	19,07	15,21
19	La Veta, CO	1085,90	1934,20	06/13/2014 0:32	02:08:05	19,36	17,15
18	Alamosa, CO	1027,60	1992,50	06/12/2014 00:00	02:04:41	19,51	21,02
17	South Fork, CO	981,00	2039,10	06/12/2014 18:55	02:02:28	19,44	14,26
16	Pagosa Springs, CO	933,00	2087,10	06/12/2014 15:33	01:23:06	19,81	16,88
15	Durango, CO	878,70	2141,40	06/12/2014 12:20	01:19:53	20,02	17,11
14	Cortez, CO	834,50	2185,60	06/12/2014 09:45	01:17:18	20,21	16,05
13	Montezuma Creek, UT	784,20	2235,90	06/12/2014 06:37	01:14:10	20,55	1673
12	Mexican Hat, UT	744,60	2275,50	06/12/2014 04:15	01:11:48	20,80	18,50
11	Kayenta, AZ	699,90	2320,20	06/12/2014 01:50	01:09:23	20,97	21,01
10	Tuba City, AZ	628,10	2392,00	06/11/2014 22:25	01:05:58	20,96	24,00
9	Flagstaff, AZ	556,10	2464,00	06/11/2014 19:25	01:02:58	20,62	15,82
8	Cottonwood, AZ	487,00	2533,10	06/11/2014 15:03	0:22:36	21,55	18,77
7	Prescott, AZ	445,40	2574,70	06/11/2014 12:50	0:20:23	21,85	17,82
6	Congress, AZ	395,00	2625,20	06/11/2014 10:00	0:17:33	22,51	20,63
5	Salome, AZ	342,30	2677,80	06/11/2014 07:27	0:15:00	22,82	18,98
4	Parker, AZ	286,30	2733,80	06/11/2014 04:30	0:12:03	23,76	23,91
3	Blythe, CA	234,90	2785,20	06/11/2014 02:21	0:09:54	23,73	24,35
2	Brawley, CA	145,20	2874,90	06/10/2014 22:40	0:06:13	23,36	27,92
1	Lake Henshaw, CA	56,80	2963,30	06/10/2014 19:30	0:03:03	18,62	18,62
0	Oceanside, CA	0,00	3020,00	06/10/2014 16:27	0:0:0	0,00	0,00

ANALYSIS 24H ROAD 2015

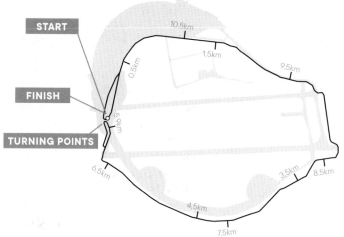

POWER DATA AND FACTS

Body weight [lbs/kg]	172/78
FTP [W]	380
Duration of the ride [h]	24
Length of one lap [mi/km]	7.33/11.8
Laps ridden	76
Total distance [mi/km]	556.75/896.2
TSS	1050
Cadence average [rpm]	79.6
Speed average [mph/kph]	23.20/37.3
Power average [W]	250
Normalized power [W]	254
ø Watt/kg [W]	3.2
Heartrate average [bpm]	137

In the 24-hour world record ride in Berlin one thing is obvious: the pace and performance in the second half decreased significantly, although a constant power curve was sought. The reason for this were the damp weather and the cold at night, which costed energy. Because of the bad weather I also had to wear a rain-jacket and leg-warmers, which decline aerodynamics. But also the mental component was a big factor, because the hoped-for limit of 900 kilometers was no longer possible and I got motivation problems. Only with the mood of the audience and the final spurt in the last hour, I could raise my performance again. The average power of 254 watts NP equals 66% of the FTP threshold.

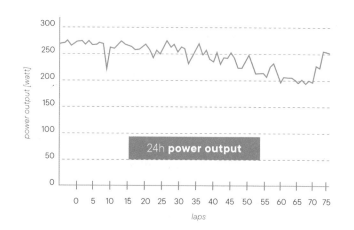

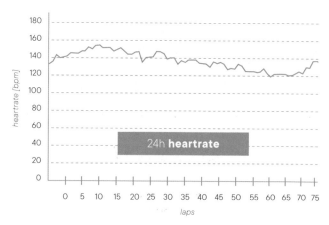

ANALYSIS 24H TRACK 2017

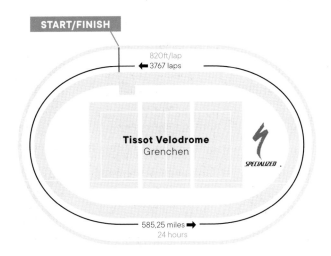

START/FINISH

820ft/lap
← 3767 laps

Tissot Velodrome
Grenchen

SPECIALIZED .

585,25 miles →
24 hours

POWER DATA AND FACTS

Body weight [lbs/kg]	172/78
FTP [W]	375
TSS - Traing Stress Score	836
Length of one lap [m]	250
Laps ridden	3767
Total distance [mi]	585.25
Total distance [km]	941.9
Cadence average [rpm]	75
Speed average [mph/kph]	24.40/39.2
Normalized power [W]	218
Heartrate average [bpm]	139

#track24h

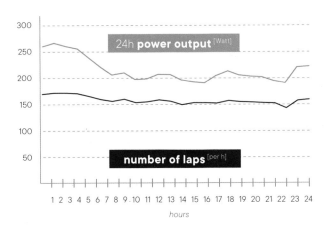

24h **power output** [Watt]

number of laps [per h]

hours

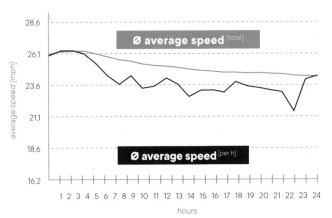

Ø **average speed** [total]

average speed [mph]

Ø **average speed** [per h]

hours

I will always remember the world record ride on the indoor-track as the toughest 24 hours of my life. Due to the centrifugal force in the curves, the aerodynamic position and the slight dizziness, it was not possible for me to hold the performance at a constant high level I was aiming for. I had problems with the food intake and the mental monotony was grueling and energy-consuming. Originally, I planned with the same wattage output as in Berlin 2015, but I fell in a physical low very soon, which also shows in the performance numbers. Thus, the 1000 kilometer benchmark, I was dreaming of, or even the hoped-for average speed of 40km/h could not be achieved. Meanwhile, there have been several attempts to beat the record, but all of them were unsuccessful.